W9-BGH-521

HOMELESSNESS IN
AMERICA, 1893–1992

HOMELESSNESS IN AMERICA, 1893–1992

An Annotated Bibliography

Compiled by
Rod Van Whitlock, Bernard Lubin,
and Jean R. Sailors

Foreword by Irene S. Levine

Bibliographies and Indexes in Sociology, Number 22

GREENWOOD PRESS
Westport, Connecticut • London

Library of Congress Cataloging-in-Publication Data

Homelessness in America, 1893-1992 : an annotated bibliography /
  compiled by Rod Van Whitlock, Bernard Lubin, and Jean R. Sailors ;
  foreword by Irene S. Levine.
      p.   cm.—(Bibliographies and indexes in sociology, ISSN
  0742-6895 ; no. 22)
    Includes bibliographical references and index.
    ISBN 0-313-27623-4 (alk. paper)
    1. Homelessness—United States—History—Bibliography.
    2. Homeless persons—United States—History—Bibliography.   I. Van
  Whitlock, Rod.   II. Lubin, Bernard.   III. Sailors, Jean R.
  IV. Series.
  Z7164.H72H66   1994
  [HV4505]
  016.3625'0973—dc20   93-11876

British Library Cataloguing in Publication Data is available.

Library of Congress Catalog Card Number: 93-11876
ISBN: 0-313-27623-4
ISSN: 0742-6895

First published in 1994

Greenwood Press, 88 Post Road West, Westport, CT 06881
An imprint of Greenwood Publishing Group, Inc.

Printed in the United States of America

The paper used in this book complies with the
Permanent Paper Standard issued by the National
Information Standards Organization (Z39.48-1984).

10 9 8 7 6 5 4 3 2 1

Contents

Foreword

The tragedy of homelessness has an impact on the lives of many Americans. Over the past decade, there have been multiple responses to this complex problem, both publicly and privately, at national, state, and local levels. Yet it is obvious that more needs to be done to address the root causes of homelessness.

Research can play an integral role in developing long-term solutions to end and abate homelessness. Past research, in fact, has contributed to our present understanding of this multi-faceted problem. But more needs to be learned. We need to clearly understand and acknowledge the causes of homelessness for any given individual as well as the housing and social welfare policies that create and perpetuate homelessness among the vulnerable poor. While the availability of low-cost housing is essential to solve the homelessness problem, alone it is often an insufficient response to the needs of many segments of the homeless population. For these individuals, housing needs to be coordinated with a range of health and social welfare services.

I am certain that this bibliography will serve as a useful resource for students, researchers, program providers, and policymakers alike. Carefully cataloging what we know will assist our current efforts to meet the needs of homeless persons and chart directions for what we need to study in the future.

Irene S. Levine, Ph.D., Director
Office of Programs for the Homeless Mentally Ill
National Institute of Mental Health

Preface

Interest in the problem of homelessness in America has led to a great increase in research and publication in this field over the past decade. Although the problem of homelessness is ancient and worldwide, we have limited our literature search to the past century in America. During that period a wide range of scholarly disciplines and publication outlets are represented in the literature.

We have attempted to keep in mind the variety of research and scholarship needs of those who work in this field; this perspective has guided our selection of items to include and to abstract. Items with an empirical component had a better chance to be abstracted. We hope also that many of the more important items have been abstracted. "Importance," however, being in the eye of the beholder, some deserving items undoubtedly were overlooked.

This bibliography contains a total of 1,703 citations (140 books and 1,563 articles, book chapters, and dissertations). Of the 717 annotations, 74 are books and 643 are articles, book chapters, and dissertations. Eleven topical areas provide an organization for this bibliography. These are: early research: 1893-1965; mental health; alcohol and drug abuse; single homeless; health and health care; families and children; legal issues; social and historical perspectives; special populations: elderly, minorities, veterans; programs and services; and housing. Two indices (an author index and a subject index) are provided.

We hope that this bibliography will encourage further research and scholarship concerning this tragic human problem.

We wish to thank the many people who assisted us in the complex process of bringing this selectively annotated bibliography to completion. We would like to express our special appreciation to Carol Rust for her invaluable efforts in many areas.

R.V.W.
B.L.
J.R.S.

HOMELESSNESS IN AMERICA, 1893–1992

1

Early Research: 1893–1965

1. Allardyce, A. (1934). Wandering minds and wandering feet. Occupations, 13, 153-155.

2. Anderson, H.E. (1931). Centralized care of the homeless. The Family, 11, 318-319.
    Based on interviews with a small number of homeless people, the author argues for differentiating types of homeless persons in order to more effectively cope with the homelessness problem.

3. Anderson, H.E. (1928). Travelers and non-residents. The Family, 9, 75-79.
    Presents an argument for greater administrative cooperation among welfare agencies serving transients and the homeless, supported with critical descriptions of existing relief agencies.

4. Anderson, N. (1923). The hobo: The sociology of the homeless man. Chicago, IL: University of Chicago Press.
    Describes Chicago's "hobohemia" based on the author's own observations and experiences which include data from over 400 interviews and case histories.

5. Anderson, N. (1931). The milk and honey route: A handbook for hoboes. New York: Vanguard.
    Discusses being a hobo as a profession, with rules and standards of behavior not unlike other professions.

6. Anderson, N. (1932). Report on the municipal lodging house of New York City. New York: Welfare Council of New York City, Research Bureau.

7. Anderson, N. (1934). Homeless in New York City. New York: Board of Charity.
    This description of the homeless population of New York and the agencies that work with them explores the police practices on skid row and the work histories,

health, and mental health of a sample of 900 homeless men. Methodological problems associated with estimating the numbers of homeless are discussed.

8.   Anderson, N. (1935). Vagrancy. Encyclopedia of the Social Sciences, 15, 205-208.

9.   Anderson, N. (1940). Highlights of the migrant problem today. Proceedings of the National Conference of Social Work. New York: NCSW.
The labor surplus created by extensive unemployment during the depression created a new class of migrants that differed greatly from their predecessors. The author argues for continuation and expansion of federal works programs to limit the number of "depression era" migrants. The author supports the argument with a comparison of pre-depression "knight of the road" and depression era migrants, using statistics from a variety of studies of transients.

10. Anderson, N. (1940). Men on the move. Chicago, IL: University of Chicago Press.
This argument for an extended role for the federal government in solving the problems created by extensive migration is supported with a review of literature that attempts to describe the total scope of migrancy from its beneficial function of balancing employment needs to its darker side of poverty.

11. Bain, H.G. (1950). A sociological analysis of the Chicago Skid-row lifeway. Unpublished master's thesis, University of Chicago.

12. Baker, M.A. (1965). An estimate of the population of homeless men in the Bowery area, New York City, February 26, 1965. New York: Bureau of Applied Social Research, Columbia University.
Describes procedures and findings from two yearly censuses of homeless men in the Bowery area of New York in 1964 and 1965. The findings suggest about a 5% drop in the number of homeless men over the two year period.

13. Bauer, C., & McEntire, D. (1953). Redevelopment in Sacramento's West End, report # 5: Relocation study, single male population. Sacramento, CA: Redevelopment Agency of the City of Sacramento.
Describes a plan to relocate 4,500 skid row men, two-thirds of whom are transients who find low-skill employment in agriculture or industry. The focus of the plan is on relocation without destroying important relationships and ensuring job availability; little emphasis is put on employment or skills training programs for these men.

14. Beasley, R.W. (1933). Care of destitute men in Chicago. Unpublished master's thesis, University of Chicago.

15. Bendiner, E. (1961). The bowery man. New York: Thomas Nelson.
Presents a history of the Bowery and a description of its contemporary atmosphere and conditions and includes accounts of the author's own experiences with homeless men.

16. Blumberg, L. (1960). The men on skid row. Philadelphia, PA: Department of Psychiatry, Temple University School of Medicine.

Report findings from interviews conducted by 200 medical students with 2,249 skid row men. Data is presented concerning: (1) current drinking patterns, (2) living accommodations, (3) physical health status, (4) perceptions of themselves and their community, and (5) educational, employment and family histories.

17.   Bogue, D.J. (1963). Skid row in American Cities. Chicago, Il: Community and Family Study Center, University of Chicago.
Results from a 1957-58 survey of all of Chicago's skid row areas are reported. The sample (N=613) includes residents of SRO hotels, missions, and skid row area jails, as well as county hospital patients with skid row addresses, and persons living on the streets. The author discusses respondent's daily activities, drinking behavior, social mobility, employment history, family background, and personality structure.

18.   Bogue, D.J., & Schusky, J.W. (1958). The homeless man in skid row. Chicago, IL: Tenants Relocation Bureau.

19.   Bradwin, E.W. (1928). The bunkhouse man. Unpublished doctoral dissertation, Columbia University, New York.

20.   Brantner, J.P. (1958). Homeless men: A psychological and medical survey. Unpublished doctoral dissertation. University of Minnesota, Minneapolis, MN.

21.   Brissenden, P.F. (1919). The I.W.W.: A study of American syndicalism. New York: Russell & Russell.

22.   Caplow, T. (1940). Transiency as a cultural pattern. American Sociological Review, 5, 731-739.
Transiency has become a normal phase of life for many Americans and may represent social mobility rather than social pathology.   Drawing upon observations made while "on the road" in 1939, the author concludes that the new transients differ from both traditional vagrants and depression-era transients.

23.   Caplow, T., Lovald, K., & Wallace, S.E. (1958). A general report on the problem of relocating the population of the lower loop redevelopment area. Minneapolis, MN: Minneapolis Housing and Redevelopment Authority.

24.   Carpenter, N., & Haenszel, W.M. (1930). Migratoriness and criminality in Buffalo. Social Forces, 9, 254-255.

25.   Cecil, W. (1904). A plea for the tramp. National Review, 43, 964-971.

26.   Chambliss, W.J. (1964). A sociological analysis of the law of vagrancy. Social Problems, 12, 67-77.
Discusses the history of vagrancy law from the 14th century to the 19th century, focusing on the changing conceptions of the vagrant and subsequent changes in vagrancy law. Vagrancy law is seen as reflecting the interests of powerful groups in society, initially powerful landowners and later merchants.

27.   Chicago Tenants Relocation Bureau. (1961). The homeless man on skid row. Chicago, IL: Author.

28. Collins, H.H., Jr. (1941). America's own refugees: Our 4,000,000 homeless migrants. Princeton, NJ: Princeton University Press.

29. Cook County Service Bureau for Men. (1935). Characteristics of unattached men on relief. Chicago, IL: Illinois Emergency Relief Commission.

30. Cross, D.E. (1924). A behavior study of Abraham Bernstein, one of the 123 so-called homeless men who were interviewed at the Chicago municipal lodging house in 1924. Chicago, IL: Chicago Unemployment Bureau.
    This portrayal of the homeless as a willfully wretched lot is based on an interview with a single man whom the author feels is characteristic of the majority of homeless men she had contact with while associated with the Chicago Unemployment Bureau.

31. Cross, W.T. (1937). The poor migrant in California. Social Forces, 15, 423-427.
    Discusses the problem of rising numbers of homeless and destitute migrants in California and describes state and federal initiatives on behalf of the homeless.

32. Cross, W.T., & Cross, D.E. (1937). Newcomers and nomads in California. Stanford: Stanford University Press.
    The authors describe the federal emergency legislation to aid transients and discuss the policy implications of the California experience with the destitute homeless. The discussion also includes several shelter and rehabilitation programs for homeless individuals and families.

33. Culver, B.F. (1933). Transient unemployed men. Sociology and Social Research, 17, 519-535.
    From the data collected on a study of 136 clients of a shelter in Palo Alto, California, the author constructs a profile of the "average unemployed transient man."

34. Dees, J.W. (1948). Flophouse: An authentic undercover study of the flophouses, cage hotels including missions, shelters and institutions serving unattached (homeless) men. Francestown, NH: Marshall Jones.
    This review of the relief policies in 11 American cities compares American policies with British relief policies from the reign of James I. The author also provides a history of homeless shelters in Chicago and describes their conditions. The recommendation is for increasing pressure to reintegrate homeless men.

35. Demone, H.W. & Blacker, E. (1961). The unattached and socially isolated resident on skid row. Boston, MA: Boston Community Development Program.
    Describes the problem of homelessness and skid row and the resources available to resolve the problem in accordance with the city's urban renewal plan. The authors suggest that unless homeless men are involved in community training and rehabilitation programs, they will merely gravitate to other marginal areas in the city.

36. Department of Psychiatry, Temple University School of Medicine (1960). The men on skid row. Philadelphia, PA: Temple University.

37.   Devine, E.T. (1897). The shifting and floating city population. Annals of the American Academy of Political and Social Sciences, 10, 149-164.
A German program is cited as an example of a successful program to eradicate the begging problem in U.S. cities. Formation of anti-begging societies, centralized control of shelters, creation of labor colonies and imprisonment of beggars and those who help them are suggested as appropriate measures to end begging.

38.   DiBella, E.E. (1934). Mental hygiene aspects of the transient program. Indiana Bulletin of Characterology and Corrections, March, 55-60.

39.   Dubin, G.V., & Robinson, R.H. (1962). The vagrancy concept reconsidered: Problems and abuses of status criminality. New York University Law Review, 37, 102-136.
The history and evolution of vagrancy law in English and American society is reviewed. The authors argue for reform, noting that most vagrancy laws are inconsistent with the constitution.

40.   Dunham, H. (1953). Homeless men and their habitats: A research planning report. Detroit, MI: Wayne State University Press.
Reviews the literature on homelessness and skid row, suggesting that the major causes include: (1) being from a broken or unstable home, (2) lack of education, (3) history of institutionalization, and (4) wandering. Abuse of alcohol is seen as a coping response to life on skid row.

41.   Feeney, F.E., Mindlin, D.F., Minear, V.H., & Short, E.E. (1955). The challenge of the skid row alcoholic: A social, psychological and psychiatric comparison of chronically jailed alcoholics and cooperative alcoholic patients. Quarterly Journal of Studies on Alcohol, 16, 645-667.
Compared 50 alcoholics referred to treatment from municipal courts and 50 volunteer patients and found that the referred group, though relatively lacking in education, intelligence, quantity of family affiliations and in consistent employment, had fewer serious alcoholic reactions.

42.   Gillin, J.L. (1929). Vagrancy and begging. American Journal of Sociology, 35, 424-432.
The author describes the history of vagrancy and begging and the social responses to them. Private and public responses are reviewed, with the establishment of labor colonies according to European models viewed as desirable.

43.   Gilmore, H.W. (1929). Social control of begging. The Family, 10, 179-181.
Argues that the street begging problem will continue to grow as long as the public continues to give money directly to beggars rather than to social agencies and the police take a sympathetic stand on arresting them.

44.   Gilmore, H.W. (1932). Five generations of a begging family. American Journal of Sociology, 37, 768-774.

45.   Gilmore, H.W. (1940). The beggar. Chapel Hill: University of North Carolina Press.
This review of the history of begging in western society and types of beggars and

their behavior suggests that control of mendicancy depends on understanding its causes.

46. Goldberg, M.M. (1941). A qualification of the marginal man theory. American Sociological Review, 6, 52-58.

47. Goldsborough, E.W., & Hobbs, W.E. (1956). The petty offender. The Prison Journal, 36, 3-26.
     Findings of a study of 35 males released from jail who were part of a program designed to make them self-sustaining citizens are reviewed. A comprehensive approach to the problem of the homeless man is advocated. Characteristics of homeless men that must be addressed include: (1) lack of income, (2) family problems, (3) lack of a trade or marketable skill, (4) health and mental health problems, and (5) problems with the law. The authors argue for the development of more community resources including halfway houses.

48. Gordon, C.W. (1956). Social characteristics and life career patterns of the skid row alcoholic. Institute on the Skid Row Alcoholic, Annual Conference. New York: National Committee on Alcoholism.

49. Governor's Commission on Unemployment Relief. (1936). Public Relief for transient and non-settled persons in the state of new York: A study of the nature and administration of the care extended destitute persons not having legal settlement in the community where they receive aid. Albany, NY: Author

50. Green, A.W. (1947). A re-examination of the marginal man concept. Social Forces, 26, 167-171.

51. Guild, J.P. (1939). Transient in a new guise. Social Forces, 17, 366-372.
     Examined case records of 858 male transients served by the Travelers Aid Society in Virginia in 1938 in order to study the role of social casework in aiding homeless transients.

52. Hachtel, E. (1933). A study of one hundred and thirty one young transient women. Unpublished master's thesis, University of Tulane, Tulane, GA.

53. Hallwachs, G.M. (1931). Decentralized care of the homeless in a crisis. The Family, 12, 314-317.
     Suggests that decentralized services for the homeless leads to establishment of soup kitchens by charitable groups which only leads to increased vagrancy.

54. Harlow, H.F. (1931). Old bowery Days. New York: Appleton.

55. Harrington, M. (1963). The other America. Baltimore, MD: Penguin Books.
     The author's experiences as a member of the Catholic Worker group in New York City's bowery in the early 1950s and his encounters with alcoholic derelicts during these years are described.

56. Health and Welfare Council of Philadelphia (1952). What about Philadelphia's Skid Row. Philadelphia, PA.

57.   Hirt, J.V. (1939). <u>The transient problem as reflected by a study of short contact cases in a Buffalo agency</u>. Unpublished master's thesis, University of Buffalo, Buffalo, NY.

58.   Hoffman, V.F. (1953). <u>The American tramp, 1870-1900</u>. Unpublished master's thesis, University of Chicago.

59.   Holtz, D.O. (1963). <u>A report on the relocation of residents, business and institutions for the Gateway Center Project Area</u>. Minneapolis, MN: Minneapolis Housing and Redevelopment Authority.
      Reports findings of an analysis of the relocation of 2,400 single unattached skid row men in Minneapolis. The relocation plan, which involved the establishment of an office of relocation to help these men find housing within the existing housing market, was an alternative to building of new low-rent SRO hotels. The effects of the relocation on businesses and missions in the area are discussed.

60.   Hoy, W.R. (1928). Care of the homeless in St. Louis. <u>The Family</u>, <u>9</u>, 209-219.
      This discussion of the strengths and weaknesses of agencies and programs to serve the homeless in St.Louis suggests that there is great need for additional housing for the employed homeless and free employment services for those who are not.

61.   Hunter, R. (1904). <u>Poverty</u>. New York: Macmillan.
      A chapter on vagrancy and skid row offers a classification of vagrants and a discussion of each type. The competitive industrial system which requires a surplus of labor available for "casual" employment is suggested as the primary cause of vagrancy.

62.   Illinois Emergency Relief Commission (1932). <u>Men in the crucible</u>. Chicago, IL.
      Explores the characteristics of men receiving shelter services based on 6,009 life histories collected by the agency and describes services and programs for homeless men provided by the commission's shelters.

63.   Jackson, J.K. (1956). The problem of alcoholic tuberculous patients. In P.J. Sparer (Ed.), <u>Personality, stress, and tuberculosis</u>. New York: International Universities Press.

64.   Jackson, J.K. (1956). Some aspects of the sanatorium adjustment difficulties of white male Skid Row alcoholic tuberculous patients. In P.J. Sparer (Ed.), <u>Personality, stress, and tuberculosis</u>. New York: International Universities Press.

65.   Jackson, J.K., & Connor, R. (1953). The skid row alcoholic. <u>Quarterly Journal of Studies on Alcohol</u>, <u>18</u>, 468-486.
      This article discusses the informal social groupings among wine-drinking alcoholic males on skid row. These small groups may exist for relatively long periods of time and provide emotional support for continuing drinkers who do not acknowledge that they are dependent on alcohol.

66. Jackson, J.K., & Fergus, E.B. (1959). The tuberculous alcoholic before and during hospitalization. <u>American Review of Tuberculosis and Respiratory Disease, 79</u>, 659-662.

67. Johnson, G.H. (1937). <u>Relief and health problems of a selected group of non-family men</u>. Chicago, IL: University of Chicago Press.
Findings of a study of 144 single men under the care of the Cook County Relief Administration are used to describe Chicago's approach to the problem of homeless men and to argue for better coordination of the professions and organizations involved in serving this population.

68. Kean, G.G. (1965). <u>A comparative study of negro and white homeless men</u>. Unpublished doctoral dissertation, Yeshiva University.
Compared 3 groups of males: (1) 30 homeless black males, (2) 30 homeless white males, and (3) 30 non-homeless black male controls. For the most part, differences between the groups were non-significant.

69. Kelley, E. (1908). <u>The elimination of the tramp</u>. New York: G.P. Putnam's Sons.

70. Kellner, F. (1965). Public intoxication in Rochester. <u>Quarterly Journal of Studies on Alcohol, 26</u>, 117.

71. Kimble, G.E. (1935). <u>Social work with travelers and transients: A study of traveler's aid work in the United States</u>. Chicago, IL: University of Chicago.

72. Lacey, F.W. (1953). Vagrancy and other crimes of personal condition. <u>Harvard Law Review, 66</u>, 1203-1266.
Punitive measures in dealing with crimes such as vagrancy are useless since such crimes are actually "crimes of condition" rather than crimes of action or inaction.

73. Laubach, F.C. (1916). <u>Why there are vagrants: A study based on examination of one hundred men</u>. Unpublished doctoral dissertation, Columbia University, New York.

74. Levinson, B.M. (1947). <u>A comparative study of certain homeless and unattached domiciled men</u>. Unpublished doctoral dissertation, New York University.
Compared 50 homeless white males and 50 non-homeless white males on public assistance on intelligence, personality characteristics, family background, home environment, criminal behavior, health and public assistance history. Men from both samples tended to have similar health and employment problems, while homeless men tended to be more likely to be "downwardly mobile" and to be experiencing greater psychological disturbance. The author concludes that the lack of differences between the two groups does not warrant differential treatment by welfare or public assistance agencies.

75. Levinson, B.M. (1955). The intelligence of middle-aged white homeless men in receipt of public assistance. <u>Psychological Reports, 1</u>, 35-36.
Based on findings that the intelligence test scores of 50 randomly selected homeless male residents of an urban shelter fell within the normal intelligence

range, the author concludes that the causes of homelessness must be sought in factors other than intelligence.

76. Levinson, B.M. (1956-1957). The socio-economic status, intelligence, and personality traits of Jewish homeless men. YIVO Annual of Jewish Social Science, 11, 122-141.

77. Levinson, B.M. (1957). The socioeconomic status, intelligence, and psychonometric pattern of native-born white homeless men. Journal of Genetic Psychology, 91, 205-211.

78. Levinson, B.M. (1958). Some aspects of the personality of the native born white homeless man as revealed by the Rorschach. Psychiatric Quarterly Supplement, 32, 278-286.
    Assessed the personality structure of 40 homeless males who were administered the Rorschach and concluded that homeless men are emotionally immature, depressed, lack drive or definite goals, have feeling of worthlessness, have few interests, are passive and feel insecure. The author argues that the condition of homelessness has intensified emotional problems which have their roots in early life experiences and concludes that homelessness is a natural outcome of "latent personality trends."

79. Levinson, B.M. (1963). The homeless man: A psychological enigma. Mental Hygiene, 47, 590-601.
    Explored differences in the personality structure of the homeless man and the alcoholic. The personality of the homeless man is seen as a consequence of aversive learning experiences and the internalization of indifference and detachment from life. The author concludes that there is a need for interdisciplinary research on the origins and problems of the homeless man.

80. Levinson, B.M. (1964). The beat phenomenon in Weschler tests. Journal of Clinical Psychology, 20, 118-120.
    This attempt to determine the extent of the relationship between feelings of hopelessness among the culturally disadvantaged and performance on I.Q. tests is based on a study of 182 skid row men who were administered the Weschler intelligence test.

81. Levinson, B.M. (1964). A comparative study of the WAIS Performance of Native-born Negro and white homeless. Journal of Genetic Psychology, 105, 211-218.
    This study of black and white homeless men attempts to demonstrate that homeless men, regardless of background, have aversive learning experiences and that these experiences lead to certain personality traits that lead to homelessness. Similar psychometric patterns were found for both groups.

82. Levinson, B.M. (1965). Note on the intelligence and WAIS pattern of white first time applicants for shelter care. Psychological Reports, 16, 524.
    Reports findings of 41 administrations of the WAIS to first time applicants for shelter care in New York City. Although the results were found to be within the established normal range, the author suggests that psychologically healthy and psychologically maladapted males will respond differently to homelessness.

83.   Levinson, B.M. (1965). The homeless man. Psychological Reports, 17, 391-
      394.
      Reviews the literature, identifying major themes in the contemporary literature.
      Problems in defining homelessness are discussed. However, the author's primary
      interest is in identifying characteristics of the homeless personality.

84.   Levinson, B.M., & Baron, S. (1956). Responses of homeless men to Baron M-
      limits blots. Psychological Reports, 2, 431.

85.   Lewis, O.F. (1912). The tramp problem. Annals of the American Academy of
      Political and Social Science, 40, 217-227.
      A national program to study transients and to assist them in securing employment
      is suggested. Alcohol problems and vagrancy are seen as the principle problems
      of transients.   Three groups of transients based on employment problems are
      discussed: (1) transients who do not want to work, (2) disabled transients who are
      unable to work, and (3) transients who seek employment but cannot find it.

86.   Lilliefors, M. (1928). Social casework and the homeless man. The Family, 9,
      294-303.
      The author discriminates between the homeless who are migrant workers,
      recommending shelter as an appropriate intervention, and those who are beggars,
      vagrants, or thieves, for whom personal counseling is viewed as the intervention
      of choice.

87.   Lindesmith, A.R. (1940).   The drug addict as a psychopath.   American
      Sociological Review, 5, 914-920.

88.   Lisle, J. (1915). Vagrancy law: Its faults and their remedy. Journal of Criminal
      Law and Criminology, 5, 498-513.
      Argues that reforming existing laws concerning vagrancy requires no new
      classifications, but should reflect the known differences among groups of
      vagrants. The author argues for indeterminate commitment to such institutions
      as farm colonies rather than jails.

89.   Locke, H.J. (1935). Unemployed men in Chicago shelters. Sociology and Social
      Research, 19, 420-428.
      Reports findings of participant observation research conducted in a Chicago
      shelter as well as an ecological study of 3,000 clients and 1,000 life histories of
      shelter residents.   Shelter residents are divided into 5 categories: (1) casual
      laborers, (2) steady unskilled workers, (3) bums and beggars, (4) skilled
      tradesmen, and (5) white-collar workers. The skilled tradesmen and the white
      collar workers exhibited more severe psychological disorder and demoralization
      than the other groups. Casual laborers reported satisfaction with the shelter and
      voiced little interest in living, while most bums and beggars reported resentment
      with the structure of shelter living, preferring to remain outside until adverse
      conditions forced them to seek shelter.

90.   Lovald, K.A. (1963). From hobohemia to skid row: The changing community
      of the homeless man.   Unpublished doctoral dissertation, University of
      Minnesota, Minneapolis.

91. Love, E.G. (1956). Subways are for sleeping. New York: Signet.

92. Lowrey, L.G. (1941).   Runaways and nomads.   American Journal of
     Orthopsychiatry, 11, 775-783.
     Reports findings of a study of 2,756 persons served by the New York Travelers
     Aid Society during 1935-1939. The majority were teenagers and male. Many
     of the teenagers were runaways and had felt unwanted or frustrated by parent-
     child conflicts. Few of the runaways exhibited any psychiatric disturbances. In
     the group of chronic wanderers, or nomads, many of which were aged and
     female, schizophrenic and paranoid symptoms were common.

93. Markel, N. (1964). A preliminary study of New York's legal agencies and their
     effects on homeless men and the Bowery. New York: Columbia University,
     Bureau of Applied Social Research.
     Reviews the application of penal legislation, law enforcement, and court
     procedures to homeless men.

94. Marsh, B.C. (1904). Causes of vagrancy and methods of eradication. Annals
     of the American Academy of Political and Social Sciences, 23, 445-456.
     While posing as a tramp, the author observed and interviewed vagrants in
     Philadelphia and London in order to develop a typology of vagrants.

95. McCarthy, R.G. (1950). Public health approach to the control of alcoholism.
     American Journal of Public Health, 40, 1412-1417.

96. McCook, J.J. (1893). A tramp census and its revelations. Forum, 15, 753-765.
     Compared 1,349 residents of municipal shelters in U.S. cities compared a sample
     of residents of British casualty wards. The author argues that tramps are
     suffering from a "contagious and hereditary disease" which he refers to as a
     "moral taint."

97. McCook, J.J. (1895).   The tramp problem.   Proceedings of the National
     Conference of Social Work, 1, 288-301.

98. McKinsey, J.P. (1940).   Transient men in Missouri. Unpublished doctoral
     dissertation, University of Missouri, Columbia.
     Reports findings of a study of the case records of 6,000 homeless and transient
     men, as well as, the observations of the author over a 6 year period as an
     administrator with the Federal Transient Program. Sections are devoted to an
     historical and demographic description of transients, the operation of the Federal
     Transient Program, the WPA, and the adequacy of federal programs serving
     homeless and transient males.

99. Meyerson, D.J. (1953). An approach to the skid row problem in Boston. New
     England Journal of Medicine, 249, 646-649.
     Discusses the alcohol and personality problems of skid row men and describes a
     program for skid row alcoholics developed by the Long Island Hospital in Boston.

100. Meyerson, D.J. (1956).   The skid row problem.   New England Journal of
     Medicine, 254, 1168-1173.

101. Meyerson, D.J., & Mayer, J. (1966). Origins, treatment, and destiny of skid row alcoholic men. New England Journal of Medicine, 275, 419-425.

102. Minehan, T. (1934). Boy and girl tramps of America. New York: Farrar & Rinehard.
Based on a collection of over 500 case histories of homeless and transient adolescents gathered over a two year period, the author discusses their backgrounds, attitudes, religious and moral beliefs, and goals. The author argues for youth camps and for greater public education programs for homeless youths.

103. Moore, P. (1934). Mental attitudes of transients. Indiana Bulletin of Characterology and Corrections, March, 60-62.

104. Morgan, M. (1951). Skid row: An informal portrait of Seattle. New York: Viking.

105. Morris, A. (1927). Some social and mental aspects of mendicancy. Social Forces, 5, 605-613.
Discusses factors that contribute to homelessness among men including: (1) failure to hold a steady job, (2) old age, (3), alcoholism and drugs and, (4) disabilities and illness.

106. Nascher, I.L. (1909). The wretches of Povertyville: A sociological study of the bowery. Chicago, IL: Joseph J. Lanzit.
Describes the institutions of the Bowery and case histories of some of the people living in the area, stressing the need for rehabilitation as one of the solutions to the conditions there.

107. Nash, G. (1964). The habitats of homeless men in Manhattan. New York: Columbia University, Bureau of Applied Social Research.
Explores the myth that homeless men are geographically confined to skid row. The author found that homeless men could be found in various geographical locations living in varying sites, including abandoned buildings, sewers, vehicles and parks. Factors influencing the geographical distribution of homeless men are discussed.

108. Nash, P. (1964). The methodology of the study of Bowery lodging houses. New York: Bureau of Applied Social Research, Columbia University.

109. Nash, G. & Nash, P. (1965). A preliminary estimate of the population and housing of the Bowery in New York City. New York: Columbia University, Bureau of Applied Social Research.
Discusses the estimation of New York City's bowery population, the percentage of homeless persons in that neighborhood, and the methods used to derive the estimate.

110. New York City Municipal Lodging House. (1915). The men we lodge. New York.

111. Nichols, M.S. (1933). Homeless persons. Social Work Yearbook, 1933. New York: Russell Sage Foundation.

Describes the changing mobility of homeless persons due to advances in transportation, especially the automobile. A survey of lodging houses suggests there is considerable variability in quality of services and that increased government involvement will improve the quality of lodging and social services available to homeless men.

112. Nimkoff, M.F. (1928). Personality problems of beggars. Sociology and Social Research, 12, 431-442.
Suggests that the observed personality problems among homeless men are exacerbated by long histories of begging and that persons become beggars to avoid working in mainstream society.

113. Nylander, T. (1924). The migratory population of the United States. American Journal of Sociology, 30, 129-153.
Suggests that typifications of migrants in the 1920's were biased due to the overemphasis on participant-observation research in typical literature reviews, the "neo-romantic" work ethic of many contemporary authors, and the abundant number of tales of "the road" that romanticize the tramp lifestyle. A discussion of the causes of migrancy and its solution is provided.

114. Nylander, T. (1933). Wandering youth. Sociology and Social Research, 17, 560-568.
Transient boys are categorized into four groups: (1) "single boys on the road," (2) "road kids;" groups of boys seeking work, (3) "embryonic tramps"; boys who have been on the road for some time and have developed tramp-like characteristics, and (4) boys who have come under the control of a "pervert" who has taught them to steal or beg. The author suggests that boy transiency might be eliminated by establishing a system of permanent subsistence farms throughout the country.

115. Ottenberg, D.J. (1956). T.B. on skid row. National Tuberculosis Association Bulletin, 42, 85-86.
Found that the prevalence of tuberculosis in skid row residents is 18 times greater than that in the general population and suggests that diseases like T.B. are inherent in the skid row lifestyle and that solution of the T.B. problem on skid row necessitates treatment of the skid row way of life.

116. Outland, G.E. (1934). The education of transient boys. School and Society, 40, 501-504.

117. Outland, G.E. (1935). Should transient boys be sent home? Social Service Review, 9, 511-519.
Reports findings from a follow-up study of 251 boys who were returned home by the Los Angeles Welfare Department. The findings indicate that nearly 70% had successfully resettled in their home environment.

118. Outland, G.E. (1935). Sources of transient boys. Sociology and Social Research, 19, 429-434.
Reports findings from a study of 10,000 homeless adolescent boys served by the Federal Transient Service's youth camps. The author suggests that adolescent homelessness can be traced to unstable home environments.

119. Outland, G.E. (1936). The Federal Transient Program for boys in southern California. Social Forces, 14, 427-432.
Describes group and individual treatment programs for transient boys in southern California, the extent of their success, and the need for continued federal aid for such programs.

120. Outland, G.E. (1937). The Federal Transient Service as a deterrent of boy transiency. Sociology and Social Research, 22, 143-148.
The author responds to criticisms of the Federal Transient Service that have suggested that the service and its camps encourage boy transiency. The author demonstrates that boy transiency was a significant problem before establishment of the service and argues that homeless boys are most often the product of a broken or unstable home.

121. Outland, G.E. (1938). Determinants involved in boy transiency. Journal of Educational Sociology, 11, 360-372.
Studied the Los Angeles Federal Transient Service records of 3,352 transient boys and found that the typical transient boy was white, from an urban background, and was homeless for the first time. Major reasons for leaving home included: (1) economic hardship, (2) family stressors, including being from a broken home, and (3) "love of adventure."

122. Outland, G.E. (1939). Boy transiency in America: A compilation of articles dealing with youth wandering in the United States. Santa Barbara, CA: Santa Barbara State College.
This is a compilation of the author's previously published articles concerning adolescent homelessness during the depression. The book is divided into 3 sections: (1) educational and social histories of homeless boys, (2) the work of the Federal Transient Service, and (3) causes of homelessness among adolescent boys.

123. Pascal, G.R. & Jenkins, W.O. (1960). A study of the early environments of workhouse inmate alcoholics and its relationship to adult behavior. Quarterly Journal of Studies on Alcohol, 21, 40-50.
The authors differentiate between the childhood experiences with parents and siblings between skid row alcoholics and matched non-alcoholic controls (N = 38). The alcoholic group differed from controls in levels of early childhood social and emotional deprivation.

124. Peterson, W.J., & Maxwell, M.A. (1958). The skid row wino. Social Problems, 5, 308-316.
Data from interviews with 33 skid row "winos" suggest that these men are not socially isolated, but are socially integrated with their peers and help each other secure shelter, food, and companionship.

125. Philadelphia Prison Society (1956). The homeless man: A Philadelphia study. Philadelphia, PA.

126. Pittman, D.J., & Gordon, C.W. (1958). Criminal careers of the chronic police case inebriate. Quarterly Journal of Studies on Alcohol, 9, 255-268.

127. Pittman, D.J. & Gordon, C.W. (1958). The revolving door: A study of the chronic police case inebriate. New York: The Free Press.
Describes the dependency careers of 187 chronic inebriates jailed in Rochester, New York in the early 1950's using an "undersocialization" hypothesis to explain chronic drunkenness. According to this view, these men are unable to meet the demands placed on adults in contemporary society due to "stressful" family experiences (i.e., as growing up in broken homes) which give rise to emotional handicaps. Thus, drinking is seen as a secondary cause of homelessness.

128. Plunkert, W.J. (1934). Public responsibility for transients. Social Service Review, 8, 421.

129. Plunkert, W.J. (1960). Is skid row necessary? Canadian Journal of Corrections, 2, 200-208.
Describes the characteristics of skid row and the men living there. Skid row men are characterized by lack of skills necessary for competition in the contemporary labor market, high rates of hostility, and problems with interpersonal relationships. The author argues that there is a great need for empirical research in order to provide a data base for developing programs to eliminate and prevent skid row.

130. Pollak, F. (1949). On the psychopathology of impulsive wandering. Journal of Nervous and Mental Diseases, 110, 215-217.

131. Potter, E.C. (1937). After five years. New York: Committee on Care of the Transient and Homeless.

132. Potter, E.C. (1934). The problem of the transient. Annals of the American Academy of Political and Social Science, 176, 66-73.
Presents a brief history of transiency in the U.S. and a discussion of the sudden increase in the numbers of homeless persons following the panic of 1929. The author compares the findings of two censuses of homeless men undertaken by the Committee on the Care of Transient and Homeless in 1933 and evaluates various governmental programs aimed at the transient.

133. Reckless, W.C. (1934). Why women become hoboes. American Mercury, 31, 175-180.

134. Reed, E.F. (1934). Federal transient program: An evaluative survey, May to July, 1934. New York: Committee on Care of Transient and Homeless.
Reviews 3 months of administrative records from the New York office of the Federal Emergency Relief Administration. The author discusses the need for greater emphasis on health care and food programs.

135. Rice, S.A. (1918). The homeless, Annals of the American Academy of Political and Social Science, 77, 140-153.
Describes four types of homeless men: (1) the self-supporting, (2) the temporarily dependent, (3) the chronically dependent, and (4) the parasitic. The general characteristics of each type are discussed.

136. Rice, S.A. (1922). The failure of the Municipal Lodging House. National Municipal Review, 11, 358-362.
Compared the New York City Municipal Lodging House and a privately owned facility for housing homeless men and found that the failure of the municipal center was due to inadequate organization and poorly defined responsibilities. Further, the success of a shelter depended on its ability to address the needs of clients as they perceived them.

137. Ricker, C.S. (1932). A study of 300 inmates of a state farm. Journal of Juvenile Research, 16, 102-124.

138. Riis, J.A. (1957). How the other half lives. New York: Hill & Wang.
The author's classic account of living conditions on New York's lower east side includes a history of tenement housing in New York City and an inventory of tenement areas classified according to prevalent ethnic groups. A description of the bowery and the lifestyle of its homeless residents is included.

139. Rooney, J.F. (1961). Group processes among skid row winos: A reevaluation of the undersocialization hypothesis. Quarterly Journal of Studies on Alcohol, 22, 444-460.
Based on participant observation of skid rows and their inhabitants, the author argues that skid row inhabitants are socially organized, rather than socially isolated, and take deliberate steps to structure social relationships around the purchasing and drinking of alcohol.

140. Rosenman, S. (1955). The skid row alcoholic and the negative ego image. Quarterly Journal of Studies on Alcohol, 16, 447-473.
This is primarily a detailed psychoanalytic case history of a skid row alcoholic, focusing on his self image as unworthy and degraded and how this self image determines his behavior.

141. Rubington, E. (1958). The chronic drunkenness offender. The Annals of the American Academy of Political and Social Science, 315, 65-72.

142. Ryan, P.E. (1940). Migration and social welfare. New York: Russell Sage Foundation.

143. Sands, I.J. (1927). Manifestations of mental disorders in Traveler's Aid Society clients. Mental Hygiene, 11, 728-744.

144. Schubert, H.J.P. (1934). Some characteristics of our transient population. Psychological Bulletin, 31, 695.

145. Schubert, H.J.P. (1935). The school achievement and acceleration of transients. School and Society, 41, 846-848.

146. Schubert, H.J.P. (1935). Twenty thousand transients: A one year's sample of those who apply for aid in a northern city. Buffalo, NY: Emergency Relief Bureau.
Differentiates between three groups of transients based on records from various

intake locations of the Emergency Relief Bureau in Buffalo, New York: (1) Homeless men, (2) seamen, and (3) families.

147. Shandler, I.W. (1965). <u>Philadelphia's skid row: A demonstration in human renewal</u>. Philadelphia, PA: Redevelopment Authority of the City of Philadelphia. Describes the programs and services provided by the Diagnostic and Relocation Center in Philadelphia's skid row area. Some of the services provided included: (1) medical and dental evaluations, (2) psychological screening, (3) psychiatric evaluation, (4) development of a workable relocation plan, and (5) post-relocation follow-up interviews. Effectiveness of the services is assessed.

148. Shaw, A. (1891). Municipal lodging houses. <u>The Charities Review: A Journal of Practical Sociology</u>, <u>1</u>, 20-26.

149. Shaw, C.R. (1930). <u>The jack-roller</u>. Chicago, IL: University of Chicago Press. The author draws on the writings of a 17 year-old boy to discuss the social, cultural, and psychological background of a homeless adolescent.

150. Solenberger, A.W. (1911). <u>One thousand homeless men: A study of original records</u>. New York: Charities Publications Committee.
This study of types, characteristics and origins of homeless men was based on official records of 1,000 males who applied for public assistance from the Chicago Bureau of Charities between 1901 and 1903.

151. Sorenson, K., & Fagan, R.F. (1963). Who's on skid row: The hospitalized skid row alcoholic. <u>Nursing Forum</u>, <u>2</u>, 86-112.
Discusses the dynamics of patient-staff interaction of chronically ill skid row men with histories of pathological drinking. The process of social and physical debilitation which leads to dereliction among such men is described.

152. Strauss, R. (1946). Alcohol and the homeless man. <u>Quarterly Journal of Studies on Alcohol</u>, <u>7</u>, 360-404.
Results of interviews with 203 clients of a Salvation Army Men's Social Service Center provided the basis for this discussion of the typical patterns of alcoholism and homelessness.

153. Strauss, R. (1948). Some sociological concomitants of excessive drinking as revealed in the life history of an itinerant inebriate. <u>Quarterly Journal of Studies on Alcohol</u>, <u>9</u>, 1-52.
Presents a detailed case history of a homeless alcoholic and discusses the relationship between his present situation and an early childhood history of being deprived of the opportunity to participate in normal social activities.

154. Strauss, R., & Bacon, S.D. (1951). Alcoholism and social stability: A study of occupational integration in 2,023 male clinic patients. <u>Quarterly Journal of Studies on Alcohol</u>, <u>12</u>, 231-260.

155. Strauss, R., & McCarthy, R.G. (1951). Non-addictive pathological drinking patterns of homeless men. <u>Quarterly Journal of Studies on Alcohol</u>, <u>12</u>, 601-606.
Results of a study of 444 users of daytime shelter services in the Bowery suggest that the majority of the respondents had considerable control over their drinking

and the amount of money they spent on alcoholic beverages.   The author compares the motives for drinking, and attitudes towards drinking of "controlled" and "uncontrolled" drinkers.

156. Strauss, R. (1955).   The homeless alcoholic: Who he is, his locale, his personality, the approach to his rehabilitation. The homeless alcoholic: Report of the First Annual Institute on the Homeless Alcoholic. Lansing, MI: Michigan State Board of Alcoholism.

157. Sutherland, E.H., & Locke, H.J. (1936).   Twenty thousand homeless men. Philadelphia, PA: Lippincott.
Results of participant-observation research conducted in Chicago shelters in the mid 1930's include discussions of the daily activities, manner of interaction between residents, and backgrounds of shelter residents. It is noted that many clients had become homeless as a result of the depression. The author includes a discussion of public policy concerns and advocates the client perspective on the inefficiencies and injustices of shelter management.

158. Swenson, C. & Davis, H.C. (1959).   Types of workhouse inmate alcoholics. Quarterly Journal of Studies on Alcohol, 20, 757-766.
Describes 5 basic types of skid row alcoholics based on cases histories and psychological tests from 20 public drunkenness arrestees in Knoxville, Tennessee: (1) loners who drink non-beverage alcohol and had strict mothers, (2) loners who drank non-beverage alcohol with possessive mothers, (3) loners who did not drink non-beverage alcohol, (4) loners who were paranoid schizophrenics, and (5) sporadic drinkers.   Drinking behavior is discussed as a result of father-son relationships, while other pathological symptoms are viewed as deriving from mother-son relationships.

159. Vanderkooi, R.C. (1963).   Skid row and its men: An exploration of social structure, behavior, and attitudes (Technical Bulletin B-39).   East Lansing MI: Michigan State University.
Reports findings of a participant observation study of 71 skid row residents in Chicago. A description of social characteristics, leisure activities, and reasons for being on skid row, as well as, a discussion of respondents powerlessness, social isolation, and normlessness are provided.

160. Vexliard, A. (1956).   The hobo: Myths and realities. Diogenes, 16, 59-67.

161. Wattenberg, W.W., & Moir, J.B. (1954).   Counseling homeless alcoholics. Lansing: Michigan State Board of Alcoholism.

162. Wattenberg, W.W., & Moir, J.B. (1954).   Factors linked to success in counseling homeless alcoholics. Quarterly Journal of Studies on Alcohol, 15, 587-594.
Reviewed 770 cases of involving attempts to counsel homeless alcoholics.   70 cases were judged to have had successful outcomes.   The factors that distinguished between successes and failures included: (1) intact social relationships such as being married, attending church, and being employed, (2) having positive attitudes, and (3) cooperation with agency counselors and Alcoholics Anonymous.

163. Webb, J.N. (1935). The transient unemployed. Washington, DC: W.P.A.
An exhaustive study of 25,000 single transients and 1,900 transient families drawn from the relief roles in 13 U.S. cities provides in depth descriptions of the characteristics of the transient population, their mobility and reasons for migration, and problems of reintegration into the work force. The author concludes that the problem of transiency will be solved only when business and industry provide the employment necessary to provide stability.

164. Webb, J.N. (1937). The migratory casual worker. Washington, DC: W.P.A., Division of Social Research.
Results of interviews with 500 casual workers in 13 U.S. cities conducted by the Federal Emergency Relief Program found that migratory casual workers constitute only a small proportion of transient relief recipients and that a national employment assistance program, unemployment insurance, and public works projects are the most feasible federal programs for migratory workers.

165. Webb, J.N. (1938). Migratory families. Washington, DC: W.P.A.

166. Weltman, R.E. (1964). A comparative study of institutionalized and non-institutionalized homeless men. Unpublished doctoral dissertation, Yeshiva University.
Compares a non-representative sample of 39 permanent residents of Camp LaGuardia, a custodial institution for homeless men, with 29 men who had not remained with the camp. The permanent residents were found to be more likely to be married, of middle class background, less heavy drinkers, and higher in I.Q. test scores.

167. Wilensky, H.L., & Edwards, H. (1959). The skidder: Ideological adjustments of downward mobile workers. American Sociological Review, 24, 215-231.

168. Willard, E.B. (1928). Psychopathic vagrancy. Welfare Magazine, 19, 565-573.
Based on observations of 4 homeless derelicts, the author suggests mobilizing such social institutions as psychiatry and police in order to confine or segregate homeless vagrants from society.

169. Willard, J.F. (1899). Tramping with the tramps: Studies and sketches of vagabond life. New York: The Century Company.

170. Wilson, R.S. (1930). Transient families. The Family, 11, 243-251.
Discusses of the employment, health, and attitude problems of homeless families during the depression. The author presents a typology of homeless families based on a process of social disaffiliation.

171. Wilson, R.S. (1931). Community planning for homeless men and boys. New York: Family Welfare Association of America.
Outlines a general program for care and rehabilitation of men and boys made homeless by the depression. Data from 14 cities and 2 rural counties involving providing services for homeless men and boys are presented. The focus of this study is on short-term consequences of the depression on unskilled workers.

172. Wolfe, A.B. (1906). The lodging problem in Boston. Boston, MA: Houghton Mifflin.

173. Wood, S.E. (1939). Municipal shelter camps for California migrants. Sociology and Social Research, 23, 222-227.
Describes the Fresno Shelter Camp, a program designed to provide short-term lodging to migrants and "would-be-vagrants," particularly during the winter months when jobs are scarce. The author argues that provision of shelter is an inexpensive way to reduce petty crimes and meet the needs of the homeless and that similar programs should be developed in other communities.

174. Woods, M.M. (1953). Paths of loneliness. New York: Columbia University Press.

175. Zorbaugh, H.W. (1929). The Gold Coast and the slum: A sociological study of Chicago's near north side. Chicago, IL: University of Chicago Press.
This history of Chicago's Near North Side from 1865 when it was an elite residential district to 1929 when much of it had deteriorated into slums includes sections devoted to descriptions of slum derelicts and alcoholics.

2

Mental Health

176. Anonymous. (1992). Survey shows decline in city shelter beds for homeless mentally ill despite increasing need. Hospital and Community Psychiatry, 43, 189-190.

177. Abdellah, R., Chamberlain, J., & Levine, I.S. (1986). The role of nurses in meeting the health/mental health needs of the homeless: Summary of a workshop for service providers, researchers and educators. Public Health Reports, 101, 494-498.
    The role of nursing in providing services to the homeless mentally ill is the subject of this summary of an American Public Health Association workshop. Summaries of presentations and recommendations from participants on how nurses, educators, administrators, and researchers can improve services and meet the needs of the homeless are presented.

178. Aiken, L.H. (1987). Unmet needs of the chronically mentally ill: Will nursing respond? Image: Journal of Nursing Scholarship, 19, 121-125.
    Discusses the nursing needs of the chronically mentally ill in community settings. Trends in mental hospital admissions, percentages of homeless patients with psychiatric disabilities, and proportions of urban populations receiving mental health services are presented. The authors recommend several strategies for improving the mental health system including: (1) consolidating decision making and accountability in local government, (2) developing alternative service settings outside the mental health hospital, (3) and attracting more professionals into public service.

179. Albee, G. (1990). The futility of psychotherapy. Special Issue: Challenging the therapeutic state: Critical perspectives on psychiatry and the mental health system. Journal of Mind and Behavior, 11, 369-384.

180. Alger, I. (1985). Depicting the plight of our American homeless. Hospital and Community Psychiatry, 36, 709-710.
Reviews three videotapes depicting the plight of the homeless.

181. American Psychiatric Association Task Force on the Homeless Mentally Ill. (1984). Recommendations of APA's task force on the homeless mentally ill. Hospital and Community Psychiatry, 35, 908-909.
According to the American Psychiatric Association's (APA's) task force on the homeless mentally ill, in order to address the multiple problems of the homeless mentally ill, a comprehensive and integrated system of care, with designated responsibility, accountability, and adequate fiscal resources must be established.

182. American Psychological Association. (1985). Psychologists working on homelessness. Washington, DC: American Psychological Association.
Reports findings of an APA survey of 15 psychologists conducting research or practice with the homeless.

183. American Public Health Association. (1984). National leadership workshop on the homeless mentally ill. Washington, DC.
In these proceedings of a workshop sponsored by the American Public Health Association, synopses of four presentations on support services, housing, legal issues, and coordination of programs are provided. Participants called for a comprehensive, long-term approach to the problems of the homeless mentally ill, increased federal and state funding, and the creation of a coalition of organizations concerned with this population.

184. American Public Health Association (1985). National leadership workshop on the homeless mentally ill: Proceedings of the workshop. Washington, DC: APHA.
This summary of workshop proceedings attempts to: (1) clarify the existing activities and policies of 14 national organizations concerned with mental health and homelessness, (2) to identify the unmet needs of the homeless populations, and (3) to make recommendations for future actions and policy directions. The participants agreed to a policy statement recommending a comprehensive, long-term approach to the problem of the homeless mentally ill, increased state and federal funding, and the support of a coalition of organizations participating.

185. Appleby, L. (1981). The urban nomad: Is it a psychiatric problem? Paper presented at the annual meeting of the American Psychiatric Association, New Orleans, May.

186. Appleby, L., & Desai, P. (1985). Documenting the relationship between homelessness and psychiatric hospitalization. Hospital and Community Psychiatry, 36, 732-737.
Analyzed data from Illinois statistical reports and the admission reports of a major Illinois state hospital in Chicago and found that the rate of homelessness has increased dramatically among both psychiatric and general hospital admissions over the past 10 years. Further, the homeless had lower admission rates than non-homeless persons. Nearly twenty percent of the homeless left the hospital against advice, and few of the homeless were referred to long-term care facilities. The authors argue that this data supports the contention that homelessness is increasing

among the chronically mentally ill, and will continue to increase until the mental health system becomes more responsive to the needs of their homeless clients.

187. Appleby,L., & Desai, P. (1987). Residential instability: A perspective on system imbalance. American Journal of Orthopsychiatry, 57, 515-524.

188. Appleby, L., Slagg, M.S., & Desai, P.N. (1982). The urban nomad: A psychiatric problem? In, J.H. Masserman (Ed.), Current psychiatric therapies, vol. 21. New York: Grune & Stratton.
Studied residential instability and recidivism in chronic mental patients. 215 psychiatric admissions were followed for a year after their initial hospitalization. In addition to an unusually high incidence of residential mobility, a relationship between mobility and number of hospitalizations was evident, as were isolation, disruptive family situations, and homelessness. Recommended responses for the mental health system are discussed.

189. Arana, J.D. (1990). Characteristics of homeless mentally ill inpatients. Hospital and Community Psychiatry, 41, 674-676.

190. Arce, A.A. (1983). Statement before the Committee on Appropriations, in U.S. Senate Special Hearing on Street People. Washington, DC: U.S. Government Printing Office.

191. Arce, A.A., Taflock, M., Vegare, M.J., & Shapiro, S.H. (1983). A psychiatric profile of street people admitted to an emergency shelter. Hospital and Community Psychiatry, 34, 812-817.
Reviewed the records of 193 residents of an emergency shelter for the homeless operated by the city of Philadelphia. Shelter residents were grouped into 3 groups: (1) habitual homeless, (2) episodic homeless, and (3) persons undergoing an acute crisis and that were not usually homeless. Thirty-five percent of the sample reported previous psychiatric treatment. Nearly 56% reported multiple hospital admissions and nearly 5% reported having had treatment for drug or alcohol abuse.

192. Arce, A.A., & Vegare, M.J. (1984). Identifying and characterizing the mentally ill among the homeless. In H.R. Lamb (Ed.), The homeless mentally ill. Washington, DC: American Psychiatric Association Press.
This chapter reviews a number of studies of the prevalence of mental disorder in the homeless population. Profiles of the typical chronic homeless person and the typical episodic homeless person are provided. The authors argue that these two groups, as well as other groups of homeless persons, have different service needs. The authors also discuss several problems encountered when conducting research with homeless persons including: (1) differences in definitions, (2) differences in sampling criteria, (3) effects of climate and weather, and (4) differences in social and economic characteristics of the community in which research is conducted. The authors conclude by estimating that between 25 and 50 percent of the homeless population are mentally ill.

193. Arce, A.A., & Vergare, M. (1987). Homelessness, the chronically mentally ill and community mental health centers. Community Mental Health Journal, 23, 242-249.

Suggest that a midcourse correction of the community mental health center (CMHC) program is underway that will address the failure of the CMHC program to operationalize its original aims. The authors also discuss staffing, legal, and funding issues of CMHCs and conclude that there is much optimism about the future of CMHCs role in the care of the chronically mentally ill.

194. Attkisson, C.C. (1970). Suicide in San Francisco's skid row. British Journal of Social Psychology, 4, 282-294.

195. Aviram, U. (1990). Community care of the mentally ill: Continuing problems and current issues. Community Mental Health Journal, 26, 69-88.

196. Bachrach, L.L. (1978). A conceptual approach to deinstitutionalization. Hospital and Community Psychiatry, 29, 573-577.

197. Bachrach, L.L. (1984). The homeless mentally ill and mental health services: An Analytic review of the literature. In H.R. Lamb (Ed.), The homeless mentally ill: A Task Force report. Washington, DC: American Psychiatric Association Press. Examines the increase in homeless among the mentally ill and its causes. Methodological barriers to studying the population are discussed, as well as, the role of deinstitutionalization in creating the homeless mentally ill population are discussed. The author concludes with presenting 9 principles for improving services to the homeless mentally ill that stress the interaction of chronicity and homelessness in determining the needs of the homeless mentally ill population.

198. Bachrach, L.L. (1984). Interpreting research on the homeless mentally ill: Some caveats. Hospital and Community Psychiatry, 35, 914-917.
Discusses problems in interpreting research on the service needs of the homeless mentally ill, including: (1) biases in the studies, (2) the complexity of the homeless mentally ill population, and (3) differences in service needs and available resources in different communities.

199. Bachrach, L.L. (1984). Report and analytical summary of a meeting of DHHS-supported researchers studying the homeless mentally ill. Rockville, MD: NIMH. Reviews findings of 9 NIMH supported studies of the homeless mentally ill and argues for standardizing research and evaluation methods and operationalizing definitions.

200. Bachrach, L.L. (1984). Research on services for the homeless mentally ill. Hospital and Community Psychiatry, 35, 910-913.
Summarizes the proceedings of a meeting of researchers from 9 NIMH supported research programs studying the homeless mentally ill. Issues discussed included: (1) growth of the homeless mentally ill population in recent years, (2) common diagnoses (schizophrenia, affective disorders, personality disorders, and substance abuse), (3) barriers to services, and (4) lack of precise definitions of the homeless mentally ill population.

201. Bachrach, L.L. (1986). Dimensions of disability in the chronic mentally ill. Hospital and Community Psychiatry, 37, 981-982.

202. Bachrach, L.L. (1986). The homeless mentally ill in the general hospital: A question of fit. General Hospital Psychiatry, 8, 340-349.
Explores difficulties in providing services to the homeless mentally ill in the context of the general hospital psychiatric unit. Problems in defining the homeless mentally ill population and barriers to the provision of care are also discussed.

203. Bachrach, L.L. (1986). Issues in identifying and treating the homeless mentally ill. New Directions for Mental Health Services, 35, 43-62
Defining the homeless mentally ill population is difficult due to the disparity in definitions of homelessness, difficulty in establishing psychopathology, overlap with other populations, and geographic mobility. The author also discusses barriers to treatment specific to the homeless mentally ill and makes suggestions for improving service delivery.

204. Bachrach, L.L. (1987). Geographic mobility and the homeless mentally ill. Hospital and Community Psychiatry, 38, 27-28.
Identifies three patterns of geographic mobility among the homeless mentally ill population: (1) movement in and out of the homeless population itself, (2) seasonal movement within defined geographic areas, and (3) migration over wide geographic areas. Implications for provision of services to these distinct groups are discussed.

205. Bachrach, L.L.(1988). Transient patients in a western state hospital. Hospital and Community Psychiatry, 39, 123-124.

206. Bachrach, L.L. (1989). Issues in general hospital psychiatry. Hospital and Community Psychiatry, 40, 1234-1235.

207. Bachrach, L.L. (1992). The urban environment and mental health. International Journal of Social Psychiatry, 38, 5-15.

208. Bachrach, L.L. (1992). What we know about homelessness among mentally ill persons: an analytical review and commentary. Hospital and Community Psychiatry, 43, 453-464.
Noting that existing research has failed to adequately determine the extent of chronic mental illness among the homeless, the extent to which deinstitutionalization has precipitated homelessness among the chronically mentally ill, and what types of services should be provided, the author recommends that future research should use clearer definition of terms used and that future service planning should address the full array of disabilities experienced by the homeless.

209. Bachrach, L.L., Santiago, J.M., Berren, M.R., & Hannah, M.T. (1988). The homeless mentally ill in Tucson: Implications of early findings. American Journal of Psychiatry, 145, 112-113.
Using the results of psychiatric screenings of 264 adults of whom 41 (26 males and 15 females) were homeless, the authors found that the homeless group was characterized by patterns of gross geographic mobility and were unlikely to use community services provided specifically for the homeless.

210. Bachrach, L.L., Talbott, J.A., & Meyerson, A.T. (1987). The chronic psychiatric patient as a "difficult" patient: A conceptual analysis. New Directions for Mental Health-Services, 33, 35-50.
The psychiatric treatment system often fails to reach the patients in most need of treatment, those defined as "difficult patients." Difficult patients are disproportionately represented among the homeless and are said to be resistant to treatment and use services inappropriately. Program principles that address the "difficult patient" are presented.

211. Ball, F.L.J. (1982). San Francisco's homeless consumers of psychiatric services: Demographic characteristics and expressed needs. San Francisco, CA: Community Mental Health Services.

212. Ball, F.L.J., & Havassey, B.E. (1984). A survey of the problems and needs of homeless consumers of acute psychiatric services. Hospital and Community Psychiatry, 35, 918.
A survey of 112 17-67 year old homeless users of psychiatric services in San Francisco found a great disparity between the types of services traditionally offered by community mental health centers and those the homeless population feel they need. Subjects linked their inability to avoid readmissions to their lack of basic resources for survival rather than need for psychiatric treatment and social services.

213. Barker, R.L. (1990). At home with the homeless: An experience in transcultural communication. Journal of Independent Social Work, 4, 61-73.

214. Bassuk, E.L. (1984). The homelessness problem. Scientific American, 252, 40-45.
The recent rise in the number of homeless Americans, a great many of whom are mentally ill, is viewed as the result of poor implementation of deinstitutionalization, lack of affordable housing, and cuts in government benefit payments. The author suggests that full implementation and funding of the 1963 community mental health laws are essential in resolving the contemporary homelessness problem.

215. Bassuk, E.L. (1985). Emergency shelters for the homeless: Are they replacing state mental hospitals? American Journal of Social Psychiatry, 5, 45-49.
The limitations of emergency shelters in meeting the needs of the homeless mentally ill. Because of the failure of deinstitutionalization, these persons are especially vulnerable to the housing crisis and the conservative political climate. The author suggests a renewed commitment to strengthen other community services since shelters are ill equipped to provide services essential to the homeless mentally ill (e.g., 24-hr asylum, long-term treatment, etc.).

216. Bassuk, E.L. (1985). Psychiatric emergency services: Can they cope as last-resort facilities? New Directions for Mental Health Services, December, 11-20.

217. Bassuk, E.L. (Ed.) (1986). The mental health needs of homeless persons. New York: Jossey-Bass.

218. Bassuk, E.L., & Buckner, J.C. (1992). Out of mind--out of sight. American Journal of Orthopsychiatry, 62, 330-331.

219. Bassuk, E.L., & Lamb, H.R. (1986). Homelessness and the implementation of deinstitutionalization. New Directions for Mental Health Services, June, 7-14. Discusses the role of deinstitutionalization and problems with its implementation in contributing to the large numbers of severely mentally ill persons in the homeless population. Lack of affordable housing and the federal government's "crackdown on ineligibility" for Supplemental Income and Social Security Disability Insurance has also contributed to the rising numbers of homeless mentally ill. Suggestions for reversing this trend are presented.

220. Bassuk, E.L., & Lauriat, A.S. (1984). The politics of homelessness. In H.R. Lamb, (Ed.), The homeless mentally ill. Washington, DC: American Psychiatric Association.

221. Bassuk, E.L., & Lauriat, A.S. (1985-1986). Are emergency shelters the solution? International Journal of Mental Health, 14, 125-136. The authors discuss the inadequacies of emergency shelters in providing for the long-term service needs of the homeless mentally ill. The authors review programs for the homeless that have been implemented in Massachusetts as well as in other areas of the U.S.

222. Bassuk, E.L., Rubin, L., & Lauriat, A. (1984). Is homelessness a mental health problem? American Journal of Psychiatry, 141, 1546-1550. Reports findings of interviews with 78 homeless residents of an emergency shelter. 90% of those interviewed received primary psychiatric diagnoses, including psychoses (40%), chronic alcoholism (29%), and personality disorders (21%). Further, 75% of those interviewed had no friends or family relationships, while only 6% worked steadily and only 22% received public assistance. The authors argue that emergency shelters are replacing mental health departments as institutions of care for the chronically mentally ill.

223. Baumann, D.J. (1985). The Austin homeless: Final report provided to the Hogg Foundation for Mental Health. Austin, TX: Hogg Foundation for Mental Health.

224. Baumohl, J. (1992). Addiction and the American debate about homelessness. British Journal of Addiction, 87(1), 7-10. Discusses the need to find alternative ways to manage the homeless mentally ill in the community in order to prevent massive reinstitutionalization. The challenges facing policy makers is to combine strategies of hospitalization and treatment with humane and flexible supportive housing arrangements.

225. Bawden, E.L. (1990). Reaching out to the chronically mentally ill homeless. Journal of Psychosocial Nursing and Mental Health Services, 28, 6-8, 10-13.

226. Baxter, E., & Hopper, K. (1982). The new mendicancy: Homeless in New York City. American Journal of Orthopsychiatry, 52, 393-408. Reports findings of an ethnographic study of homeless persons in New York City which was undertaken to address: (1) to what extent living on the streets was self-imposed, and (2) what were the most pressing needs of the homeless and how

these needs might be met. The results suggest that the size and the composition of the homeless population has changed significantly in the past 15 years, with the number of mentally ill homeless having greatly increased. The authors suggests that successful rehabilitation is linked to safe and accessible shelter and that therapeutic and social needs are intimately linked.

227. Baxter, E., & Hopper, K. (1985). Troubled on the streets: The mentally disabled homeless poor. In J.A. Talbott (Ed.), The Chronic mental patient: Five years later. New York: Grune & Stratton.

228. Bean, G.J., Stefl, M.E., & Howe, S.R. (1987). Mental health and homelessness: Issues and findings. Social Work, 32, 411-416.
    The authors conducted interviews with 979 homeless people in order to assess their mental health status. About 1/3 were found to be in need of mental health services.

229. Begun, M.S. (1985). Crossroads. Special Issue: Deinstitutionalization. American Journal of Social Psychiatry, 5, 19-22.
    Discusses the need for an increase in development of full-time therapeutic care programs for the homeless mentally ill population. Cites growing public callousness towards street people as the primary reason that full-time therapeutic care must be addressed now.

230. Belcher, J.R. (1987). Adult foster care: An alternative to homelessness for some chronically mentally ill persons. Adult Foster Care Journal, 1, 212-225.
    Discusses the use of adult foster care in reducing the chances for homelessness in chronically mentally ill populations. Categories are presented that explain how former mental patients become homeless.

231. Belcher, J.R. (1987). Describing the process of homelessness among former hospital patients. Dissertation Abstracts International, 48, 1317 A.

232. Belcher, J.R. (1988). Defining the service needs of homeless mentally ill persons. Hospital and Community Psychiatry, 39, 1203-1205.
    Surveyed 132 psychiatric patients discharged from a state hospital to determine if they became homeless. At six months after discharge, 47 had become homeless. Four types of homelessness, based on severity of mental illness, life in the community after discharge, and reasons for becoming homeless, are presented.

233. Belcher, J.R. (1988). Exploring the struggles of homeless mentally ill persons: A holistic approach to research. Case Analysis, 2, 220-240.
    Develops a typology of homeless mentally ill persons based on data collected on 47 persons discharged from a state hospital who became homeless. The 4 categories are: (1) wanderers, (2) tenuous planners, (3) situational homeless, and (4) dropouts. Case histories are presented for each type.

234. Belcher, J.R. (1988). The future role of state hospitals. Psychiatric Hospital, 19, 79-83.
    Reports findings of a six month follow-up of 47 homeless adults following their discharge from an urban state mental hospital. Eighty percent had diagnoses of

schizophrenia or other chronic mental illnesses while the remainder had adjustment disorders of acute substance abuse problems. The findings suggest that those with chronic conditions were homeless as a direct result of their illness while the remainder were homeless because of problems with social functioning.

235. Belcher, J.R. (1988). Rights versus needs of homeless mentally ill persons. Social Work, 37, 398-402.
Discusses the moral and ethical questions that may arise in the process of providing effective intervention while attempting to maintain the rights of the homeless mentally ill. The author examines the impact of a narrow interpretation of commitment legislation upon the homeless mentally ill and urges service providers to weigh client rights of self-determination against the potential mental health restoration that might be provided through psychiatric commitment.

236. Belcher, J.R. (1989). The homeless mentally ill and the need for a total care environment. Canadian Journal of Psychiatry, 34, 186-189.
Based on findings from a naturalistic study of 132 discharged mental patients over a 6 month period, the author argues for a continuous service approach to address the needs of mental patients who are also homeless.

237. Belcher, J.R. (1989). On becoming homeless: A study of chronically mentally ill persons. Journal of Community Psychology, 17, 173-185.
The author describes a naturalistic study of the post-hospitalization adjustments of 132 mental patients, 36% of whom became homeless after hospitalization. Categories were constructed to explain differing paths to homelessness for discharged patients. Suggestions for reintegration of the homeless mentally ill into the community are discussed.

238. Belcher, J.R., & DiBlasio, F.A. (1990). The needs of depressed homeless persons: Designing appropriate services. Community Mental Health Journal, 26, 255-266.

239. Belcher, J.R., & Ephross, P.H. (1989). Toward an effective practice model for the homeless mentally ill. Social Casework, 70, 421-427.
This practice model described must be holistic, sensitive to the special needs of those with severe problems in functioning, and attuned to the social reality of homelessness. Effective practice depends on recognition of the homeless persons's dignity and right to self-determination.

240. Belcher, J.R., & First, R.J. (1988). The homeless mentally ill: Barriers to effective service delivery. Journal of Applied Social Sciences, 12, 62-78.
A qualitative analysis of 132 patients discharged from a state mental hospital revealed that 47 patients (36%) became homeless within six months of discharge. The 33 patients who were rated as most disabled had a history of homelessness prior to their last hospitalization, did not comply with aftercare, were released from the hospital without a home, displayed symptoms of mental illness at follow-up interviews, and had limited financial and social support. Findings are discussed in terms of federal guidelines for community mental health programs.

241. Belcher, J.R., & Toomey, B.G. (1988). Relationship between the deinstitutionalization model, psychiatric disability, and homelessness. Health and

Social Work, 13, 145-153.
Results of a follow-up study of state mental hospital discharges (n=133) show that 35% became homeless within 90 days, supporting the notion that deinstitutionalization contributes to the homelessness problem. Characteristics of homeless persons and the processes by which they become homeless are described. The authors report that some clients were discharged without homes or means of economic support. Homeless subjects were described as persons who formulated vague and tenuous plans for the future or as aimless wanderers who continued to decompensate.

242. Benda, B.B., & Dattalo, P. (1988). Homelessness: consequence of a crisis or a long-term process? Hospital and Community Psychiatry, 39, 884-886.

243. Bennett, M.I., Gudeman, J.E., Jenkins, L., Brown, A., & Bennett, M.B. (1988). The value of hospital-based treatment for the homeless mentally ill. American Journal of Psychiatry, 145, 1273-1276.
Of the 31 homeless mentally ill persons who were admitted to an inpatient mental health unit, 48.4% had a major mental illness with no signs of substance abuse. The remainder were diagnosed with substance abuse, brain disease, or personality disorders.

244. Blankertz, L.E., & Cnaan, R.A. (1989). Symbolic interaction: A framework for outreach. Philadelphia, PA: Horizon House, Inc.
Presents a conceptual framework to guide outreach workers in their interactions with dually diagnosed homeless persons (e.g., those with both severe mental health problems and drug and/or alcohol abuse).

245. Blankertz, L.E., Cnaan, R.A., White, K., & Fox, J. (1990). Outreach efforts with dually diagnosed homeless persons. Families in Society, 71, 387-397.
Developed an outreach model, based on a framework of symbolic interaction, for dually diagnosed homeless persons who have severe mental health problems and drug and alcohol abuse. Four case examples are presented.

246. Brady, S.M., & Carmen, E.H. (1990). AIDS risk in the chronically mentally ill: Clinical strategies for prevention. New Directions for Mental Health Services, 48, 83-95.

247. Brahams, D., & Weller, M.P. (1986). Crime and homelessness among the mentally ill. Medico-Legal Journal, 54, 42-53.
Discusses the increases in crime among the mentally ill after the closing of psychiatric hospitals. The authors argue that the release of mental patients to the streets has lead to unnecessary jail terms. Five case examples are described in which failure to issue treatment orders allowed discharged mental patients to commit crimes. The authors suggest that government policy should be adjusted to provide funds for the maintenance, repair, and rebuilding of psychiatric hospitals. Further, how interpretation of statutes has become more restrictive regarding the provision of care and shelter to the mentally ill is discussed.

248. Braun, P. (1981). Deinstitutionalization of psychiatric patients: A critical review of outcome studies. American Journal of Psychiatry, 138, 736-749.

249. Breakey, W.R., & Fischer, P.J. (1991). The epidemiology of alcohol, drug, and mental disorders among homeless persons. American Psychologist, 46, 1115-1128.

250. Breakey, W.R., Fischer, P.J., Kramer, M., Nestadt, G., Romanoski, A.J., Ross, A., Royall, R.M., & Stine, O.C. (1989). Health and mental health problems of homeless men and women in Baltimore. Journal of the American Medical Association, 262, 1352-1357.
Reports findings of a two stage study of the health and mental health service needs of homeless persons in Baltimore. In stage one, baseline interviews were conducted with 528 randomly selected residents of shelters, missions, and jails. Data from this phase of the study suggests high levels of disaffiliation and substance abuse. In the second stage, a sub-sample of 203 interview respondents received systematic psychiatric and physical examinations. Results confirm high levels of substance abuse and demonstrate a high prevalence of mental illnesses and a number of physical disorders. The high rate of co-morbidity of these conditions and the need for health and mental health services are discussed.

251. Briggs, N.A. (1989). Homelessness and mental illness: Evidence from the National Health Care for the Homeless Program. Dissertation Abstracts International, 49, 3889 A.

252. Brill, N.Q. (1985). Deinstitutionalization and the rights of society. American Journal of Social Psychiatry, 5, 54-59.
The author discusses the failure of the deinstitutionalization movement to achieve its original aims and argues that massive discharging of mentally ill patients from the state hospitals has resulted in increasing numbers of chronically mentally ill who are homeless, in jail, or in poorly managed welfare hotels and nursing homes. The author argues for establishment of asylums for the mentally ill, increased use of involuntary hospitalization when needed, and adequate financing for programs.

253. Campbell, R., & Reeves, J.L. (1989). Covering the homeless: The Joyce Brown Story. Critical Studies in Mass Communication, 6, 21-42.

254. Carling, P.J. (1990). Major mental illness, housing, and supports: The promise of community integration. American Psychologist, 45, 969-975.
Summarizes the ways in which the concept of housing and support needs for people with psychiatric disabilities is rapidly shifting in the mental health field. Based on research on the effectiveness of non-facility-based community support and rehabilitation approaches, the findings of other disability fields, and the emergence of mental health consumers' own preferences for expanded choices, normal housing, and more responsive services, including consumer-operated services, the author argues these new sources of knowledge are facilitating a paradigm shift in which people with psychiatric disabilities are no longer seen as hopeless, or merely as service recipients, but rather as citizens with a capacity for full community participation and integration.

255. Carter, J.H. (1991). Chronic mental illness and homelessness in black populations: prologue and prospects. Journal of the National Medical Association, 83, 313-317.

256. Carter, J.H. (1991). Mental health needs of rural homeless African Americans. Hospital and Community Psychiatry, 42, 981.

257. Caton, C.L., Wyatt, R.J., Grunberg, J., & Felix, A. (1990). An evaluation of a mental health program for homeless men. American Journal of Psychiatry, 147, 286-289.
    The authors conducted a before-and-after evaluation of an on-site mental health day treatment program for homeless men. Thirty-two primarily single, unemployed adult males were interviewed six or more months after placement from a crisis shelter to community housing in order to probe housing stability, after care treatment compliance, employment, rehospitalization, and criminal justice contacts. Case reports of two subjects illustrate how the program functions.

258. Chafetz, L. (1988). Perspectives for psychiatric nurses on homelessness. Issues in Mental Health Nursing, 9, 325-335.
    Since chronically mentally ill persons in urban areas are at risk for homelessness, psychiatric nurses may play important roles, both as clinicians and advocates, in preventing homelessness among this population. The authors discuss treatment issues and new treatment models being used to provide support services for the chronically mentally ill.

259. Chafetz, L. (1990). Withdrawal from the homeless mentally ill. Community Mental Health Journal, 26, 449-461.

260. Chafetz, L., & Goldfinger, S.M. (1984). Residential instability among a psychiatric emergency service clientele. Psychiatric Quarterly, 56, 20-34.
    Studied 124 admissions to a psychiatric emergency unit and found that 46% of admissions were either currently homeless or moved frequently between temporary living arrangements. Homeless and non-homeless could not be distinguished by either demographic characteristics or symptomatology. Residential instability was linked to being male, living alone, and length of hospitalization.

261. Chamberlin, J. (1985). An ex-patient's view of the homeless mentally ill. Psychosocial Rehabilitation Journal, 8, 11-15.
    The author, a former mental patient, criticizes the final report of the American Psychiatric Association's task force on the homeless mentally ill. She argues that society should address the basic economic and social causes of homelessness and that the categorization of a group of people as homeless mentally ill is irrelevant and will lead to development of unwanted services for that group.

262. Chawla, A., & Griffith, J.L. (1992). Homelessness and chronic mental illness in Mississippi. Journal of the Mississippi State Medical Association, 33, 39-42.

263. Christ, W.R., & Hayden, S.L. (1989). Discharge planning strategies for acutely homeless inpatients. Social Work in Health Care, 14, 33-45.
    Acute homeless, those who unexpectedly become homeless while in the hospital, are studied. It is found that administrative discharge planning and linkages to services are important to those homeless mentally ill if self-esteem and personal growth are important.

264. Cohen, B.E., & Burt, M.R. (1990). The homeless: Chemical dependency and mental health problems. Social Work Research and Abstracts, 26, 8-17. Investigated the characteristics of homeless people with experiences of mental hospitalization or substance abuse treatment by interviewing 1,704 homeless adult users of soup kitchens and shelters in 1987 in US cities that had populations of 100,000 or more in 1984. The need for services to meet the specific requirements of this population is emphasized.

265. Cohen, C.I., & Thompson, K.S. (1992). Homeless mentally ill or mentally ill homeless? American Journal of Psychiatry, 149, 816-823. Objecting to mainstream psychiatry's conceptualization of persons who are homeless and mentally ill as distinct from other homeless groups, the authors suggest that recent socioeconomic and political shifts contributed to homelessness among all groups, regardless of mental illness. De-emphasizing clinical solutions in favor of empowerment, entitlement and community level solutions is suggested.

266. Cohen, M.B. (1989). Interaction and mutual influence in a program for homeless mentally ill women. Dissertation Abstracts International, 49, 2282 A.

267. Cohen, M.B. (1989). Social work practice with homeless mentally ill people: Engaging the client. Social Work, 34, 505-509.

268. Cohen, N.L. (1990). Stigma is in the eye of the beholder: A hospital outreach program for treating homeless mentally ill people. Bulletin of the Menninger Clinic, 54, 255-258.

269. Cohen, N.L. (1992). What we must learn from the homeless mentally ill. Hospital and Community Psychiatry, 43, 101.

270. Conklin, J.J. (1985). Homelessness and deinstitutionalization. Journal of Sociology and Social Welfare, 12, 41-61. Discusses the history of the deinstitutionalization movement and its failure to provide for patients less well suited for community living. Excessive strain on community mental health centers due to deinstitutionalization has led to increasing numbers of homeless mentally ill. The author describes a program using unused staff residences at state hospitals for housing of the homeless mentally ill and social work interns as staff for these facilities.

271. Conklin, J.J. (1986). Therapy for deinstitutionalized patients. Psychosocial Rehabilitation Journal, 10, 49-56. Assesses the impact of deinstitutionalization in terms of the concepts of negative identity, learned helplessness, and the need for multimodal community treatment. Treatment should consider the individual, family, and community systems as well as medication.

272. Cournos, F. (1989). Involuntary medication and the case of Joyce Brown. Hospital and Community Psychiatry, 40, 736-740. Discusses the case of a homeless women who challenged the New York City plan to hospitalize mentally ill street people. This case illustrates the problems associated with involuntary hospitalization (e.g., commitment of competent persons, lack of effective approaches to persistent treatment refusal, etc.).

273. Cournos, F. (1992). Factors in homelessness among psychiatric patients. American Journal of Psychiatry, 149(2), 279.
Argues that the presence of mental illness is only one aspect of the homelessness problem, which flows from a complex series of economic and social events. The role of the mental health system should be to provide specific interventions to those homeless with psychiatric problems.

274. Crystal, S., & Goldstein, M. (1984). Correlates of shelter utilization: One day study. New York: Human Resources Administration.
This study of 911 residents of homeless shelters in New York City provides data concerning demographics, causes of homelessness, psychiatric and substance abuse history, and social and employment history are presented. Nearly 22% of males and 47% of females had either previous psychiatric hospitalizations or severe psychiatric symptoms. Those residents with psychiatric disorders remained shelter residents significantly longer than those without psychiatric disorders.

275. Crystal, S., Ladner, S., & Towber, R. (1986). Multiple impairment patterns in the mentally ill homeless. International Journal of Mental Health, 14, 61-73.
Assessed patterns of impairment due to mental illness in over 7,500 adults seeking emergency shelter in New York. Questions were asked about demographic characteristics, physical and mental health characteristics, military service, and criminal record. About one-fourth were classified as having indications of mental disorder, with women more likely to report mental disorders than men. Subjects in the mentally ill group reported more physical symptoms, had histories of previous shelter stays, and were more likely to have substance abuse problems. The authors suggest that a wide range of services are needed for the homeless mentally ill residing in shelters.

276. Dattalo, P. (1990). Widening the range of services for the homeless mentally ill. Administration and Policy in Mental Health, 17, 247-256.

277. Davies, M., Munetz, M.R., Schulz, S., & Bromet, E.J. (1987). Assessing mental illness in SRO shelter residents. Hospital and Community Psychiatry, 38, 1114-1116.
This article investigated the nature and prevalence of mental illness among 48 homeless individuals who were evicted from their temporary shelter. Results indicated that 92% met Diagnostic and Statistical Manual of Mental Disorders (DSM-III) criteria for one or more disorders.

278. Dear, M.J., & Wolch, J.R. (1987). Landscapes of despair: From deinstitutionalization to homelessness. Princeton, N.J.: Princeton University Press.

279. Dennis, D.L., Buckner, J.C., Lipton, F.R., & Levine, I.S. (1991). A decade of research and services for homeless mentally ill persons: Where do we stand? American Psychologist, 48, 1129-1138.

280. Dilley, J.W., & Boccellari, A.A. (1992). Management and residential placement problems of patients with HIV-related cognitive impairment. Hospital and Community Psychiatry, 43(1), 32-37.
Reports findings of a study of the Neuropsychiatric AIDS Rating Scale, a measure

of HIV related cognitive impairment. Moderate to severe impairment was related to residential instability and homelessness.

281. Dincin, J. (1990). Assertive case management: Special Issue: Redesigning a public mental health system. Psychiatric Quarterly, 61, 49-55.

282. Dockett, K.H. (1986). Homeless mentally ill people: An analysis of the referral network. Paper presented at the 94th Annual Convention of the American Psychological Association, Washington, DC, August.

283. Drake, R.E., Osher, F.C., & Wallach, M.A. (1991). Homelessness and dual diagnosis. American Psychologist, 46, 1149-1158.

284. Drake, R.E., Wallach, M.A., & Hoffman, J.S. (1989). Housing instability and homelessness among aftercare patients of an urban state hospital. Hospital and Community Psychiatry, 40, 46-51.
Studied the residential instability of 187 aftercare patients with chronic mental illnesses and found that 17% percent of the sample was judged by outreach workers to be predominantly homeless while another 10% were judged to be occasionally homeless over the six month period prior to their evaluations. Homelessness was associated with being younger, male, substance abuse problems treatment non-compliance, and a variety of psychosocial problems and psychiatric symptoms. Homeless subjects had higher rehospitalization rates than non-homeless subjects.

285. Drake, R.E., Wallach, M.A., Teague, G.B., & Freeman, D.H. (1991). Housing instability and homelessness among rural schizophrenic patients. American Journal of Psychiatry, 148, 330-336.

286. Dunn-Stroehecker, M. (1988). From street to treatment: An examination of five demonstration programs for persons who are homeless and mentally disabled. Dissertation Abstracts International, 48, 1886 A.

287. Durenberger, D. (1989). Providing mental health care services to Americans. American Psychologist, 44, 1293-1297.

288. Durham, M. (1989). The impact of deinstitutionalization on the current treatment of the mentally ill. Special Issue: Mental disorder and the criminal justice system. International Journal of Law and Psychiatry, 12, 117-131.

289. Elpers, J.R. (1987). Are we legislating reinstitutionalization? American Journal of Orthopsychiatry, 57, 441-446.
Provides a historical overview of attitudes and trends in the care of the chronically mentally ill with special emphasis on the contemporary movement away from community care and back to hospitalization. An outline of options for actions on behalf of the homeless mentally ill is also provided.

290. Estroff, S.E. (1985). Medicalizing the margins: On being disgraced, disordered, and undeserving. Psychosocial Rehabilitation Journal, 8, 34-38.
This article is a response to the American Psychiatric Association task force report on homelessness. The author questions whether the report actually

distinguishes two groups of homeless people: (1) the ill and deserving and (2) the willfully malfunctioning and undeserving, and the value of medicalizing the homelessness problem, which seems to reflect greater underlying social and economic relationships.

291. Farr, R.K. (1982). The skid row project. Los Angeles, CA: Los Angeles County Department of Mental Health.

292. Farr, R.K. (1984).   The Los Angeles Skid Row Mental Health Project. Psychosocial Rehabilitation Journal, 8, 64-76.
The author describes the development and efforts on behalf of the homeless mentally ill of the Los Angeles Skid Row Mental Health Project. Some of the services developed by the project include: (1) a women's center, (2) a low-cost transportation plan, and (3) a primary health care facility.

293. Farr, R.K. (1985).   A programmatic view of the homeless mentally ill in Los Angeles County. International Journal of Family Psychiatry, 6, 129-148.
Discusses the homeless mentally ill population of Los Angeles. Reasons for the rising numbers of mentally ill among the homeless include: (1) deinstitutionalization of the mentally ill, (2) failures of psychiatric drugs, and (3) barriers to access of social support systems designed for the disabled. Program planning for the homeless mentally ill should involve 2 basic approaches: (1) targeting specific subgroups among the homeless with specialized service needs and (2) conceptualizing interventions in three phases; emergency, stabilization, and long-term.

294. Farr, R.K., Koegel, P., & Burnam, A. (1986). A study of homelessness and mental illness in the Skid Row area of Los Angeles. Los Angeles County Department of Mental Health.
The findings of the first attempt to draw a probability sample of homeless persons, funded by NIMH, are presented. The methodology and instruments used are described and defended. The population was found to be primarily male, young, and minority. 28% were found to be seriously mentally ill and 34% were found to be substance abusers. Few participants were receiving disability relief or any form of relief. The authors conclude that, while methodologically sound research is necessary, appropriate action in the meantime is imperative.

295. Ferguson, M.A. (1989). Psych nursing in a shelter for the homeless. American Journal of Nursing, 89, 1060-1062.

296. First, R.J., Rife, J.C., & Kraus, S. (1990). Case management with people who are homeless and mentally ill: Preliminary findings from an NIMH demonstration project. Psychosocial Rehabilitation Journal, 14, 87-91.
The authors report preliminary findings on barriers to implementation of the intensive care management approach, based on evaluation results from a National Institute of Mental Health (NIMH) services demonstration project involving 139 people who were assessed to be homeless and mentally ill. The findings address 1) linking homeless clients to services and 2) maintaining client contact following placement in housing.

297. Fischer, P.J., & Breakey, W.R. (1986). Homelessness and mental health: An overview. International Journal of Mental Health, 14, 6-41.
A review of the literature on homelessness in America reveals two separate aspects of homelessness: (1) lack of adequate shelter, and (2) disaffiliation. Four distinct subgroups of homeless are discussed in the literature: (1) the chronically mentally ill, (2) alcoholics, (3) street people who choose isolation, and (4) the situationally distressed. Although the health status and prevalence of mental disorders within the homeless population has been addressed, the size of the homeless population and the actual prevalence of mental disorders remains unclear.

298. Fischer, P.J., Shapiro, S., & Breakey, W. (1984). Mental health and social characteristics of the homeless: A survey of mission users. Paper presented at the Annual Meeting of the American Public Health Association, Anaheim, CA, November.

299. Fischer, P.J. , Shapiro, S., Breakey, W.R., Anthony, J.C., & Kramer, M. (1986). Mental health and social characteristics of the homeless: A survey of mission users. American Journal of Public Health, 76, 519-524.
A comparison of homeless and non-homeless men found that homeless men reported higher psychological distress, had a higher prevalence of mental disorder, and were more frequently hospitalized than non-homeless men. Greater social dysfunction was observed for homeless men as indicated by fewer social contacts and higher numbers of arrests than non-homeless men.

300. Frances, A.J., & Goldfinger, S.M. (1986). Treating a homeless mentally ill patient who cannot be managed in the shelter system. Hospital and Community Psychiatry, 37, 577-579.
Uses the case of a homeless mentally ill man who underwent a series of transfers from one public health center to another to illustrate the problems of providing effective services to hard-to-manage homeless patients.

301. Frazier, S.H. (1985). Responding to the needs of the homeless mentally ill. Public Health Reports, 100, 462-469.
Presents a brief overview of the homeless problem, its history, and causes. Emphasis is placed upon the special circumstances of the homeless mentally ill. The author argues for increased coordination of services and efforts among practitioners, researchers, and policy makers. NIMH initiatives are described.

302. Frazier, S.H. (1986). Homelessness and mental health. Paper presented at Clinical Center Grand Rounds at the National Institute of Mental Health, Bethesda, MD, October.
Discusses the multiple causes of homelessness among mentally ill persons including: (1) deinstitutionalization in the absence of adequate community supports, (2) a massive decline in housing for low-income persons, (3) institutionalized unemployment, (4) fragmentation of mental health, housing and social services, and (5) disintegration of the nuclear family, and summarizes findings of 10 NIMH-funded research studies on the homeless mentally ill.

303. Frazier, S.H. (1986). Mental health policy for the homeless. Paper presented at the Harvard Medical School Conference on Homelessness: Critical Issues for

Policy and Practice, Boston, MA, March.
Addresses the difference between mental illness and homelessness and warns against attaching to the condition of being homeless the stigma associated with being defined mentally ill. This paper further discusses the relationship between deinstitutionalization and contemporary homelessness, ongoing research activities of NIMH, the need for continued NIMH involvement in the issue of homelessness and mental illness and the need to increase public awareness and understanding of the needs and problems of the homeless mentally ill.

304. Freddolino, P.P., & Moxley, D.P. (1992). Refining an advocacy model for homeless people coping with psychiatric disabilities. Community Mental Health Journal, 28, 337-352.

305. Freedman, A.M. (1989). Mental health programs in the United States: Idiosyncratic roots. International Journal of Mental Health, 18, 81-98.

306. Freeman, S.J., Formo, A., & Alampu, A.G. (1979). Psychiatric disorder in a skid-row population. Comprehensive Psychiatry, 20, 454-462.

307. French, L. (1987). Victimization of the mentally ill: An unintended consequence of deinstitutionalization. Social Work, 32, 502-505.
Discusses the failure of the community mental health movement to meet the needs of deinstitutionalized mental patients. Characteristics of the homeless mentally ill and their victimization on the streets and by the criminal justice system is described. The author argues for a more responsive clinical network to address the problems of the homeless mentally ill.

308. Gardner, J.R., & O'Hara, T.J. (1984). The homeless. Psychosocial Rehabilitation Journal, 8, 17-20.
The authors are concerned with the growing interest in "reinstitutionalization" of the chronically mentally ill. The authors discuss the implications of this position for practitioners of psychosocial rehabilitation and for the mentally disabled.

309. Garner, E.L. (1992). A study of health status and health attributions among homeless mentally ill persons: With and without substance abuse disorders. Dissertation Abstracts International, 53, 2044-B.
Significant differences in perceived health status and heath attributions between substance abusing and non-abusing homeless mentally ill persons suggest that non-abusing persons perceived their health in a more positive manner while substance abusers were more likely to see powerful others as controlling their health. Neither group made significant internal health attributions.

310. Gelberg, L., & Linn, L.S. (1989). Psychological distress among homeless adults. Journal of Nervous and Mental Disease, 177, 291-295.
Surveyed 529 homeless adults to determine factors associated with psychological distress and found that homeless respondents were more likely to report psychological distress than the general population. Level of distress was positively associated with unemployment, higher levels of cigarette and alcohol use, poorer health, fewer social supports, and perceived barriers to medical care.

311. Gelberg, L., Linn, L.S., & Leake, B.D. (1988). Mental health, alcohol and drug use, and criminal history among homeless adults. American Journal of Psychiatry, 145, 191-196.
As part of a community-based survey of 529 homeless adults, the authors analyzed factors associated with their use of mental health services. Homeless persons who had a previous psychiatric hospitalization were the least likely to sleep in an emergency shelter, had been homeless nearly twice as long as the rest of the sample, had the worst mental health status, used alcohol and drugs the most, and were the most involved in criminal activities. The majority had not made an outpatient mental health visit in 5 years. It is suggested that diverse systems of care are needed for homeless persons.

312. Gentry, B., & Ryan, M. (1990). Single room occupancy housing as residences for the homeless with mental illness. Adult Residential Care Journal, 4, 249-253.

313. Goering, P., Wasylenski, D.A., St.Onge, M., & Paduchak, D. (1992). Gender differences among clients of a case management program for the homeless. Hospital and Community Psychiatry, 43(2), 160-165.
Compared male and female clients of a case management program serving homeless shelter residents on indices of social functioning and psychopathology at the time of intake into the program and at a 9 month interval. No differences in psychopathology were found at intake or at follow-up. And although both men and women were socially isolated with limited social networks, women had higher levels of social skills, more supportive social networks, and better housing conditions than men at program intake, but these differences disappeared at follow-up.

314. Goldberg, M.M. (1972). The runaway Americans. Mental Hygiene, 56, 13-21.

315. Goldman, H.H., & Morrisey, J.P. (1985). The alchemy of mental health policy: Homelessness and the fourth cycle of reform. American Journal of Public Health, 75, 727-731.
The history of the mental health reform is viewed as a series of unrealistic, and yet, cyclical reform movements aimed at the prevention of chronic mental illness. The authors conclude that the present system of "community support" holds the most promise since it aims less at prevention than it does at providing services.

316. Gonzales, O.E. (1989). Coping with transition. Journal of Psychosocial Nursing and Mental Health Services, 27, 32-33.
Discusses the role that psychiatric nurses must play in assisting the homeless attain optimum health with emphasis on the use of crisis intervention and primary prevention strategies.

317. Goodman, L., Saxe, L., & Harvey, M. (1991). Homelessness as psychological trauma: Broadening perspectives. American Psychologist, 46, 1219-1225.

318. Greene, R.R. (1987). Case management: Helping the homeless mentally ill and persons with AIDS and their families. Silver Springs, MD: National Association of Social Workers.
Discusses case management for homeless mentally ill persons and AIDS victims

from the point of view of the NASW. The author includes recommendations to increase the number of professionally trained case managers.

319. Gullberg, P.L. (1989). A psychiatric nurse's role. Journal of Psychosocial Nursing and Mental Health Services, 27, 9-13.
Reviews pilot programs for the chronically mentally ill homeless established in Veteran's Administration hospitals and the role that psychiatric nurses may play in providing services to the homeless mentally ill. The author includes a discussion of the causes of homelessness, the proportion of those with severe emotional disorders, and obstacles to psychiatric care.

320. Haggard, L. (1983). The homeless mentally ill: A formidable challenge to policy makers. Princeton, NJ: Princeton University.

321. Hannapel, M., Calsyn, R.J., & Morse, G.A. (1989). Mental illness in homeless men: A comparison of shelter and street samples. Journal of Community Psychology, 17, 304-310.
Compared three groups of homeless men (N=152), either low-, moderate-, or high-frequency users of shelters on a battery of instruments assessing background characteristics, mental health status, and service needs. No significant differences were found for most measures. However, low-frequency respondents reported having been homeless longer and needing more social support than the other groups.

322. Harris, M., & Bachrach, L.L. (1990). Perspectives on homeless mentally ill women. Hospital and Community Psychiatry, 41, 253-254.

323. Herman, M., Galanter, M., & Lifschutz, H. (1991). Combined substance abuse and psychiatric disorders in homeless and domiciled patients. American Journal of Drug and Alcohol Abuse, 17, 415-422.
This study reports the prevalence of homelessness in a population of dually diagnosed psychiatric hospital patients. The most common substances abused in the sample were alcohol and crack cocaine. Forty-six% were homeless at the time of their admission into the hospital. The authors also note that many of the non-homeless patients in the study had also experienced homelessness and that self-help treatment programs might offer the best chance of recovery from substance abuse problems in this population.

324. Heston, L.L. (1992). Mending minds: A guide to the new psychiatry of depression, anxiety, and other serious mental disorders. New York: Freeman & Co.
Although this book provides primarily a general overview of the modern practice of psychiatry for the general reader, the author gives considerable attention to the social implications of psychiatric practice with the homeless mentally ill.

325. Hogg, L.I., Hall, J.N., & Marshall, M. (1990). Assessing people who are chronically mentally ill: New methods for new settings. Psychosocial Rehabilitation Journal, 13, 7-9.
The authors highlight the difficulties that are now emerging in understanding the changes in mental health care systems as a result of the move from hospital to

community and examine developments in formal assessment methods, particularly in relation to their usefulness in community settings.

326. Hope, M., & Young, J. (1984). From Back Wards to Back Alleys: Deinstitutionalization and the homeless. Urban and Social Change Review, 17, 7-11.

327. Hopper, K. (1988). More than passing strange: Homelessness and mental illness in New York City. American Ethnologist, 15, 155-167.
Discusses the impaired capacity model of homelessness, which assumes that homelessness is a result of individual deficit, and criticizes this approach on empirical, methodological and historical grounds. It is argued that individual failures to secure stable housing have their roots in broader developments in terms of housing, employment, household composition, and government assistance programs. It is the circumstances under which psychiatric disability is converted into social dispossession, and not deviance per se, that need to be investigated. Data for this article are derived from ethnographic research conducted in New York City and recent epidemiological literature.

328. Hopper, K. (1992). On not leaving it to the feuilletons. British Journal of Addiction, 87(1), 12-15.
This commentary discusses the negative implications of the transformation of the homeless and poor into scapegoats for society's ills and recommends analysis of the social structural causes of homelessness and in-community treatment of the homeless mentally ill.

329. Hopper, K., Baxter, E., & Cox, S. (1982). Not making it crazy: The young homeless patients in New York City. New Directions for Mental Health Services, 14, 33-42.
Focusing on the homeless of New York City, the authors argue that there has been a radical transformation in the homeless population, with a dramatic increase in the number of young and severely disabled street people. The authors suggest that the success of therapeutic efforts depends on the availability of safe and accessible shelter for the homeless.

330. Human Services Research Institute. (1985). Homelessness Needs Assessment Study: Findings and recommendations for the Massachusetts Department of Mental Health. Boston, MA: Massachusetts Department of Mental Health.
Describes the needs of long-term, seriously mentally ill homeless persons in Massachusetts. Four sample sub-populations were drawn: (1) homeless persons on the street, (2) homeless persons in shelters, (3) homeless persons in Department of Mental Health Inpatient Units, and (4) homeless clients in day programs. The findings suggest that the homeless and mentally ill sub-populations in Boston closely resembled those in other cities. Approximately 81 percent of the homeless were male, 48 percent were under 35 years of age, less than half were high school graduates, 89 percent were unemployed, and 45 percent had a previous psychiatric hospitalization. The study recommends strengthening case management services and improving housing and employment assistance services for the homeless and mentally ill.

331. Hyde, P.S. (1985). Homelessness in America: Public policy, public blame. Psychosocial Rehabilitation Journal, 8, 21-25.
Critiques the American Psychiatric Association task force report on the homeless mentally ill for over-emphasizing short-term solutions that may lead to poorly conceived public policies. Further, she objects to the notion that most of the homeless are mentally ill and points to factors other than deinstitutionalization that have led to the rise in the number of homeless in America.

332. Imperato, P.J. (1987). New York's homeless. New York State Journal of Medicine, 87, 1-3.
Examines the increase in the numbers of homeless persons in New York City, which is at least partially due to the growing number of mentally ill persons dumped on the streets without the benefit of adequate community care as had been the promise of the deinstitutionalization movement. The author recommends several long-term interventions to resolve the contemporary homelessness problem.

333. Jones, B. (Ed.) (1986). Treating the homeless: Urban psychiatry's challenge. Washington, DC: American Psychiatric Association Press.

334. Jones, R.E. (1983). Street people and psychiatry: An introduction. Hospital and Community Psychiatry, 34, 807-811.
The history of the homeless mentally ill in America is discussed, including the role of the media and reports in the scientific literature in alerting the public and the mental health profession to the plight of the homeless. The author also discusses the impact of deinstitutionalization on homelessness and the role of advocacy organizations on behalf of the homeless.

335. Kahn, M.W. (1985). An epidemiological study of mental illness and substance abuse among the homeless. Paper presented at the 93rd Annual Convention of the American Psychological Association, Los Angeles, August.

336. Kahn, M.W., Hannah, M., Hinkin, C., & Montgomery, C. (1987). Psychopathology on the streets: Psychological assessment of the homeless. Professional Psychology: Research and Practice, 18, 580-586.
Studied the incidence of psychological disorder and substance abuse in a homeless population and found that about one-third of the cases meet criterion for serious alcohol abuse, while about one-fourth met criterion for serious drug abuse. Further, severe psychopathology was indicated in about one-third of the cases. When considering overlap among the categories, over 50% of the population met criterion for severe psychological disorder.

337. Kahn, M.W., Hannah, M., Kirkland, S., & Lesnik, S. (1992). Substance misuse, emotional disturbance, and dual diagnosis in a meal-line population of mixed ethnicity. International Journal of the Addictions, 27(3), 317-330.
Studied the rates of substance misuse, affective disturbance, and dual diagnosis among a sample of adolescent and adult clients of a soup kitchen. Alcohol and drug use was reported in 93% of cases with severe misuse found in nearly 40% of cases. Severe mental illness was noted in over half of cases and nearly 30% were classified as having dual diagnoses. Three subtypes of S's were determined: (1) those with dual diagnoses, (2) those with severe substance abuse and

personality disorder, and (3) those with neither. Ethnicity did not appear to be associated with the 3 subtypes.

338. Kalifon, S.Z. (1989). Homelessness and mental illness: Who resorts to state hospitals? Human Organization, 48, 268-273.
Compared homeless (N=57) to non-homeless (N=257) persons interviewed upon admission to a state hospital and found that the two groups did not differ demographically or by psychiatric diagnosis. However, two distinct groups of homeless patients based on the reasons they sought hospitalization were identified. Type 1 homeless came to the hospital seeking shelter or to leave an unfavorable family or housing situation. Type 2 indicated that mental illness led them to seek hospitalization.

339. Kass, F., & Silver, J. (1990). Neuropsychiatry and the homeless. Journal of Neuropsychiatry and Clinical Neurosciences, 2, 15-19.

340. Kim, M.S. (1991). The relationship between risk factors and the mentally ill homeless: Predictors of homelessness in the chronically mentally ill. Dissertation Abstracts International, 53, 868-B.
Studied the prevalence of homelessness among discharges from an inpatient mental health facility, and found an 8.5% prevalence of homelessness in this population. Those found to become homeless within one-year of discharge were matched with non-homeless discharges to examine risk factors associated with homelessness. A combination of psychiatrically related assaultiveness, multiple suicide attempts, criminal activity, and lack of family support best predicted homelessness.

341. Kline, J., Harris, M., Bebout, R.R., & Drake, R.E. (1991). Contrasting integrated and linkage models of treatment for homeless, dually diagnosed adults. New Directions in Mental Health Services, Summer, 95-106.

342. Knight, K., & Christopher, M.A. (1990). A mobile clinic for the homeless and mentally ill: Meeting the needs of a target population. Caring, 9, 68-69, 75-77.

343. Koegel, P. (1992). Through a different lens: An anthropological perspective on the homeless mentally ill. Culture, Medicine and Psychiatry, 16(1), 1-22.
Criticizes the lack of understanding of homeless mentally ill persons that has resulted from researchers' preoccupation with pathology. Citing the lack of qualitative descriptions of homeless "lives in process," the failure to view homeless mentally ill individuals in the broader socioeconomic and situational contexts of their every day lives, the absence of longitudinal perspectives, and the over-reliance on self-reports, the author suggests using an anthropological perspective to increase meaningful understanding of the homeless mentally ill.

344. Koegel, P., Burnam, M.A., & Farr, R.K. (1988). The prevalence of specific psychiatric disorders among homeless individuals in the inner city of Los Angeles. Archives of General Psychiatry, 45, 1085-1092.
The authors compared a probability sample of homeless adults in Los Angeles to a household sample of adults to determine differences in the current and lifetime prevalence of mental disorder. Prevalence of every mental disorder, including substance abuse, was greater for the homeless group. Substance abuse was most

prevalent among older individuals and Native Americans, while schizophrenia was most prevalent among persons between 31 and 40 years old. Persons who had been homeless over long periods of time were characterized by high rates of both schizophrenia and substance abuse. Overall, 28% of the sample met DSM-III criteria for mental disorder.

345. Koshes, R.J. (1991). Psychiatric care of the homeless mentally ill: An opportunity for military psychiatry training. Military Medicine, 156, 121-126.
Reviews the phenomenon of homelessness in the US, particularly in Washington, D.C. Prevalence data on psychiatric illness in the homeless is presented,and the formation of a psychiatric service network to treat the homeless mentally ill is described. The development of an innovative training program in community psychiatry is described, focusing on issues inherent in understanding the work of the psychiatric resident in community-based training and service delivery. The relevance of this experience to military medicine involves training psychiatric residents to develop service-delivery schemes in times of rapidly expanding mental health needs, such as combat.

346. Lamb, H.R. (1980). Board and care home wanderers. Archives of General Psychiatry, 37, 135-137.

347. Lamb, H.R. (1982). Young adult chronic patients: The new drifters. Hospital and Community Psychiatry, 33, 465-468.

348. Lamb, H.R. (1984). Deinstitutionalization and the homeless mentally ill. Hospital and Community Psychiatry, 35, 899-907.
The failure of deinstitutionalization to provide structured living arrangements and adequate community treatment for the chronically mentally ill has led to the increasing number of mentally ill homeless. A vast expansion of community housing and revamping the mental health system might meet the needs of the chronically mentally ill for support and stability.

349. Lamb, H.R. (Ed.) (1984). The homeless mentally ill: A task force report. Washington, DC: American Psychiatric Association.
The 14 chapters of this book represent one of the first attempts to study the homeless mentally ill. This volume summarizes the problems of this population and makes several recommendations for improving programs to help them. Also included are a literature review, a discussion of deinstitutionalization and its impact on the homeless, and discussions of the medical, political, and legal aspects of homelessness.

350. Lamb, H.R. (1985). The homeless mentally ill: Some additional reflections. Psychosocial Rehabilitation Journal, 8, 38-41.

351. Lamb, H.R. (1988). The homeless mentally ill. In J.G. Howells (Ed.), Modern perspectives in psychosocial pathology. New York: Bruner/Mazel.

352. Lamb, H.R., & Grant, R.W. (1982). The mentally ill in an urban county jail. Archives of General Psychiatry, 39, 17-22.

353. Lamb, H.R., & Lamb, D. (1990). Factors contributing to homelessness among the chronically and severely mentally ill. Hospital and Community Psychiatry, 41, 301-305.

354. Lamb, H.R., & Talbott, J.A. (1986). The homeless mentally ill: The perspective of the American Psychiatric Association. Journal of the American Medical Association, 256, 498-501.

355. Leach, J. (1979). Providing for the destitute. In J.K. Wing & R. Olsen (Eds.), Community care for the mentally disabled. New York: Oxford University Press.

356. Leshner, A.I. (1992). A national agenda for helping homeless mentally ill people. Public Health Reports, 107, 352-355.

357. Leukefeld, C.G. (1991). Chronic mental illness. Health and Social Work, 16, 7-10.
Outlines three issues associated with the chronically ill population that have received public attention: 1) the connection between chronic mental illness and homelessness, 2) the complications of chemical abuse or dual diagnosis, and 3) the role that jails play in treating mentally ill people. These issues highlight dilemmas facing the general public, policymakers, and social work practitioners. Guiding principles for psychiatric services in jails are discussed.

358. Levine, I.S. (1983). Homelessness: Its implications for mental health policy and practice. Paper presented at the Annual Meetings of the American Psychological Association. Anaheim, CA, August.

359. Levine, I.S. (1984). Homelessness: Its implications for mental health policy and practice. Psychosocial Rehabilitation Journal, 8, 6-16.
Presents an overview of the problem of homelessness and discusses the relationship between deinstitutionalization and homelessness among the chronically mentally ill. A discussion of public and private sector responses to homelessness is also provided.

360. Levine, I.S., & Haggard, L.K. (1989). Homelessness as a public mental health problem. In D.A. Rochefort (Ed.), Handbook on mental health policy in the United States. Westport, CT: Greenwood Press.

361. Levine, I.S., & Kennedy, C. (1988). The homeless mentally ill: A consultation challenge. Consultation: An International Journal, 4, 52-63.
Presents an overview of homelessness in the U.S. and the unique service needs of the chronically mentally ill homeless. The authors discuss consultation efforts in three areas (e.g., shelter-based populations, street populations, and systems change) aimed at improving opportunities and services for the homeless mentally ill.

362. Levine, I.S., Lezak, A.D., & Goldman, H.H. (1986). Community support systems for the homeless mentally ill. New Directions for Mental Health Services, June, 27-42.
Discusses ways in which the federal Community Support Program's (CSS) can be adapted to meet the special needs of the homeless mentally ill. Before CSS's

can be implemented, major structural barriers to understanding the unique needs of the homeless mentally ill must be addressed.

363. Levine, I.S., & Rog, D.J. (1990). Mental health services for homeless mentally ill persons: Federal initiatives and current service trends. American Psychologist, 45, 963-968.
Describes the population of homeless single adults who suffer from severe mental illnesses targeted by National Institute of Mental Health research. Particular emphasis is given to two mental health programs established under the Stewart B. McKinney Homeless Assistance Act. Also discussed are proposed future directions for federal research and evaluation efforts in this area.

364. Levine, I.S., & Stockdill, J.W. (1986). Mentally ill and homeless: A national problem. In B. Jones (Ed.), Treating the homeless: Urban psychiatry's challenge. Washington, DC: American Psychiatric Association Press.
Discusses the changing nature of the homeless population and the unique needs and problems of the homeless mentally ill. The authors report that national studies indicate that between 22 and 66 per cent of the homeless population suffer from some sort of mental illness. These persons suffer when mental health programs do not reach out to those on the streets and the available shelters do not provide mental health services. The homeless mentally ill not only must contend with economic hardship and lack of low-income housing, but also with vulnerability to stress and difficulties in obtaining access to needed services.

365. Linhorst, D.M. (1990). A redefinition of the problem of homelessness among persons with a chronic mental illness. Journal of Sociology and Social Welfare, 17, 43-56.

366. Lipton, F.R., & Micheels, P. (1983) Down and out in New York: The homeless patient. Paper presented at the Annual Meeting of the American Psychiatric Association, New York.

367. Lipton, F.R., Nutt, S., & Sabatini, A. (1988). Housing the homeless mentally ill: A longitudinal study of a treatment approach. Hospital and Community Psychiatry, 39(1), 40-45.
Studied 49 homeless chronic mentally ill patients, who were randomly assigned to one of two groups. One group was placed in an experimental residential treatment program following discharge, and the other group received standard post-discharge care. Subjects were interviewed every four months during the year as well as at index hospitalization and discharge. The authors found that, compared with the control group, the subjects in the residential treatment program spent significantly more nights in adequate shelter, spent fewer nights in hospitals or undomiciled, and were more satisfied with and committed to their living arrangements.

368. Lipton, F.R., & Sabatini, A. (1984). Constructive support systems for homeless chronic patients. In R. Lamb (Ed.), The homeless mentally ill. Washington, DC: American Psychiatric Association.

369. Lipton, F.R., Sabatini, A., & Katz, S. (1983). Down and out in the city: The homeless mentally ill. Hospital and Community Psychiatry, 34, 818-821.

Studied of 100 homeless persons treated in a psychiatric hospital's emergency room and found that 72% were diagnosed with schizophrenia and another 13% were diagnosed with personality disorders.

370. Louks, J.L., & Smith, J.R. (1988). Homeless: Axis I disorders. Hospital and Community Psychiatry, 39, 670-671.

371. Lovell, A.M., & Barrow, S.M. (1981). Psychiatric disability and homelessness: A look at Manhattan's upper west side. Paper presented at the Conference on the Community Support Population: Designing Alternatives in Uncertain Environments, Syracuse, NY, November.

372. Luchins, A.S. (1986). What should be done about the homeless mentally ill? Clinical Psychologist, 39, 54.

373. Lurigio, A., & Lewis, D. (1989). Worlds that fail: A longitudinal study of urban mental patients. Journal of Social Issues, 45, 79-90.

374. McQuistion, H.L., D'Ercole, A., & Kopelson, E. (1991). Urban street outreach: using clinical principles to steer the system. New Directions in Mental Health Services, Winter, 17-27.

375. Marcos, L.R. (1989). Media power and public mental health policy. American Journal of Psychiatry, 146, 1185-1189.
Uses the highly publicized New York City policy of involuntary hospitalization of the homeless mentally ill to illustrate the functions of the news media and their influence on mental health policymaking and suggests strategies for effective interactions with the news media.

376. Marcos, L.R. (1989). Mentally ill and homeless: The plight of freedom. Issues in Ego Psychology, 12, 20-28.

377. Marcos, L.R. (1990). Political psychiatry: The New York City homeless mentally ill initiative. Administration and Policy in Mental Health, 18, 81-90.
Illustrates the concept of political psychiatry by describing a recent New York City policy to involuntarily remove from the streets and hospitalize mentally ill homeless people. Emphasis is on the need for mental health professionals to effectively interact with the political process to influence government policies that constantly shape the delivery of psychiatric care.

378. Marcos, L.R., & Cohen, N.L. (1986). Taking the suspected mentally ill off the streets to public general hospitals. New England Journal of Medicine, 315, 1158-1161.
Discusses issues involved in involuntary treatment and hospitalization of the homeless mentally ill. A historical overview of involuntary treatment and statistics for New York City are included.

379. Marcos, L.R., Cohen, N.L., Nardacci, D., & Brittain, J. (1990). Psychiatry takes to the streets: The New York City initiative for the homeless mentally ill. American Journal of Psychiatry, 147, 1557-1561.
Discusses New York City's program to remove seriously mentally ill homeless

people from the streets to a public hospital, and a report on the 298 patients (aged 16-80) hospitalized during the first year of the program. Most subjects were male, single, from outside of New York City, previously admitted to a psychiatric hospital, and homeless for more than one year. Most also suffered from schizophrenia and had additional medical diagnoses. Follow up contact two years after initiation of the program revealed that 55% of the subjects either were living in a community setting or were under institutional care.

380. Martin, M.A. (1990). The homeless mentally ill and community-based care: Changing a mindset. Special Issue: The homeless mentally ill. Community Mental Health Journal, 26, 435-447.
Discusses issues and assumptions that influence the development of a comprehensive system of community-based care for the homeless mentally ill. A task force created to reconceptualize a comprehensive system of care for the homeless mentally ill is described. It includes full participation from government, the nonprofit community, and the private sector.

381. Martin, M.A., & Nayowith, S.A. (1988). Creating community: Groupwork to develop social support networks with homeless mentally ill. Social Work With Groups, 11, 79-93.
Describes the creation of social networks through social group work with homeless mentally ill men and women in shelters, drop-in centers, and SRO hotels in New York City and how such networks can contribute to the effective maintenance of the homeless mentally ill in the community.

382. Mechanic, D., & Rochefort, D.A. (1992). A policy of inclusion for the mentally ill. Health Affairs, 11, 128-150.

383. Mellen, V. (1985). A response to the American Psychiatric Association report on the homeless mentally ill. Psychosocial Rehabilitation Journal, 8, 3-10.
The author generally agrees with the major task force report, but warns that many homeless people could be needlessly reinstitutionalized if a careful definition of "treatment resistance" is not made.

384. Michaels, D., Zoloth, S.R., Alcabes, P. & Braslow, C.A. (1992).Homelessness and indicators of mental illness among inmates in New York City's correctional system. Hospital and Community Psychiatry, 43(2), 150-155.
The prevalence of homelessless among detainees in the New York City correctional system was assessed is 3 samples of male inmates. One quarter to one third of each sample reported being homeless at some time in the 2 months prior to their arrest. Further, 20% were found to have been homeless the night before their arrest, and nearly twice as many of those who reported having been homeless in the past 3 years were positive to at least one mental health screening question than those who had not been homeless.

385. Miller, W.H., Resnick, M.P., Williams, M.H., & Bloom, J.D. (1990). The pregnant psychiatric inpatient: A missed opportunity. General Hospital Psychiatry, 12, 373-378.

386. Morrison, J. (1989). Correlations between definitions of the homeless mentally ill population. Hospital and Community Psychiatry, 40, 952-954.

Categorized 100 short-stay psychiatric patients as either not homeless or as meeting 1 of six different definitions of homelessness. Overall, 42% had a diagnosis of schizophrenia and 36% had a diagnosis of affective disorder. The percentage of persons defined as homeless ranged from 22% (90 or more days on the street) to 57% (homeless the previous night) depending on the definition of homelessness employed. Implications of differing definitions of homelessness on clinical practice are discussed.

387. Morrissey, J.P., & Dennis, D.L. (1986). NIMH-funded research concerning homeless mentally ill persons: Implications for policy and practice. Washington, DC: Alcohol, Drug Abuse and Mental Health Administration.
Summarizes the proceedings of a meeting of 10 principal investigators of NIMH-funded research programs studying the homeless mentally ill, as well as, many others from various private and public agencies. Recommendations for reforms in policy and practice included a need for multiple interventions and a range of housing options to help the homeless mentally ill.

388. Morrissey, J.P., & Levine, I.S. (1987). Researchers discuss latest findings, examine needs of homeless mentally ill persons. Hospital and Community Psychiatry, 38, 811-812.
Summarizes the proceedings of a meeting of NIMH researchers involved in studying the prevalence of mental illness among the homeless.

389. Morse, G.A., & Calsyn, R.J. (1985-1986). Mentally disturbed homeless people in St. Louis: Needy, willing, but underserved. International Journal of Mental Health, 14, 74-94.
Studied the mental health service needs of 248 homeless adults in St. Louis, Missouri and found that 25% of participants had a history of psychiatric hospitalizations. About half reported significant psychiatric symptoms according to the Brief Symptom Inventory (BSI) and over one-third appeared to have significant alcohol abuse problems. The authors make recommendations concerning the service needs of the homeless population.

390. Mossman, D., & Perlin, M.L. (1992). Psychiatry and the homeless mentally ill: a reply to Dr. Lamb. American Journal of Psychiatry, 149, 951-957.

391. Mowbray, C.T., Johnson, V.S., & Solarz, A. (1987). Homelessness in a state hospital population. Hospital and Community Psychiatry, 38, 880-882.
Reports findings of a study of 388 admissions to a state mental hospital conducted to determine the characteristics and service needs of the homeless mentally ill population.

392. Mowbray, C.T., Johnson, V.S., Solarz, A., Phillips-Smith, E., & Coombs, C.J. (1985). Mental health and homelessness in Detroit: A research study. Lansing, MI: Michigan Department of Mental Health.
Findings from five studies of homeless mentally ill persons in Detroit are reported. The studies included: (1) a survey of shelter operators, (2) observations and interviews at soup kitchens, (3) a survey of admissions to a state hospital, (4) interviews with homeless patients at a state hospital, and (5) physical and mental health screenings at emergency shelters. The authors conclude that the typical stereotypes of homeless persons are inaccurate, that most homeless people have

multiple health, mental health, social and employment problems, that interventions must address the multiplicity of these problems, and that future research should be more focused.

393. Mowbray, C.T., Solarz, A., Combs, C., & Johnson, V.S. (1986). Mental illness and homelessness in Detroit: Research and case studies. Psychosocial Rehabilitation Journal, 10, 5-13.
Findings of interviews with 72 residents of emergency shelters for the homeless suggest that the homeless are a diverse population with multiple health and mental health problems, as well as, problems with vocational and interpersonal functioning.

394. Moxley, D.P., & Freddolino, P.P. (1991). Needs of homeless people coping with psychiatric problems: Findings from an innovative advocacy project. Health and Social Work, 16, 19-26.

395. Mulkern, V., Bradley, V.J., Spence, R., Allein, S., & Oldham, J.E. (1985). Homelessness needs assessment study: Findings and recommendations for the Massachusetts Department of Mental Health. Boston, MA: Massachusetts Department of Mental Health.

396. Nakdimen, K.A. (1990). Multiple personality. Hospital and Community Psychiatry, 41, 566-567.

397. National Association of State Mental Health Program Directors. (1984). NASMHPD's position paper on homeless people. Washington, DC.
This summary of NASMHPD's opinions and recommendations concerning the homeless mentally ill discusses several approaches state mental health departments can take to address the problem of the homeless mentally ill. The authors agree that mental health professionals must be a part of an integrated effort with other health and human service providers to assess the extent of the homeless problem and to develop appropriate policies, programs and interventions geared towards long-term solutions.

398. National Association of State Mental Health Program Directors (1985). State mental health agency role in meeting the problems of homeless people. Washington, DC: NASMHPD.
Describes the role of state mental health agencies in meeting the needs of the homeless and suggests that state mental health agencies participate in low-cost housing task forces, provide service coordination, and encourage and support improved research and training. The report concludes that the role of the state mental health agency is to ensure that the chronically mentally ill are given adequate housing opportunities and that all homeless persons have access to mental health services.

399. National Institute of Mental Health. (1988). Synopses of NIMH-funded mental health services demonstration projects for the homeless mentally ill. Rockville, MD.

400. National Mental Health Association. (1986). The role of community foundations in meeting the needs of homeless individuals with mental illnesses. Alexandria,

VA.
This summary of the proceedings of NMHA sponsored conference on the homeless mentally ill discusses the impact of the fragmentation of mental health, housing, and other human services on the homeless mentally ill and recommends a 3-part course of action for community foundations in addressing the needs of the homeless mentally ill. First, they should provide community leadership by gathering and distributing information, generate private resources and channel them to service providers, offer consultation and focus on long-term systemic change. Second, they should focus on strengthening the infrastructure of available services by striving to reduce legal and regulatory barriers, and by building constituencies. Finally, community foundations should support collaborative efforts with each other as well as with local coalitions, advocacy groups, service providers, public agencies and the media.

401. National Mental Health Association Task Force. (1985). Mentally ill people who are homeless: Recommendations for action by MHA affiliates. Rosslyn, VA.
Seven recommendations are made for Mental Health Association affiliates to resolve the problems of the homeless mentally ill, including advocating comprehensive, community wide interventions, recognizing that housing an income support are integral elements in any solution, and emphasizing community-based services rather than in-hospital treatment.

402. Nores, J.M., & Dalayeun, J. (1987). Homelessness in Paris. New York State Journal of Medicine, 87, 411-415.
The authors compare the role of unemployment, alcoholism, and mental illness in homeless persons in New York City and in Paris.

403. Oroomiefar, G. (1992). The homeless mentally ill: A study of a public mental health system. Dissertation Abstracts International, 53, 962-A.
Examined differences between homeless and non-homeless clients of a county mental health system. Homeless clients were more likely to be referred by police or courts, to be admitted involuntarily, and to present with thought disorders than non-homeless clients. Services also differed between the 2 groups, with homeless clients typified by case management services and non-homeless clients typified by more treatment-oriented services. Recommendations for improving mental health policy making are provided.

404. Padgett, D., Struening, E.L., & Andrews, H. (1990). Factors affecting the use of medical, mental health, alcohol, and drug treatment services by homeless adults. Medical Care, 28, 805-821.

405. Paterson, A., & Craig, R.T. (1985). The homeless mentally ill: No longer out of sight and out of mind. State Legislative Report, 10, 1-20.

406. Pepper, B., & Ryglewicz, H. (1982). Testimony for the neglected: The mentally ill in the post-deinstitutionalized age. American Journal of Orthopsychiatry, 52, 390-393.

407. Perr, I.N. (1985). The malignant neglect of the mentally ill street people. American Journal of Psychiatry, 142, 885-886.
Uses the case of a 41 year old mentally ill homeless woman to demonstrate the

failure of policies regarding involuntary hospitalization of the chronically mentally ill. The author regards the problem of the homeless mentally ill to be a result of deinstitutionalization and its over-reliance on social theories of mental disorder.

408. Piliavin, I., Westerfelt, H., & Elliott, E. (1989). Estimating mental illness among the homeless: The effects of choice-based sampling. Social Problems, 36, 525-531.

409. Priest, R.G. (1978). The epidemiology of mental illness: Illustrations from the single homeless population, Psychiatric Journal of the University of Ottawa, 3, 27-32.
Epidemiological studies have consistently shown high rates of mental illness (particularly schizophrenia) in inner city and homeless populations. An excess of psychiatric morbidity among the homeless was demonstrated in findings from a study of 79 homeless persons in Edinborough, Scotland and 50 homeless persons in Chicago, Illinois.

410. Reich, R., & Seigal, L. (1978). The emergence of the bowery as a psychiatric dumping ground. Psychiatric Quarterly, 50, 191-201.

411. Rhoden, N.K. (1982). The limits of liberty: Deinstitutionalization, homelessness, and Libertarian theory. Emory Law Journal, 31, 375-440.

412. Rife, J.C., First, R.J., Greenlee, R.W., & Miller, L.D. (1991). Case management with homeless mentally ill people. Health and Social Work, 16, 58-67.

413. Robertson, M.J. (1986). General welfare assistance: Barriers to mentally disabled homeless adults. Paper presented at the 114th Annual Meeting of the American Public Health Association, Las Vegas, Nevada, September.

414. Robertson, M.J. (1986). Mental disorder among homeless persons in the United States: An overview of recent empirical literature. Administration in Mental Health, 14, 14-27.
Reviews research literature on homelessness published after 1974. High rates of psychiatric disorder, psychological distress, and psychiatric hospitalization were found throughout the literature. The author concludes that the lack of reliable estimates of the prevalence of mental disorder among the homeless results from the lack of standardized methodologies and inconsistent findings across studies.

415. Robertson, M.J. (1989). The prevalence of mental disorder among the homeless: A review of the empirical literature. In R. Jahiel (Ed.), Homelessness: A prevention-oriented approach. Baltimore, MD: Johns Hopkins University Press. Discusses the prevalence and distribution of mental disorder among the homeless, including critiques of indicators of psychiatric disorders and research methods used.

416. Rog, D. (1988). Engaging homeless persons with mental illness into treatment. Alexandria, VA: National Mental Health Association.

417. Romanoski, A.J., Nestadt, G., Ross, A., Fischer, P.J., & Breakey, W.R. (1988). Alcoholism and psychiatric comorbidity in the homeless: The Baltimore study. Paper presented at the 116th Annual Meeting of the American Public Health Association, Boston, November.
Reports the findings of a study that attempted to use standardized and reliable clinical examinations performed by psychiatrists in order to diagnose specific psychiatric conditions and make recommendations for specific psychiatric treatments among an unselected sample of homeless persons in missions, shelters and jails.

418. Rosenfeld, S. (1991). Homelessness and rehospitalization: The importance of housing for the chronic mentally ill. Journal of Community Psychology, 19, 60-69.

419. Rosnow, M., Shaw, T., & Stapleton-Concord, D. (1985). Listening to the homeless: A study of mentally ill persons in Milwaukee. Milwaukee, WI: Human Services Triangle, Inc.
Conducted in-depth interviews with 338 persons living in shelters or on the streets in Milwaukee in order to examine the social and demographic characteristics of the homeless population and to assess the needs of the seriously mentally ill homeless. Of those interviewed, 40% were considered mentally ill, while 24% had alcohol or drug abuse problems. Forty-two percent had at least one previous hospitalization for mental illness or alcohol/drug abuse. Recommendations are offered to meet the needs of the mentally ill homeless and to prevent further homelessness among the mentally ill.

420. Roth, D., Bean, G.J., & Hyde, P.S. (1986). Homelessness and mental health policy: Developing an appropriate role for the 1980's. Community Mental Health Journal, 22, 203-214.
Based on 979 interviews with rural and urban homeless in Ohio, the authors conclude that, although the rate of psychiatric disorder was relatively low, the homeless mentally ill were only marginally served by the mental health system. Implications for community mental health policy makers and program designers are discussed.

421. Sacks, J.M., Phillips, J., & Cappelletty, G. (1987). Characteristics of the homeless mentally disordered population in Fresno County. Community Mental Health Journal, 23, 114-119.
Results of interviews with 61 homeless adults conducted to assess the need for mental health programs for the homeless found that nearly 80% met DSM III criteria for psychiatric diagnosis. Further, 34% were found to be severely impaired and 33% were found to be moderately impaired. Participants reported they would prefer to work with counselors rather than psychiatrists, psychologists or social workers, and preferred service locations in or near shelters, rather that in hospital or clinic settings.

422. Sangueneti, V.R., & Brooks, M.O. (1992). Factors related to emergency commitment of chronic mentally ill patients who are substance abusers. Hospital and Community Psychiatry, 43(3), 237-241.
Of 247 chronic mentally ill patients committed for emergency involuntary hospitalization, those who tested positive for at least one psychoactive substance

at admission were found to be more likely to live alone, to be homeless, to have made threats, and to have a diagnosis of organic disorder or substance abuse. Those who tested negative were more likely to being living in a supervised setting, to have been committed for assaults or suicidal behavior, and to have a diagnosis of schizophrenia.

423. Santiago, J.M., Bachrach, L.L., Berren, M.R., & Hannah, M.T. (1988). Defining the homeless mentally ill: a methodological note. Hospital and Community Psychiatry, 39, 1100-1102.
Categorized 106 adults referred for psychiatric screening as homeless (e.g., living on the street or in a shelter). An additional 53 persons were defined as homeless when a time dimension was included (e.g., had lived on the street or in a shelter in the past 3 months). Implications of findings for research with homeless populations are discussed.

424. Searight, H.R., & Searight, P.R. (1988). The homeless mentally ill: Overview, policy implications, and adult foster care as a neglected resource. Adult Foster Care Journal, 2, 235-259.
Based on a review of the literature, which suggests that about 30% of the homeless have been psychiatric inpatients, while about 80% exhibit serious mental health impairment, the authors conclude that the primary response to the problem of homelessness, the provision of emergency, short-term shelter is inadequate. The use of adult foster care and other types of long-term residential facilities is discussed.

425. Seeger, C. (1990). Reflections on working with the homeless. New Directions for Mental Health Services, 46, 47-55.

426. Segal, S.P., & Baumohl, J. (1980). Engaging the disengaged: Proposals on madness and vagrancy. Social Work, 25, 358-365.

427. Segal, S.P., Baumohl, J., & Johnson, E. (1977). Falling through the cracks: Mental disorder and social margin in a young vagrant population. Social Problems, 24, 387-400.

428. Shaner, A. (1989). Asylums, asphalt, and ethics. Hospital and Community Psychiatry, 40, 785-786.
Discusses the ethical dilemmas associated with providing emergency psychiatric treatment for homeless mentally ill persons. The author argues that choice of treatment is essentially an ethical decision, rather than a decision based on technical medical issues alone.

429. Shanks, N.J. (1989). Previously diagnosed psychiatric illness among inhabitants of common lodging houses. Journal of Epidemiology and Community Health, 43, 375-379.

430. Shore, M.F. (1989). The perversion of research and the paralysis of action. American Journal of Orthopsychiatry, 59, 482.

431. Simons, R.L., Whitbeck, L.B., & Bales, A. (1989). Life on the streets: Victimization and psychological distress among the adult homeless. Journal of Interpersonal Violence, 4, 482-501.

432. Snow, D.A., Baker, S.G., & Anderson, L. (1988). On the precariousness of measuring insanity in insane contexts. Social Problems, 35, 192-196.
This article is a reply to James D. Wright's (1988) comment on the authors' previous paper (Snow, Baker, Anderson & Martin, 1986) which questions the typification of homeless persons as mentally ill. The authors dispute Wright's assertion that the "true" incidence of mental illness in the homeless population is 2 to 3 times higher than what the authors found.

433. Snow, D.A., Baker, S.G., Anderson, L. & Martin, M. (1986). The myth of pervasive mental illness among the homeless. Social Problems, 33, 407-423.
Data presented from a field study of 911 unattached homeless persons contradicts the notion that homelessness is primarily a result of deinstitutionalization. The authors suggest that this view results from medicalization of the homelessness problem, misplaced emphasis on the causal role of deinstitutionalization, the greater visibility of the homeless mentally ill, and conceptual and methodological shortcomings research assessing the mental status homeless persons. The authors conclude that the most common face on the street is not of the mentally ill, but of one enmeshed in a cycle of low-paying, dead-end jobs that fail to provide the means to get off and remain off the streets.

434. Solarz, A., & Mowbray, C. (1985). An examination of physical and mental health problems of the homeless. Paper presented at the 113th Annual Meeting of the American Public Health Association, Washington, DC.

435. Solomon, P.L., Draine, J.N., Marchenko, M.O., & Meyerson, A.T. (1992). Homelessness in a mentally ill urban jail population. Hospital and Community Psychiatry, 43(2), 169-171.
A study of homelessness among mentally ill detainees found that nearly one third had been homeless at the time of detention and that persons with the most severe psychiatric disabilities were at greater risk for homelessness.

436. Spaniol, L., & Zipple, A. (1985). NIMH-supported research on the mentally ill who are homeless: A second meeting of researchers sponsored by the Division of Education and Service Systems Liaison, National Institute of Mental Health. Rockville, MD: NIMH.
This report summarizes the research design, status and current findings of ten NIMH-supported research projects concerning the homeless mentally ill. This report also includes a discussion of the methodological, funding, and political barriers to research on the homeless mentally ill and presents recommendations to NIMH on how to encourage research with this population.

437. Spaniol, L., & Zipple, A.M. (1986). NIMH supported research on the mentally ill who are homeless. Boston, MA: Boston University Sargent College of Allied Health Professions Center for Psychiatric Rehabilitation.

438. Spitzer, R., Cohen, G., & Miller, J.D. (1969). The psychiatric status of 100 men on skid row. International Journal of Social Psychiatry, 15, 230-234.

439. Stark, L.R. (1985-1986). Stranger in a strange land: The chronically mentally ill homeless. International Journal of Mental Health, 14, 95-111.
Based on 4 case histories, the author discusses the self-discipline and street-knowledge that is necessary for homeless mentally ill women to survive on the streets. The author believes that many could adapt to a structured environment in a supervised setting.

440. Surber, R.W., Dwyer, E., Ryan, K.J., Goldfinger, S.M., & Kelly, J. (1988). Medical and psychiatric needs of the homeless: A preliminary response. Social Work, 33, 116-119.
Reports findings from two independent studies conducted by the San Francisco Department of Public Health to assess the medical and psychiatric needs of the homeless in San Francisco. The authors report on a program designed to meet the needs of the homeless population and advocate further programmatic and policy considerations to respond to the problem of homelessness.

441. Susnick, L.C. (1992). Stigma, fear, and dreams: An interview-observation study of persons who are homeless and mentally ill and their service providers. Dissertation Abstracts International, 53, 3397-B.

442. Susser, E., Conover, S., & Struening, E.L. (1990). Mental illness in the homeless: Problems of epidemiologic method in surveys of the 1980s. Special Issue: The homeless mentally ill. Community Mental Health Journal, 26, 391-414.
Reviews surveys of mental illness in homeless adults in the 1980s to address problematic aspects of this research, including sampling, use of comparison groups, and measures of mental health status. Sampling in only a few of many shelters in a given area, with no attempt to estimate differences between homeless persons who use shelters and those who do not, is a practice that should be avoided. Comparison with community samples from other studies that bear no correspondence to the homeless sample is not recommended. Diagnostic interviews without evidence of reliability and validity also should be avoided.

443. Susser, E., Goldfinger, S., & White, A. (1990). Some clinical approaches to the homeless mentally ill. Special Issue: The homeless mentally ill. Community Mental Health Journal, 26, 463-480.

444. Susser, E.S., Lin, S.P., & Conover, S.A. (1991). Risk factors for homelessness among patients admitted to a state mental hospital. American Journal of Psychiatry, 148, 1659-1664.

445. Susser, E.S., Lin, S.P., Conover, S.A., & Struening, E.L. (1991). Childhood antecedents of homelessness in psychiatric patients. American Journal of Psychiatry, 148, 1026-1030.

446. Susser, E.S., & Struening, E.L. (1990). Diagnosis and screening for psychotic disorders in a study of the homeless. Schizophrenia Bulletin, 16, 133-145.

447. Susser, E., Struening, E.L., & Conover, S. (1989). Psychiatric problems in homeless men: Lifetime psychosis, substance use, and current distress in new arrivals at New York City shelters. Archives of General Psychiatry, 46, 845-

850.
Findings of a study of 177 male first-time users of homeless shelters indicate that length of time homeless was associated with higher levels of psychopathology on several measures of psychiatric distress and substance abuse.

448. Sweeney, D., Garrison, J., & Dabrowski, D. (1982). Mapping urban hotels: Life space of the chronic mental patient. Journal of Psychosocial Nursing and Mental Health Services, 20, 9-14.

449. Szasz, T. (1989). Madness and homelessness. Issues in Ego Psychology, 12, 13-19.

450. Talbott, J.A. (1983). The shame of the cities. Hospital and Community Psychiatry, 34, 773.

451. Talbott, J.A. (1984). Statement of the American Psychiatric Association on the nation's homeless mentally ill. Washington, DC: U.S. Senate, December.
In his testimony before the Senate Special Committee on Aging, the author argues that the homeless mentally ill are a distinct subpopulation of homeless with special needs. He suggests developing a comprehensive support system for the chronically mentally ill based on recommendations of the APA Task Force on the Homeless. Talbott concludes by asking the federal government to take a leadership role in solving the problems of the homeless mentally ill.

452. Talbott, J.A., & Lamb, H.R. (1987). The homeless mentally ill. Archives of Psychiatric Nursing, 1, 379-384.

453. Tessler, R.C. & Dennis, D.L. (1989). A synthesis of NIMH-funded research concerning persons who are homeless and mentally ill. Amherst, MA: University of Massachusetts.
Reviews research conducted by 10 groups awarded grants by NIMH to study the relationship between homelessness and mental illness. The authors summarize findings of these studies, critique methods employed, and discuss implications for future research.

454. Toomey, B., First, R., Rife, J., & Belcher, J. (1989). Evaluating community care for homeless mentally ill people. Social Work Research and Abstracts, 25, 21-26.

455. Toro, P.A., & Wall, D.D. (1991). Research on homeless persons: Diagnostic comparisons and practice implications. Professional Psychology: Research and Practice, 22, 479-488.

456. Torrey, E.F. (1988). Nowhere to go: The tragic odyssey of the homeless mentally ill. New York City: Harper & Row.

457. Towber, R., & Ladner, S. (1985). Psychiatric indication and alcohol abuse among public shelter clients. Paper presented at MSIS Ninth Annual Users' Conference, November.

458. Trotter, R. (1983). <u>Alcohol, drug abuse, and mental health problems of the homeless: Proceedings of a roundtable</u>. Rockville, MD: Alcohol, Drug Abuse and Mental Health Administration.

459. U.S. Department of Health and Human Services, Public Health Service, Alcohol, Drug Abuse, and Mental Health Administration. (1987). <u>The homeless mentally ill: Reports available from the National Institute of Mental Health</u>. Rockville, MD: DHHS
This annotated bibliography includes abstracts of 49 papers and reports available from NIMH that address the problem of the homeless mentally ill. The citations are grouped into 3 sections: (1) policy, (2) research, and (3) services.

460. U.S. General Accounting Office. (1988). <u>Homeless mentally ill: Problems and options in estimating numbers and trends</u>. Washington, DC.
Examines the soundness of current estimates of the numbers of homeless mentally ill persons in the U.S. Strategies for arriving at better estimates are suggested.

461. Vicic, W. (1986). Sum of the parts: A memory of a homeless man. <u>Psychotherapy Patient</u>, <u>2</u>, 147-152.
Discusses the case of a homeless man in a New York City shelter whose medical records and interactions with medical and psychiatric staff reveal the inadequacies of medical and psychiatric interventions with the homeless, as well as, the short lived benefits of meaningful human interactions with homeless men.

462. Westermeyer, J. (1988). Resuming social approaches to psychiatric disorder: A critical contemporary need. <u>Journal of Nervous and Mental Disease</u>, <u>176</u>, 703-706.
The homeless mentally ill are used as one of three examples of the need for social approaches to psychiatric disorder. Such a perspective considers the demographic, geographic, and sociopolitical aspects of psychiatric disorder.

463. Whitehead, T. (1990). Closure of psychiatric hospitals. <u>Lancet</u>, <u>335</u>, 172-173.

464. Whitley, M.P., Osborne, O.H., Godfrey, M.A., & Johnston, K. (1985). A point prevalence study of alcoholism and mental illness among downtown migrants. <u>Social Science and Medicine</u>, <u>20</u>, 579-583.
Compared residents of an urban emergency shelter and an SRO hotel on demographic characteristics, physical and mental health status, and alcohol abuse. Few differences were found between the two groups.

465. Windle, C. (1991). What mental health services research does NIMH support? <u>Administration and Policy in Mental Health</u>, <u>18</u>, 199-203.
Summarizes the state of knowledge in several areas of the National Institute of Mental Health (NIMH) supported services research (SR). Currently, SR focuses on persons with severe mental illness, mentally ill homeless persons, mentally ill persons with human immunodeficiency virus (HIV) infection, children and adolescents, and minorities. The topic areas discussed include clinical level SR, systems level SR, research on mental health services in primary health care, and research in mental health economics.

466. Worley, N.K., Drago, L., & Hadley, T. (1990). Improving the physical health-mental health interface for the chronically mentally ill: Could nurse case managers make a difference? Archives of Psychiatric Nursing, 4, 108-113.

467. Wright, J.D. (1988). The mentally ill homeless: What is myth and what is fact. Social Problems, 35, 182-191.
Although the rate of mental illness in the homeless population has been exaggerated, Snow, Baker, Anderson and Martin's (1986) assertion that only 10 to 15 per cent of the homeless are mentally ill is too low. The author suggests that a more accurate "best estimate" is that about one-third of the homeless are mentally ill.

468. Wyatt, R.J., & DeRenzo, E.G. (1986). Scienceless to homeless. Science, 234, 1309.
The homelessness crisis is viewed as a result of the deinstitutionalization of the mentally ill. The authors criticize proponents of the deinstitutionalization movement for performing no large scale efficacy trials and for not monitoring adverse consequences. The authors also argue for well-designed and replicated controlled experiments to provide data for the initiation of welfare system change.

469. Zozus, R.Y., & Zax, M. (1991). Perceptions of childhood: exploring possible etiological factors in homelessness. Hospital and Community Psychiatry, 42, 535-537.

3

Alcohol and Drug Abuse

470. Alcohol Drug Abuse and Mental Health Administration. (1983). Alcohol, drug abuse and mental health problems of the homeless: Proceedings of a round table. Washington, DC: ADAMHA.

471. Anderson,S.C. (1987). Alcoholic women on skid row. Social Work, 32, 362-365.
Examined twenty skid-row women in alcoholism treatment in Portland, Oregon. Most of the women had histories of problem drinking and had been in treatment for alcoholism on more that one occasion. Most had been married and had children. Further, despite being homeless, the majority of these women maintained contact with friends and relatives.

472. Ashley, M.J., Olin, J.S., le Riche, W.H., Kornaczewski, A., Schmidt, W., & Rankin, J.G. (1976). Skid row alcoholism: A distinct sociomedical entity. Archives of Internal Medicine, 136, 272-278.

473. Bahr, H.M. (1969). Lifetime affiliation patterns of early- and late-onset heavy drinkers on skid row. Quarterly Journal of Studies on Alcohol, 30, 645-656.

474. Baumohl, J. (Ed.) (1987). Research agenda: The homeless population with alcohol problems. Rockville, MD: National Institute on Alcohol Abuse and Alcoholism.
Reports on six papers presented at a meeting to review current research on the homeless with alcohol problems sponsored by the National Institute on Alcohol Abuse and Alcoholism. Also discusses: (1) the relationship between research and service delivery, (2) pending legislation, (3) relevant current research supported by NIAAA, (4) methodological issues in research with homeless persons with alcohol problems, and (5) mechanisms for implementing research programs.

475. Bennett, R.W., Weiss, H.L., & West, B.R. (1990). Alameda County Department of Alcohol and Drug Programs Comprehensive Homeless Alcohol

Recovery Services (CHARS). Special Issue: Treating alcoholism and drug abuse among homeless men and women: Nine community demonstration grants. Alcoholism Treatment Quarterly, 7, 111-128.
Describes a federally funded community demonstration project for homeless individuals with alcohol and drug problems in Oakland, California. System components include an alcohol crisis center, 2 multipurpose drop-in centers, 7 residential recovery centers, a transitional housing program, and permanent sober housing. A comparison of initial participant service projections with actual services shows that the drop-in centers, recovery centers, and transitional housing programs are performing at a capacity significantly above that originally projected.

476. Bernstein, S.B. (1975).   Escape from custody: Study of alcoholism and institutional dependency as reflected in the life record of a homeless man. Social Science and Medicine, 9, 51-56.

477. Blankertz, L., & White, K.K. (1990). Implementation of rehabilitation program for dually diagnosed homeless. Special Issue: Treating alcoholism and drug abuse among homeless men and women: Nine community demonstration grants. Alcoholism Treatment Quarterly, 7, 149-164.

478. Blumberg, L., Shipley, T.F., & Barsky, S.F. (1978). Liquor and poverty: Skid row as a human condition. New Brunswick, NJ: Rutgers Center of Alcohol Studies.

479. Blumberg, L., Shipley, T.E., & Shandler, I.W. (1973).   Skid row and its alternatives. Philadelphia, PA: Temple University Press.

480. Bonham, G.S., Hague, D.E., & Abel, M.H. (1990).   Louisville's Project Connect for the homeless alcohol and drug abuser. Special Issue: Treating alcoholism and drug abuse among homeless men and women: Nine community demonstration grants. Alcoholism Treatment Quarterly, 7, 57-78.

481. Breakey, W.R. (1987). Treating the homeless. Alcohol Health and Research World, Spring, 42-47.
Discusses the implications of the interaction of characteristics of the client and clinician in treating homeless persons with substance abuse problems.

482. Breakey, W.R., & Fischer, P.J. (1987). Alcoholism and homeless people. Paper presented at the 140th Annual Meeting of the American Psychiatric Association, Chicago, May.

483. Calsyn, R.J., & Morse, G.A. (1991). Correlates of problem drinking among homeless men. Hospital and Community Psychiatry, 42, 721-725.
A study of 165 homeless males found that the most salient predictors of problem drinking in homeless men included, degree of pre-homeless stress, age current life satisfaction, psychopathology, and a history of mental hospitalizations. In contrast with findings from much research, length of time homeless. degree of transience, and social support had no impact on problem drinking.

484. Cohen, C.I., & Adler, A. (1975). A storefront clinic on the Bowery. Quarterly Journal of Studies on Alcohol, 37, 1336-1340.

485. Comfort, M., Shipley, T.E., White, K., & Griffith, E.M. (1990). Family treatment for homeless alcohol/drug-addicted women and their preschool children. Special Issue: Treating alcoholism and drug abuse among homeless men and women: Nine community demonstration grants. Alcoholism Treatment Quarterly, 7, 129-147.

486. Corrigan, E.M., & Anderson, S.C. (1984). Homeless alcoholic women on Skid Row. American Journal of Drug and Alcohol Abuse, 10, 535-549.
      Reports findings of a study comparing homeless alcoholic women (N=31) to non-homeless alcoholic women (N=150). The homeless group were more likely to be black, never married, protestant and older than controls. Controls were over-represented in clerical, sales and professional occupational categories. Many of the homeless alcoholics did not report life-long histories of marginality. For many of these women, their drinking problems did not begin until their mid-thirties.

487. Department of Health Services (1985). Responses to problems of homeless alcoholics in Los Angeles County. Los Angeles: DHHS.

488. Dexter, R.A. (1990). Treating homeless and mentally ill substance abusers in Alaska. Special Issue: Treating alcoholism and drug abuse among homeless men and women: Nine community demonstration grants. Alcoholism Treatment Quarterly, 7, 25-30.

489. Docter, R.F. (1967). Drinking practices of skid row alcoholics. Quarterly Journal of Studies on Alcohol, 28, 700-708.
      Results of a study of 172 male alcoholics interviewed in one of three settings: (1) sheriff's office rehabilitation units, (2) Salvation Army centers, or (3) out-patient clinics. The purpose of the study was to determine: (1) what type of beverage was preferred at a particular phase of the respondents' drinking history, (2) why a particular beverage was preferred, (3) the effects of moderate intoxication, and (4) subjects beliefs about their ability to control drinking. Beer was the most preferred beverage at the onset of subjects' drinking histories. The preference for beer gave way to whiskey in the middle phases of drinking histories and was replaced by wine at the end of their drinking histories. While the primary reason for beverage preference in the early phases was "taste," at the wine phase it had changed to "price."

490. Dunne, F.J. (1990). Alcohol abuse on skid row: In sight out of mind. Alcohol and Alcoholism, 25, 13-15.

491. Feldman, J., Su, W.H., Kaley, M., & Kissin, B. (1974). Skid-row and inner city alcoholics: A comparison of drinking patterns and medical problems. Quarterly Journal of Studies on Alcohol, 35, 565-576.

492. Fiddle, S. (1980). Catting: A synoptic view of addicts living outside conventional shelters. International Journal of the Addictions, 15, 39-45.

493. Fischer, P.J., & Breakey, W.R. (1987). Characteristics of the homeless with alcohol problems in Baltimore: Some preliminary results. Paper presented at the NIAAA Conference on the Homeless Population with Alcohol Problems, Rockville, Maryland, March.

494. Fischer, P.J. & Breakey, W.R. (1987). Profile of the Baltimore homeless with alcohol problems. Alcohol Health and Research World, 11, 36-37.
Reports findings of a study comparing homeless men living in missions to community controls. Significant differences in mental health status, service utilization, and social dysfunction were found.

495. Fischer, P.J., & Breakey, W.R. (1991). The epidemiology of alcohol, drug, and mental disorders among homeless persons. American Psychologist, 46, 1115-1128.
A review of current research found that prevalence of alcohol and mental illness among the homeless was greater than that in the general population. Homeless persons who are substance abusers or who are mentally ill are characterized by extreme poverty, isolation from all types of social support, have frequent contact with the criminal justice system, and are generally in poor health. Methodological problems in homelessness research are also addressed.

496. Fry, L.J. (1975). Responding to skid row alcoholism: Self-defeating arrangements in an innovative treatment program. Social Problems, 22, 675-688.

497. Garrett, G.R. (1987). Alcohol and the homeless: An overview of research. Paper presented at the NIAAA Conference on the Homeless Population with Alcohol Problems, Rockville, MD.

498. Garrett, G.R., & Schutt, R.K. (1987). Social services for homeless alcoholics: Assessment and response. Alcohol Health and Research World, 11, 50-53.
Case management may provide the critical link in the delivery of services to the homeless. The authors describe the use of a number of assessment techniques to determine alcohol abuse among the homeless by case managers as well as describe the work of case managers in providing services to this population.

499. Goldfarb, C. (1970). Patients nobody wants: Skid row alcoholics. Diseases of the Nervous System, 31, 274-281.

500. Graham, B.J., & Linehan, M.M. (1987). Group treatment for the homeless and chronic alcoholic woman. In C.M. Brody (Ed.), Women's therapy groups: Paradigms of feminist treatment. New York: Springer.

501. Grief, G.L., Price, C., & Johnson, F. (1990). Establishing a house for the HIV-positive intravenous drug abuser who is homeless: Analysis of closing. Journal of Psychoactive Drugs, 22, 351-353.
The authors provide a description of how staff persons at the Health Education Resource Organization established a temporary residence for drug abusers with the human immunodeficiency virus (HIV). Some of the problems and benefits of house maintenance are discussed.

502. Halikas, J.A., Lyttle, M.D, & Morse, C.L. (1984). Skid row alcoholism: An objective definition for use in detoxification and treatment planning. Journal of Clinical Psychiatry, 45, 214-216.

503. Hart, L. (1975). Attitudes towards alcoholism among a group of hospitalized skid-row alcoholics. International Journal of the Addictions, 10, 369-371.

504. Hobfoll, S.E., Kelso, D., & Peterson, W.J. (1989). When are support systems support systems: A study of skid row. In S. Einstein (Ed.), Drug and alcohol use: Issues and factors. New York: Plenum Press.

505. Knight, J.W. (1988). Alcohol abuse among the homeless. Dissertation Abstracts International, 49, 633 A.

506. Koegel, P., & Burnam, A.M. (1987). The epidemiology of alcohol abuse and dependence among homeless individuals: Findings from the inner-city of Los Angeles. Los Angeles: University of California Department of Psychiatry.
Reports findings of a secondary analysis of data collected from interviews with 379 homeless persons in the skid row area of Los Angeles. The four sets of analyses of alcohol abuse and alcoholism data performed were: (1) prevalence of alcohol abuse and dependency, (2) relationships between patterns of alcohol abuse and homelessness, (3) a comparison of homeless and non-homeless alcoholics, and (4) prevalence of dual diagnoses. Findings indicate that over 40% of those interviewed were diagnosed with alcoholism, that alcohol abuse precedes homelessness, and that about 12% of the sample presented dual diagnoses.

507. Koegel, P., & Burnam, A.M. (1987). Traditional and non-traditional homeless alcoholics. Alcohol Health and Research World, 11, 28-34.
Compares "pure alcoholics" and dual diagnosed homeless persons in Los Angeles County. Pure alcoholics are similar to the profile that dominates the historical literature on homeless. Although many demographic differences exist between the two groups, both were likely to have long-term experience with homelessness and to cite lack of employment as the primary cause of their homelessness. Alcoholism was found to precede homelessness in most cases.

508. Koegel, P., & Burnam, M.A. (1988). Alcoholism among homeless adults in the inner city of Los Angeles. Archives of General Psychiatry, 45, 1011-1018.
Compared to a matched household sample, the rate of alcoholism was higher among a probability sample of homeless adults in Los Angeles. Further, homeless alcoholics had higher rates of psychiatric disorder, more severe and long-term drinking patterns, and lower levels of social and vocational functions than alcoholics in the comparison group. Discusses the need for alcohol rehabilitation services that consider the unique situation of the homeless alcoholic.

509. Korenbaum, S., & Burney, G. (1986). Alcohol-free living environments for homeless individuals: Final report. Rockville, MD: National Institute of Alcohol Abuse and Alcoholism.
Reports the findings of detailed interviews with program staff at five alcohol-free living centers in California. Discusses issues of importance to those interested in the development of such resources, including: (1) needs assessment, (2)

financing, (3) program development, and (4) evaluation. Also provides detailed descriptions of the five programs studied.

510. Koroloff, N.M., & Anderson, S.C. (1989). Alcohol-free living centers: Hope for homeless alcoholics. Social Work, 34, 497-504.

511. Linn, L.S., Gelberg, L., & Leake, B. (1990). Substance abuse and mental health status of homeless and domiciled low-income users of a medical clinic. Hospital and Community Psychiatry, 41, 306-310.

512. Lipton, D.S. (1983). Drug use among tenants of single room occupancy (SRO) hotels in New York City. New York State Division of Substance Abuse Services.

513. Lubran, B. (1990). Alcohol and drug abuse among the homeless population: A national response. Special Issue: Treating alcoholism and drug abuse among homeless men and women: Nine community demonstration grants. Alcoholism Treatment Quarterly, 7, 11-23.

514. McCarty, D. (1990). Nine demonstration grants: Nine approaches. Special Issue: Treating alcoholism and drug abuse among homeless men and women: Nine community demonstration grants. Alcoholism Treatment Quarterly, 7, 1-9.

515. McCarty, D., Argeriou, M., Huebner, R.B., & Lubran, B. (1991). Alcoholism, drug abuse, and the homeless. American Psychologist, 46, 1149-1158.

516. McCarty, D., Argeriou, M., Krakow, M., & Mulvey, K. (1990). Stabilization services for homeless alcoholics and drug addicts. Special Issue: Treating alcoholism and drug abuse among homeless men and women: Nine community demonstration grants. Alcoholism Treatment Quarterly, 7, 31-45.

517. Mulkern, V., & Spence, R. (1984). Alcohol abuse/alcoholism among homeless persons: A review of the literature. Boston, MA: Human Services Research Institute.
Summarizes the findings of research on alcohol abuse and alcoholism among homeless persons. Issues addressed include: (1) the prevalence of alcoholism and alcohol abuse among the homeless, (2) demographic characteristics, health, and mental health problems of homeless alcoholics, (3) differences between homeless alcohol abusers and homeless alcoholics, (4) improving research methods for studying alcohol problems of the homeless, and (5) exemplary treatment programs for homeless alcoholics.

518. Mulkern, V., & Spence, R. (1984). Alcohol abuse/alcoholism among homeless persons: A review of the literature. Final report. Washington, DC: Superintendent of Documents, U.S. Government Printing Office.

519. Mulkern, V., & Spence, R. (1984). Illicit drug use among homeless persons: A review of the literature. Rockville, MD: National Institute of Drug Abuse.
Reviews the research literature on drug use among the homeless in order to estimate the prevalence of drug use in this population, and to identify demographic and clinical correlates of drug use. Estimates of drug use among 7

studies reviewed ranged from 9 to 55 per cent.   Differences in definitions, sampling techniques, and instrumentation account for this disparity.

520. Newton, S.P., & Duffy, C.P. (1987).   Old town Portland and an oldtime problem. Alcohol Health and Research World, Spring, 62-65.

521. Nimmer, R. (1972).   Two million unnecessary arrests. Proceedings of the Joint Conference on Alcohol Abuse and Alcoholism (Pp. 86-97).   Rockville, MD: National Institute of Mental Health.

522. Nores, J.M., & Dalayeun, J. (1987).   Homelessness in Paris. New York State Journal of Medicine, 87, 411-415.
Compares the role of unemployment, alcoholism, and mental illness in homeless persons in New York City and in Paris.

523. Pastor, P.A. (1978).   Mobilization of public drunkenness control: A comparison of legal and medical approaches. Social Problems, 25, 373-384.

524. Pratt, A.D. (1975).   Mandatory treatment program for skid row alcoholics: Its implication for the uniform alcoholism and intoxication treatment act. Journal of Studies on Alcohol, 36, 166-170.

525. Ridgely, M.S., McNeil, C.T., & Goldman, H.H. (1988).   Alcohol and other drug abuse among homeless individuals: An annotated bibliography. Rockville, MD: Row Sciences, Inc.

526. Ridlen, S., Asamoah, Y., Edwards, H.G., & Zinner, R. (1990).   Outreach and engagement for homeless women at risk of alcoholism. Special Issue: Treating alcoholism and drug abuse among homeless men and women: Nine community demonstration grants. Alcoholism Treatment Quarterly, 7, 99-109.

527. Roth, D., & Bean, J. (1985).   Alcohol problems and homelessness: Findings from the Ohio study. Alcohol Health and Research World, 10, 14-15.

528. Spinner, G.F., & Leaf, P.J. (1992).   Homelessness and drug abuse in New Haven. Hospital and Community Psychiatry, 43(2), 166-168.
Of 181 homeless persons residing in homeless shelters in New Haven, Connecticut, 54% reported using drugs in the 30 days prior to being interviewed, while 66% reported using drugs within the previous year.   Cocaine was the most used drug and 20% of the sample cited drug use as the primary reason for their homelessness. Drug use was most prevalent among persons who had been homeless between 6 months and 3 years.

529. Stall, R. (1984).   Disadvantages of eclecticism in the treatment of alcoholism: The problem of recidivism. Journal of Drug Issues, 14, 437-448.

530. Stark, L.R. (1987).   A century of alcohol and homelessness: Demographics and stereotypes. Alcohol Health and Research World, 11, 8-13.

531. Struening, E.L. & Padgett, D.K. (1990). Physical health status, substance use and abuse, and mental disorders among homeless adults. Journal of Social Issues, 46, 65-81.

532. Struening, E., Padgett, D.K., Pittman, J., Cordova, P., & Jones, M. (1991). A typology based on measures of substance abuse and mental disorder. Journal of Addictive Diseases, 11, 99-117.

533. Szuster, R.R., Schanbacher, B.L., & McCann, S.C. (1990). Characteristics of psychiatric emergency room patients with alcohol or drug induced disorders. Hospital and Community Psychiatry, 41, 1342-1345.
Describes the demographic and clinical characteristics of 343 consecutive patients referred to a general hospital's emergency psychiatry service. The 114 subjects diagnosed as having an alcohol or drug induced disorder were younger and were more of the male, unemployed, and homeless than subjects with disorders not induced by substance abuse.

534. Trotter, R. (1983). Alcohol, drug abuse, and mental health problems of the homeless: Proceedings of a roundtable. Rockville, MD: Alcohol, Drug Abuse and Mental Health Administration.

535. Weinreb, L. & Bassuk, E. (1990). Substance abuse: A growing problem among homeless families. Family and Community Health, 13, 55-64.

536. Welte, J.W., & Barnes, G.M. (1992). Drinking among homeless and marginally housed adults in New York State. Journal of Studies on Alcohol, 53, 303-315.
A comparison of interviews with randomly selected homeless persons and data from a sample of 5,952 domiciled adults found that although nearly 40% abstained from any alcohol use, 13% reported having more than 20 drinks a day. Heavy drinking among the homeless was more common among men than women and higher for blacks than whites. It is concluded that drinking is a contributory cause of homelessness for a minority of the homeless.

537. Whitley, M.P., Osborne, O.H., Godfrey, M.A., & Johnston, K. (1985). A point prevalence study of alcoholism and mental illness among downtown migrants. Social Science and Medicine, 20, 579-583.
Compared residents of an urban emergency shelter and an SRO hotel on demographic characteristics, physical and mental health status, and alcohol abuse. Few differences were found between the two groups.

538. Willenbring, M.L., Whelan, J.A., Dahlquist, J.S., & O'Neal, M.E. (1990). Community treatment of the chronic public inebriate: I. Implementation. Special Issue: Treating alcoholism and drug abuse among homeless men and women: Nine community demonstration grants. Alcoholism Treatment Quarterly, 7, 79-97.

539. Wiseman, J.P. (1970). Stations of the lost: The treatment of skid row alcoholics. Englewood Cliffs, NJ: Prentice Hall.

540. Wiseman, J.P. (1987). Studying the problem of alcoholism in today's homeless. Paper presented at the NIAAA Conference on the Homeless Population with Alcohol Problems, Rockville, Maryland, March.

541. Wittman, F.D. (1985). The homeless with alcohol-related problems: Proceedings of a meeting to provide research recommendations to the National Institute on Alcohol Abuse and Alcoholism. Rockville, MD: NIAAA.
Discusses an NIAAA sponsored meeting to identify research issues concerning alcohol abuse among the homeless. Presents summaries of several presentations and recommendations for future research in the area.

542. Wittman, F.D. (1989). Housing models for alcohol programs serving homeless people. Berkeley, CA: CLEW Associates.

543. Wittman, F.D., & Arch, M. (1987). Alcohol, architecture, and homelessness. Alcohol Health and Research World, Spring, 74-79.
Discusses the impact of architectural design on the character and social functioning of individuals housed there with special emphasis on housing and facilities for the homeless alcoholic. Argues that service providers and government agency administrators alike may have to take on new roles if appropriate housing and service facilities for this population are to be developed.

544. Wittman, F.D., & Madden, P.A. (1988). Alcohol recovery programs for homeless people: A survey of current programs in the U.S. Washington, DC: National Institute on Alcohol Abuse and Alcoholism.
Describes exemplary alcohol recovery programs for homeless people from across the U.S. and attempts to identify models of alcohol recovery programs that might facilitate further research, policy making, and program development.

545. Wright, A., Mora, J., & Hughes, L. (1990). The Sober Transitional Housing and Employment Project (STHEP): Strategies for long-term sobriety, employment and housing. Special Issue: Treating alcoholism and drug abuse among homeless men and women: Nine community demonstration grants. Alcoholism Treatment Quarterly, 7, 47-56.

546. Wright, J.D., & Knight, J.W. (1987). Alcohol abuse in the National "Health Care for the Homeless" client population. Amherst, MA: University of Massachusetts Social and Demographic Research Institute.

547. Wright, J.D., Knight, J.W., Weber-Burdin, E., & Lam, J. (1987). Ailments and alcohol: Health status among the drinking homeless. Alcohol Health and Research World, 11, 22-27.
Based on data from nearly 30,000 homeless persons in 16 cities participating in the Health Care for the Homeless program, the authors discuss patterns of comorbidity (alcohol/drug abuse and mental illness) among the homeless and the problems such patterns present for successful rehabilitation.

548. Young, T.J. (1989). Indigent alcoholics on skid row. In G.W. Lawson & A.N. Lawson (Eds.), Alcoholism and substance abuse in special populations. Rockville, MD: Aspen Publishers.

4

Single Homeless

549. Allsop, K. (1967). Hard travellin': The hobo and his history. New York: The New American Library.

550. Angus, A. (1974). Nomads slum. New Society, 28, 627.

551. Argensinger, J.E. (1982). Assisting the loafers: Transient relief in Baltimore, 1933-1937. Labor History, 23, 228-230.

552. Bachrach, L.L. (1984). Deinstitutionalization and women: Assessing the consequences of public policy. American Psychologist, 39, 1171-1177.

553. Bachrach, L.L. (1985). Chronic mentally ill women: Emergence and legitimation of program issues. Hospital and Community Psychiatry, 36, 1063-1069.
Previous research on homeless women has consisted mainly of descriptions or personal accounts of the lives of homeless women. Little empirical research has been conducted. The author argues for developing and disseminating research literature on the needs of homeless women.

554. Bachrach L.L. (1987). Homeless women: a context for health planning. Milbank Quarterly, 65, 371-396.
Reviews the literature on homelessness and women and argues that homelessness among women is a complex sociological phenomenon with devastating effects; resulting health problems are profound and complex and require a comprehensive response from health planners and service providers.

555. Bahr, H.M. (1967). Drinking, interaction, and identification: Notes on socialization into skid row. Journal of Health and Social Behavior, 8, 272-285.
Reports findings of a secondary analysis of data from an earlier survey of 92 randomly selected skid row men. The author concludes that adult socialization

into a deviant subculture such as the skid row community operates according to the same general principles as socialization into "normal" groups.

556. Bahr, H.M. (1968). Homelessness and disaffiliation. New York: Bureau of Applied Social Research, Columbia University.

557. Bahr, H.M. (1968). Worklife mobility among bowery men. Southwestern Social Science Quarterly, 49, 128-141.
Studied 66 randomly selected lodgers in Bowery hotels and compared the worklife mobility of his sample to that in Bogue's earlier research, concluding that the mobility histories of Bowery men are quite similar to those of men on Chicago's skid row. Unlike the popular conception of skid row residents as former middle class or working class persons, the author's sample consists primarily of persons who have spent their entire worklives in low status employment. Among those who have been downwardly mobile, problems such as illness and disability, family dissolution and alcoholism are associated with status loss.

558. Bahr, H.M. (1969). Institutional life, drinking, and disaffiliation, Social Problems, 16, 365-375.

559. Bahr, H.M (ed.) (1970). Disaffiliated man: Essays and bibliography on skid row, vagrancy, and outsiders. Toronto, University of Toronto Press.

560. Bahr, H.M. (1971). Birth order and failure: The evidence from skid row. Quarterly Journal of Studies on Alcohol, 32, 669-686.

561. Bahr, H.M. (1971). Drinking behavior among homeless women. Dissertation Abstracts International, 32, 547 A.

562. Bahr, H.M. (1973). Skid row: An introduction to disaffiliated man. New York: University Press.

563. Bahr, H.M., & Caplow, T. (1968). Homelessness, affiliation, and occupational mobility. Social Forces, 47, 28-33.
Compares the affiliation and employment histories of 203 bowery men and a control group of 125 residents of a low income census tract. Compared to controls, the skid row residents had long histories of disaffiliation both before and after their arrival on skid row. The 2 samples did not differ extensively in occupational mobility. Due to the weak association between downward mobility and loss of affiliation, the authors conclude that the homelessness of Bowery men is not attributable to downward mobility.

564. Bahr, H.M. & Caplow, T. (1974). Old men drunk and sober. New York: New York University Press.

565. Bahr, H.M. & Garrett, G.R. (1976). Women alone: The disaffiliation of urban females. Lexington, MA: D.C. Heath & Co.

566. Bahr, H.M., & Langfur, S.J. (1967). Social attachment and drinking in Skid-row life histories. Social Problems, 14, 464-472.
Investigates the extent of current alcohol consumption and lifetime affiliation with

organizations in a population of residents of lodging houses in the Bowery. The life histories of heavy drinkers on skid row are characterized by higher degrees of attachment to society than are those of abstainers or moderate drinkers on skid row. The heavy drinker is most likely to suffer losses of affiliation during adulthood while the abstainer is more likely to have never "attached" to the social order.

567. Bard, M.B. (1989). Domestic abuse and the homeless woman: Paradigms in personal narratives for organizational strategists and community planners. Dissertation Abstracts International, 49, 2346 A.

568. Barge, F.C., & Norr, K.F. (1991). Homeless shelter policies for women in an urban environment. Image Journal of Nursing Scholarship, 23, 145-149.
A survey of shelters serving women in Chicago found that nearly 2/3 of the women using shelters were African American and that a great deal of variance existed in admission criteria, policies, and services. Women with male children over 7 years of age, pregnant women, and substance users were generally less likely to be admitted to shelters.

569. Baxter, E. & Hopper, K. (1981). Private lives/public spaces: Homeless adults on the streets of New York. New York: Community Service Society.
Reports findings of an ethnographic study of homeless persons in New York City. Most homeless persons were located outside of emergency shelters, living on the streets, in abandoned buildings, or in lobbies of bus and train stations. Most of those interviewed attributed their situation to the withdrawal of family supports, with women reporting that abuse or abandonment by their spouses had led to their homelessness. Many women refused to seek support or assistance for fear of "being a burden."

570. Beall, R. (1973). A survey of persons who use social services on skid road. Portland, OR: Burnside Projects, Inc.

571. Berman-Rossi, T. & Cohen, M.B. (1988). Group development and shared decision making working with homeless mentally ill women. Social Work With Groups, 11, 63-78.
Describes the work of an on-site community support system team with homeless mentally ill women in an SRO hotel. The focus of the program is on rehabilitation through empowerment. By building on resident's strengths, the effects of alienation, hopelessness, and despair resulting from their lives on the street can be counteracted.

572. Bibby, R.W., & Mauss, A.L. (1974). Skidders and their servants: Variable goals and functions of a skid row rescue mission. Journal for the Scientific Study of Religion, 13, 421-436.

573. Birch, E.L. (1985). The unsheltered woman: Women and housing in the 80's. New Brunswick, NJ: Center for Urban Policy Research, Rutgers University.

574. Blumberg, L., Shipley, T.E., & Moor, J.O. (1971). The skid row man and the skid row status community. Quarterly Journal of Studies on Alcohol, 32, 909-941.

575. Blumberg, L., Shipley, T.E., & Shandler, I.W. (1966). The development, major goals, and strategies of a skid row program: Philadelphia. Quarterly Journal of Studies on Alcohol, 27, 242-258.
Describes a Philadelphia program started in 1952 that attempts to rehabilitate and relocate skid row men without recreating new skid row areas.

576. Breton, M. (1988). The need for mutual-aid groups in a drop-in center for women: The Sistering case. Social Work With Groups, 11, 47-61.
The author describes a drop-in center for homeless and transient women. Homelessness among these women is viewed as a result of the "feminization of poverty." Mutual-aid groups are seen as a necessary component of programs for oppressed persons.

577. Bruns, R. (1980). Knights of the road. New York: Methuen.

578. Bunston, T. & Breton, M. (1990). The eating patterns and problems of homeless women. Women and Health, 16, 43-62.

579. Burt, M., & Cohen, B. (1989). Differences among homeless single women, women with children, and single men. Social Problems, 36, 508-524.

580. Butler, S.S. (1991). Perspectives on the lives and service needs of homeless middle-aged women. Dissertation Abstracts International, 52, 1893 A.

581. Calsyn, R.J., & Morse, G. (1990). Homeless men and women: Commonalities and a service gender gap. American Journal of Community Psychology, 18, 597-608.

582. Caplow, T., Bahr, H.M., & Sternberg, D. (1968). Homelessness. International Encyclopedia of the Social Sciences, 6, 494-499.
A description of the dominant forms of contemporary homelessness include: the refugee, the migratory farm worker, and the skid-row man. The authors argue that the thread that links these groups is their detachment from the affiliative bonds characteristic of the "settled" person. Suggested causes of homelessness include industrialization, urbanization and social change.

583. Chavkin, W., Kristal, A., Seaborn, C., & Guigli, P.E. (1987). The reproductive experience of women living in hotels for the homeless in New York City. New York State Journal of Medicine, 87, 10-13.

584. Cinnater, N. (1984). Women hoboes of the great depression: Survival in hard times. Paper presented at the 6th Berkshire Conference on the History of Women.

585. Cohen, C.I. (1984). The aging men of Skid Row: A target for research and service intervention. Portions of this paper were presented at the 37th Annual Scientific Meeting of the Gerontological Society, San Antonio, November.
Reports findings of a study comparing 281 aged homeless men (Mean age=61.5 years) to a national community sample of the elderly. The findings suggest high rates of psychiatric illness and alcohol abuse. Further, many had insufficient money for food and few received public assistance or medicaid. The author also

describes Project Rescue, a program developed as an outgrowth of the research which provides several services for aging homeless men.

586. Cohen, C.I. (1989). Social ties and friendship patterns of old homeless men. In R.G. Adams & R. Blieszner (Eds.), Older adult friendship: Structure and process. Newberry Park, CA: Sage Publications.

587. Cohen, C.I., & Sokolovsky, J. (1981). A reassessment of the sociability of long-term skid-row residents: A social network approach. Social Networks, 3, 93-105.

588. Cook, T. (ed.). (1979). Vagrancy: Some new perspectives. New York: Academic Press.

589. Coston, C.T.A. (1989). The original designer label: Prototypes of New York City's shopping bag ladies. Deviant Behavior, 10, 157-172.
Based on data from interviews with 35 homeless women, the author discusses: (1) reasons for homelessness among women, (2) modes of survival on the streets, and (3) incidence of crime. The primary reason given for homelessness was unemployment. Survival strategies included using soup kitchens, sleeping in abandoned buildings, and using emergency rooms for health care. Further, three-fourths of those interviewed reported being victims of crime. A typology of styles of homelessness among women is presented.

590. Crouse, J.M. (1986). The homeless transient in the great depression: New York State, 1929-1941. Albany, NY: State University of New York Press.

591. Crystal, S., & Goldstein, M. (1982). Chronic and situational dependency: Long-term residents in a shelter for men. New York: Human Resources Administration.

592. Depp, F.C., & Ackiss, V. (1983). Assessing needs among sheltered homeless women. Paper presented at the Conference on Homelessness: A Time for New Directions, Washington, July.

593. D'Ercole, A., & Struening, E. (1990). Victimization among homeless women: Implications for service delivery. Journal of Community Psychology, 18, 141-152.

594. Diamond, G.M. (1973). Single homeless. New Society, 26, 421-424.

595. Downing, C.K., & Cobb, A.K. (1990). Value orientations of homeless men. Western Journal of Nursing Research, 12, 619-628.

596. Drake, M., & Biebuych, T. (1977). Policy and provision for the single homeless. Washington, DC: National Institute of Social Work.

597. Dumont, M.P. (1967). Tavern culture, the sustenance of homeless men. American Journal of Orthopsychiatry, 37, 938-945.

598. Farrell, E. (1981). Service needs as perceived by shelter men. Master's thesis, Washington, DC, Howard University.

599. Farrell, E. (1982). A descriptive study of some homeless women. Master's thesis, College Park, MD, University of Maryland.

600. First, R.J., & Toomey, B.G. (1989). Homeless men and the work ethic. The Social Service Review, 63, 113-126.

601. Garfield, E. (1982). On beggars, bagladies, and bums. Current Contents, 6, 5-15.

602. Garrett, G.R., & Bahr, H.M. (1973). Women on skid row. Quarterly Journal of Studies on Alcohol, 34, 1229.
Compared homeless women (N=52) and men (N=199) admitted to homeless shelters in New York City. Women differed from men on several demographic variables as well as on several measures of alcohol consumption. Homeless women were more likely than homeless men to be light drinkers, to have started heavy drinking at a later age, and to drink alone. The findings suggest that homeless women may be the most isolated and disaffiliated Skid Row residents.

603. Garrett, G.R., & Bahr, H.M. (1976). The family backgrounds of skid row women. Signs, 2, 369-381.
Compared homeless women (N=52), homeless men (N=199), and non-homeless low-income women (N=185) to determine factors related to the etiology of homelessness and excessive drinking among homeless women. The findings indicate that the background of homeless women is qualitatively different than that of homeless men, with failed marriages and histories of family instability being critical factors leading to homelessness for women.

604. Goering, P., Paduchak, D., & Durbin, J. (1990). Housing homeless women: A consumer preference study. Hospital and Community Psychiatry, 41, 790-794.

605. Golden, S. (1991). Women outside: Meanings and myths of homelessness. Berkeley, CA: University of California Press.
Presents cases studies of homeless women and discusses historical attitudes towards women living apart (hoboes, witches, prostitutes, etc.). It is forbidden female power and sexuality that made such women appear threatening and the contemporary homeless woman is the modern fulfillment of this myth.

606. Graham, B.J., & Linehan, M.M. (1987). Group treatment for the homeless and chronic alcoholic woman. In C.M. Brody (Ed.), Women's therapy groups: Paradigms of feminist treatment. New York: Springer.

607. Grunberg, J. (1989). Early recollections and criminal behavior in mentally-ill homeless men. Individual Psychology: Journal of Adlerian Theory, Research and Practice, 45, 289-299.

608. Gunn, J. (1974). Prisons, shelters, and homeless men. Psychiatric Quarterly, 48, 505-512.
Argues against the incarceration or institutionalization of homeless men and

suggests alternative approaches to the homelessness problem. The author also discusses the importance of tailoring services to meet the needs and wishes of the homeless.

609. Hand, J.E. (1982). Shopping bag women of Manhattan. New York: New School for Social Research.
Reports findings of observations of 25 homeless women on the streets of New York. Three types of homeless women are presented that represent distinct views of the self, modes of self-representation and strategies for survival.

610. Hannappel, M., Calsyn, R.J., & Morse, G.A. (1989). Mental illness in homeless men: A comparison of shelter and street samples. Journal of Community Psychology, 17, 304-310.

611. Harper, D.A. (1976). The homeless man: An ethnography of work, trains and booze. Dissertation Abstracts International, 37, 1063 A.

612. Henshaw, S.K. (1968). Camp LaGuardia: A voluntary total institution for homeless men. New York: Bureau of Applied Social Research, Columbia University.

613. Henshaw, S.K. (1971). Structure and inmate responses in a voluntary total institution for homeless men. Dissertation Abstracts International, 32, 3443 A.

614. Herman, D.B. (1991). Homeless men in New York City's public shelters: A life course perspective. Dissertation Abstracts International, 52, 3076-A.
A secondary analysis of data collected during a needs assessment conducted in New York City shelters explores similarities and differences between phases in the life histories of homeless men. Findings indicate support for the contemporary view of the homeless population as quite heterogeneous. Implications for policy making and professional practice are presented.

615. Hobfoll, S.E., Kelso, D., & Peterson, W.J. (1980). The Anchorage skid row. Quarterly Journal of Studies on Alcohol, 41, 94-99.

616. Hodnicki, D.R.L. (1992). Being homeless: An ethnographic study of women's experiences in a shelter. Dissertation Abstracts International, 53, 1785-B.
Using a feminist perspective, valuing women and the knowledge women can share, women's experiences of homelessness was studied. The 2 domains of experiences found involved disconnection and rebuilding. Typical of the first domain were disaffiliation, significant losses, hurt, uncertainty, and pressure. Rebuilding was typified by heightened awareness, making adjustments, living with limitations, growth, and being proactive. Vulnerability is typical of the experiences of homeless women once major sources of support are lost. However, vulnerability lessens as rebuilding begins.

617. Hopper, K. (1989). A bed for the night: Homeless men in New York City, past and present. Dissertation Abstracts International, 49, 3408 A.

618. Imam, H., & Redd, S. (1985). The Elizabethan Stone House: A residential mental health program for women. SAGE: A Scholarly Journal on Black

Women, 2, 65-68.

The authors describe an alternative to traditional residential mental health programs for women that was established by former mental patients. The program focuses on how women's problems are intensified by the societal pressures they experience, with black women experiencing greater psychological distress than white women due to the effects of institutionalized racism. Causes of psychological distress include low self-esteem, homelessness, poverty, and violence.

619. Imbimbo, J. & Pfeffer, R. (1987). The Olivieri Center: A study of homeless women and their concept of home. New York, NY: City University.

620. Johnson, A.K. & Kreuger, L.W. (1989). Toward a better understanding of homeless women. Social Work, 34, 537-540.

Reviews what is known about homeless women. Although there has been little systematic research, some recent research has begun to identify gender differences among the homeless. The authors offer some initial empirical evidence for whether women are alone or with children as a key discriminating factor.

621. Koegel, P. (1987). Ethnographic perspectives on homeless and homeless mentally ill women. Rockville, MD: NIMH.

Summarizes proceedings from a 1985 meeting of ethnographic researchers who have studied homeless and homeless-mentally-ill women. Methodological problems arising from conducting ethnographic or qualitative research are discussed and summaries of group discussions on the antecedents of homelessness, social support networks of homeless women, mental health problems of homeless women, and interactions of homeless women with social service systems are presented.

622. Kot, J.A. (1992). A psychological assessment of homeless men. Dissertation Abstracts International, 53, 3778-B.

Compared samples of homeless men, chronically mentally ill psychiatric inpatients, and chronically indigent men and found that the homeless men were more like the chronically indigent men than the chronically mentally ill men on personality, cognitive functioning, and several demographic and historical variables.

623. Lam, J.A. (1988). Homeless women in America: Their social and health characteristics. Dissertation Abstracts International, 49, 633 A.

624. Lamb, H.R., & Grant, R.W. (1982). Mentally ill women in a county jail. Archives of General Psychiatry, 40, 363-368.

Explores the reasons for incarcerating women with psychiatric disabilities. Forty-two percent of the women had been transient or homeless prior to their incarceration. The authors argue for increased emphasis on involuntary treatment to reduce the numbers of mentally ill women in jails.

625. Laufer, W.S. (1981). The vocational interests of homeless, unemployed men. Journal of Vocational Behavior, 18, 196-201.

Reports findings of a study of the vocational interests and personality characteristics of 69 homeless males. Although the vocational interests of the participants were comparable to those of employed persons, personality characteristics were indicative of possible behavioral and employment problems.

626. Maitra, A.K. (1982). Dealing with the disadvantaged single homeless: Are we doing enough? Public Health Reports, 96, 141-144.

627. Manuel, P.D.P. (1987). Sheltering homeless women. Dissertation Abstracts International, 47, 3205 A.

628. Maurin, J.T., Russell, L., & Memmott, R.J. (1989). An exploration of gender differences among the homeless. Research in Nursing and Health, 12, 315-321. Interviews with 337 homeless persons (266 males and 71 females) were conducted to assess gender differences in family relationships, length of homelessness, psychological disorder, health status, and employment. Males were most likely to be alone. Females were more likely to have children with them or had recent contact with their absent children. Further, women were more likely than men to be psychologically distressed. Of respondents with children, over 60% were in 2-parent families. Respondents without children reported having been homeless longer than those with children.

629. Men's Shelter Study Group. (1976). Report on men housed for one night. New York: Human Resources Administration.

630. Merves, E.S. (1986). Conversations with homeless women: A sociological examination. Dissertation Abstracts International, 47, 188 A. The author summarizes life histories of 15 homeless women (Mean age=37). The women reported either a precipitous slide into homelessness or a family or marital crisis which caused them to be homeless. The author concludes that our national economic and housing crises have led many persons to become homeless and that affordable housing in the most pressing need for homeless women.

631. Milburn, N., & D'Ercole, A. (1991). Homeless women: Moving toward a comprehensive model. American Psychologist, 46, 1161-1169.

632. Mitchell, J. C. (1987). The components of strong ties among homeless women. Social Networks, 9, 37-47. Studied the social relationships of 10 homeless women to determine the validity of Marsden & Campbell's (1984) view that a measure of closeness or emotional intensity of a relationship is the best indicator of the concept of tie strength.

633. Moore, R.E. (1988). Characteristics of homeless CSS male clients in the New York City Shelter system. New York: New York State Psychiatric Institute. Compared male homeless City Shelter System (CSS) clients and male homeless non-CSS clients in an effort to determine if these differences suggest differential service needs for the two groups. The findings support the author's contention that CSS clients are a unique subgroup of the homeless. CSS clients were found to have poorer mental health status and to have stayed longer in the shelter than non-CSS clients.

634. Morrissey, J.P., Dennis, D.L., & Gounis, K. (1985). The development and utilization of the Queens Mens's Shelter. Albany, NY: New York State Office

of Mental Health.
Report findings of a study of a shelter for men who need mental health services.
Extensive data on the demographics and psychiatric treatment history of residents
was collected through participant observation, interviews with staff and residents,
and reviews of shelter records.

635. Morse, G.A. (1982). Homeless men: A study of service needs, predictor
variables, and subpopulations. St. Louis, University of Missouri, Department of
Psychology.

636. Morse, G.A., Calsyn, R.J., & Burger, G.K. (1991). A comparison of taxonomic
systems for classifying homeless men. International Journal of Social Psychiatry,
37, 90-98.
A comparison of two taxonomic systems for classifying homeless men based on
either their past history of psychiatric disability or current psychiatric impairment
found that, although both displayed adequate discriminating power, the system
based on current psychiatric impairment was superior.

637. Multnomah County Department of Human Services. (1985). Homeless women.
Portland, OR: Department of Human Services.

638. New York State Office of Mental Health. (1982). Who are the homeless? A
study of randomly selected men who use the New York City Shelters. New York
State Office of Mental Health, Albany.

639. Novak, M.M. (1988). Innovations in family and community health. Family and
Community Health, 11, 76-81.
The author discusses the roles that community health nurses can play in providing
guided assistance to homeless women during periods of self-care deficits.

640. Nyamathi, A.M. (1991). Relationship of resources to emotional distress, somatic
complaints, and high-risk behaviors in drug recovery and homeless minority
women. Research in Nursing and Health, 14, 269-277.
In a sample of 581 homeless or drug-abusing minority women, the relationship
of self-esteem, sense of coherence, and support availability to emotional distress,
somatic complaints, and high-risk behavior were investigated. The author's
findings revealed that women who were high in self-esteem and stronger in sense
of coherence reported significantly less emotional distress, and significantly fewer
high-risk behaviors. In addition, women who were high in any of the three
resources reported lower somatic complaints. Regression analyses revealed that
coherence, self-esteem and support availability jointly accounted for 49% of the
variance in emotional distress, 10% of the variance in high-risk activities, and
26% of the variance in somatic complaints. Implications for empowering women
at risk for HIV infection are also discussed.

641. Nyamathi, A.M., & Flaskerud, J. (1992). A community-based inventory of
current concerns of impoverished homeless and drug-addicted minority women.
Research in Nursing and Health, 15(2), 121-129.
Evaluated the psychometric properties of the Community-based Inventory of
Current Concerns (CICC) with homeless and/or drug addicted minority women.

The current concerns of impoverished women were found to be complex and multidimensional.

642. Nyamathi, A., & Vasquez, R. (1989). Impact of poverty, homelessness, and drugs on Hispanic women at risk for HIV infection. Hispanic Journal of Behavioral Sciences, 11, 299-314.

643. O'Connor, A. (1987). A female bail hostel. Medicine Science and the Law, 27, 136-140.

644. Paterson, K.J. (1984). Shelters and statistics: A new face to an old problem. Urban and Social Change Review, 17, 14-17.
The author describes the collaboration of a United Way chapter and 3 shelters for battered women to address funding of services for battered and homeless women.

645. Priest, R.G. (1970). Homeless men: A USA-UK comparison. Proceedings of the Royal Society of Medicine, 63, 441-445.

646. Roth, D, Toomey, B.G., & First, R.J. (1987). Homeless women: Characteristics and needs. AFFILIA, 2, 7-19.

647. Rousseau, A.M. (1981). Shopping bag ladies: Homeless women speak about their lives. New York: Pilgrim Press.
Based on many hours on the street and in shelters with homeless women, this collection of personal narratives stresses the abuse and victimization of homeless women, as well as, pointing out that many of these women suffer from long-term mental illnesses.

648. Ryback, R.F., & Bassuk, E.L. (1986). Homeless battered women and their shelter network. New Directions for Mental Health Services, June, 55-61.

649. Salzberg, A. (1992). Behavioral phenomena of homeless women in San Diego. Dissertation Abstracts International, 52, 4482-A.
Used in depth interviews with 10 homeless women to further understanding of the experience and meaning of homelessness among women. Typically, homeless women came from unstable backgrounds, experienced frequent emotional problems, and often were substance abusers. Although 80% wanted to find employment, most said they were physically or emotionally unable to work.

650. Schein, L. (1979). A hard-to-reach populations: Shopping bag women. Journal of Gerontological Social Work, 2, 29-41.

651. Schwam, K. (1979). Shopping bag ladies: Homeless women. New York: Manhattan Bowery Corporation.

652. Slavinsky, A., & Cousins, A. (1982). Homeless women. Nursing Outlook, 30, 358-362.
Questions the popular myths about homeless women and discusses the special problems the homeless woman faces. Contrary to popular belief, few homeless women are alcoholic. However, women are prone to abuse and victimization, especially elderly women who are vulnerable to harassment from landlords and

are at great risk for becoming homeless. Emergency shelter is viewed as an inadequate intervention for homeless women. A description of a model shelter for homeless women that attempts to restore personal dignity is included.

653. Smith, J.P. (1987). Single homeless people [editorial]. Journal of Advances in Nursing, 12, 403-404.

654. Stefl, M.E., & Roth, D. (1986). Homeless women and mental illness. Paper presented at the Annual Meeting of the American Public Health Association, Las Vegas, NV.

655. Stone, L.H. (1986). Shelters for battered women: A temporary escape from danger or the first step toward divorce. In J. Erickson & C. Wilhelm (Eds.). Housing the homeless. New Brunswick, NJ: Center for Urban Policy Research, Rutgers University.

656. Stoner, M.R. (1983). The plight of homeless women. Social Service Review, 57, 4-11.
Discusses changes in the homeless population, which has become increasingly young, female, and black. The author argues that lack of documentation of the special needs and problems of homeless women has led to inadequate services for women and recommends transitional and long-term housing be added to the housing options for homeless women. Finally, the author argues for increased litigation on behalf of homeless women and presents a list of 9 issues that must be addressed to solve the problems of homeless women.

657. Stoner, M.R., Alessi, J.J., & Hearn, D. (1984). The plight of homeless women. In A.R. Roberts (Ed.), Group treatment of children in shelters for battered women. New York: Springer.

658. Strasser, J.A. (1978). Urban transient women. American Journal of Nursing, 78, 2076-2079.
Posing as a hospice worker on skid row, the author observed 34 homeless women over a six week period. Findings suggest that the stereotype of willful wanderer is inaccurate, and that physical health problems were common, but the women's perceptions of the causes of their health problems were distorted. Finally, although many had contact with health care providers, they expressed distrust of official health care providers.

659. Sullivan, P.A., & Damrosch, S.P. (1985). Correlates of successful completion of a residential rehabilitation program for homeless women. Paper presented at the annual meeting of the American Public Health Association, November.

660. Susser, E., Struening, E.L., & Conover, S. (1987). Childhood experiences of homeless men. American Journal of Psychiatry, 144, 1599-1601.
Interviews with 695 homeless men, of which 1/3 were first time shelter users, were conducted to identify childhood experiences that were correlated with homelessness. Results show a high frequency of institutionalization (e.g., delinquency and running away) among homeless men. The authors conclude that scarce family resources and chronic family conflict are important determinants of adult homelessness.

661. Susser, E., Struening, E.L., & Conover, S. (1989). Psychiatric problems in homeless men: Lifetime psychosis, substance use, and current distress in new arrivals at New York City shelters. Archives of General Psychiatry, 46, 845-850.

662. Tierney, G. (1991). Spoiled goods: Profiles of skid row women. Dissertation Abstracts International, 52, 2610-A.
Although women and men in this participant observation research shared similar problems, including mental illness, substance abuse, poor health, unemployment, few job skills, and high levels of physical, emotional and sexual abuse, women were more likely to be underserved by social services agencies, to be victims of sexual harassment, and to be discriminated against on the basis of their sex than were men.

663. Vera Institute of Justice. (1981). First time users of women's shelter services: A preliminary analysis. New York: Vera Institute of Justice.

664. Walsh, B., & Davenport, D. (1983). The long loneliness in Baltimore: A study of homeless women. Homelessness in America. Washington, DC: U.S. Government Printing Office.

665. Weitzman, B.C. (1989). Pregnancy and childbirth: Risk factors for homelessness? Family Planning Perspectives, 21, 175-178.
Compared 704 homeless families on public assistance with 524 non-homeless families on public assistance and found that being pregnant or recently giving birth, especially for women younger than age 18, was significantly correlated with becoming homeless.

666. Wynne, J. (1987). Women in San Diego: A new perspective on poverty and despair in America's finest city. San Diego, CA: County of San Diego Department of Health Services Alcohol Program.

5

Health

667. Anonymous. (1991). Deaths among homeless persons--San Francisco, 1985-1990. Morbidity and Mortality Weekly Report, 40, 877-880.

668. Anonymous. (1991). Tuberculosis among residents of shelters for the homeless--Ohio, 1990. Morbidity and Mortality Weekly Report, 40, 869-871.

669. Anonymous. (1992). Prevention and control of tuberculosis among homeless persons. Recommendations of the Advisory Council for the Elimination of Tuberculosis. Morbidity and Mortality Weekly Report, 41, 13-23.
Provides guidelines for prevention and control of tuberculosis among the homeless to health-care providers, health departments, shelter operators, and social service agencies. Among the suggestions are the need for voluntary testing of tuberculosis patients for HIV and the creation of special shelters or long-term care arrangements for homeless persons with TB.

670. Afzal, N., & Wyatt, A. (1989). Long term care of AIDS patients. QRB, 15, 20-25.
Institutional long term care may be an important service for AIDS patients because they frequently survive acute illness episodes yet remain severely incapacitated. The authors further argue that, because many AIDS patients are also homeless, often because families or friends are unwilling or unable to care for them, institutional long term care may be the preferred method to accommodate the AIDS patients' fluctuating care needs.

671. Alley, J., & McConnell, S. (1988). Providing health care to the homeless: Another important role for NP's (Interview by L.J. Peterson). Nurse Practitioner, 13, 38-45.

672. Anderson, H.J. (1992). Health care for the homeless: what role should hospitals play? Hospitals, 66, 44-48.

Hospitals should take a lead role in the increasingly collaborative provision of health care services to homeless individuals.

673. Andrade, S.J. (1988). Living in the gray zone: Health care needs of homeless persons. San Antonio, TX: Benedictine Health Resource Center.
Conducted a statewide needs assessment to obtain basic planning information for determining if new, more effective, initiatives on behalf of the homeless population of Texas are needed. Interviews with homeless people, service providers, advocates, and key decision makers from across the state were conducted. Implications for health care services for the homeless population are discussed.

674. Athey, J.L. (1991). HIV infection and homeless adolescents. Child Welfare, 70, 517-528.
This review of the literature asserts that homeless adolescents are at extremely high risk for HIV infection due to sexual and drug use behaviors and describes several innovative service models for homeless youth.

675. Barry, M., Wall, C., Shirley, L., Bernardo, J., Schwingl, P., Bringandi, E., & Lamb, G. (1986). Tuberculosis screening in Boston's homeless shelters. Public Health Reports, 101, 487-493.
Reports findings of tuberculosis screenings in homeless shelters in Boston over a one year period. Twenty-six cases were confirmed, fifteen of which were probably the result of a common source exposure to one or two highly infectious persons. Five cases were persons who had previously tested positive but had not received adequate treatment. The authors conclude that the homeless are at high risk for tuberculosis and require intensive intervention and outreach.

676. Baum, J., Fedukowicz, H.B., & Jordan, A. (1980). A survey of Moraxella corneal ulcers in a derelict population. American Journal of Opthamology, 90, 476-480.

677. Belcher, J.B., Scholler, J.A., & Drummond, M. (1991). Three stages of homelessness: A conceptual model for social workers in health care. Health and Social Work, 16, 87-93.
Studied 40 homeless people and their health care needs in Baltimore and found that as the length of the homelessness episode increased, the person's health care needs became more complex. Health care services must be appropriate to three stages of homelessness--marginal, recent, and chronic. An understanding of these stages can help social workers ensure that homeless people receive correct medical treatment and that they are assisted in reconnecting with mainstream society.

678. Bennett, D. (1989). District 13 nurses involved in coalition to meet health care needs of homeless. Georgia Nurse, 49, 5.

679. Berne, A., Dato, C., Mason, D., & Rafferty, M. (1990). The authors respond: A nursing model for addressing the health needs of homeless families. Image: Journal of Nursing Scholarship, 22, 263-264.

680. Bird, J. (1992). Helping Billy move on. Nursing Times, 88, 42-44.

681. Blakeney, B. (1991). Old, homeless and sick. Geriatric Nursing-New York, 12, 220-222.

682. Blakeney, B. (1989). She cares for the ones no one cares about. Massachusetts Nurse, 59, 1, 11.

683. Bowdler, J.E., & Barrell, L.M. (1987). Health needs of homeless persons. Public Health Nursing, 4, 135-140.
     Using indicator, key informant, and survey methods, this study attempts to study the health care needs of homeless of Richmond, Virginia. The findings indicate a high prevalence of mental disorders, alcohol and drug abuse, and infectious/parasitic diseases among the sample. Implications of the research for programming and evaluation are discussed.

684. Bowering, J., Clancy, K.L., & Poppendieck, J. (1991). Characteristics of a random sample of emergency food program users in New York: II. Soup kitchens. American Journal of Public Health, 81, 914-917.

685. Brickner, P.W. (1985). Health care and homeless people. New York: Springer.

686. Brickner, P.W. (1985). Health issues in the care of the homeless. In P.W. Brickner, L.K. Scharer, B. Conanan, A. Elvy, & M. Savarese (Eds.), Health care of homeless people. New York: Springer.

687. Brickner, P.W., Filardo, T., Iseman, M., Green, R., Conanan, B., & Elvy, A. (1984). Medical aspects of homelessness. In H.R. Lamb (Ed.), The homeless mentally ill: A task force report. Washington, DC: American Psychiatric Association.
     Addresses a wide number of issues related to the medical problems common to the homeless and the problems in providing treatment to this population. Problems in providing treatment to the homeless include: (1) bureaucratic barriers, (2) stigma of homelessness, and (3) vulnerability of the population.

688. Brickner, P.W., Greenbaum, D., Kaufman, A., O'Donnell, F., O'Brian, J.T., Scalice, R., Scandizzi, J., & Sullivan, T. (1972). Clinic for male derelicts: Welfare hotel project. Annals of Internal Medicine, 77, 565-569.

689. Brickner, P.W., & Kaufman, A. (1973). Case finding of heart disease in homeless men. Bulletin of the New York Academy of Medicine, 49, 475-484.

690. Brickner, P.W., Scanlan, B., Conanan, B., Elvy, A., McAdam, J., Scharer, L.K., & Vivic, W.J. (1986). Homeless persons and health care. Annals of Internal Medicine, 104, 405-409.
     The homeless are subject to a wide range of acute and chronic diseases, magnified by poor living conditions, stress, and sociopathic behavior. Conditions common among the homeless include: (1) trauma, (2) pulmonary tuberculosis, (3) vascular disease, and (4) infestations. Innovative outreach programs may be the best solution to establishing and maintaining health care services to the homeless.

691. Brudney, K., & Dobkin, J. (1991). Resurgent tuberculosis in New York City. Human immunodeficiency virus, homelessness, and the decline of tuberculosis control programs. American Review of Respiratory Diseases, 144, 745-749.

692. Bryant, M. (1990). Health problems of the homeless: A challenge for nurses. Virginia Nurse, 58, 10-13.

693. Buff, D.D., Kenney, J.F., & Light, D., jr. (1980). Health problems of residents in single-room occupancy hotels. New York State Journal of Medicine, 80, 2000-2005.

694. Cass, R. (1987). Miracle on Times Square. Journal of Christian Nursing, 4, 4-8.

695. Centers for Disease Control. (1992). Deaths among homeless persons--San Francisco. Journal of the American Medical Association, 267, 484-485.

696. Centers for Disease Control. (1992). Tuberculosis among homeless. Journal of the American Medical Association, 267, 483-484.

697. Chaves, A.D., Robins, A.B., & Abeles, H. (1967). Tuberculosis case finding among homeless men in New York City. American Review of Respiratory Diseases, 74, 900-901.

698. Christ, W.R., & Hayden, S.L. (1989). Discharge planning strategies for acutely homeless inpatients. Social Work in Health Care, 14, 33-45.

699. Clark, M., & Rafferty, M. (1988). The sickness that won't heal: Health care for the nation's homeless. Health Policy Advisory Center Bulletin, 16, 20-28. Reviews health data on the homeless and the high incidence of physical and mental disorders and discuss the extensive use of emergency rooms for health care and problems in developing coordinated systems of care. Descriptions of several innovative health care programs for the homeless are provided.

700. Clore, E.R. (1992). NAPNAP president's message. Address unknown: the homeless. Journal of Pediatric Health Care, 6, 171-172.

701. Crystal, S. (1985). Health care and the homeless: Access to benefits. In P.W. Brickner, L.K. Scharer, B. Conanan, A. Elvy, & M. Savarese (Eds.), Health care of homeless people. New York: Springer.

702. Cuoto, R.A., Risley, P.L., & Lee, B.A. (1985). Healthcare and the homeless of Nashville: Dealing with a problem without a definition. Urban Resources, 2, 17-23.

703. Daly, G. (1990). Health implications of homelessness: Reports from three countries. Journal of Sociology and Social Welfare, 17, 111-125.

704. Daly, G. (1989). Homelessness and health: A comparison of British, Canadian, and U.S. cities. Cities, 6, 22-38.

705. Daniels, J.S. (1990). Measuring accomplishments: A review of two OSMA committees. Ohio Medical, 86, 389, 392.

706. Derstine, J.B. (1990). Community nursing and rehabilitation nursing using community agencies. Home Healthcare Nurse, 8, 13-16.

707. Dickinson, E.J., & Dickinson, R. (1987). Medical care for the homeless [letter]. Lancet, 1, 980-981.

708. Dluhy, M. (1990). Community perceptions of the homeless: Factors in intervention strategies with the homeless. Social Work Research and Abstracts, 26, 18-24.

709. Doblin, B.A., Gelberg, L., & Freeman, H.E. (1992). Patient care and professional staffing patterns in McKinney Act clinics providing primary care to the homeless. Journal of the American Medical Association, 267, 698-701.
Based on telephone interviews with clinical medical directors of 157 clinics receiving federal funding to provide health services to the homeless, this study found that, although nearly half of the estimated homeless population received health care services through these clinics, most were understaffed. Nearly 1/3 of the clinics had a physician present no more than 5 hours weekly, while an additional 10% had no physician at all. Barriers to recruitment of physicians and recommendations for future research on provision of health care to homeless persons are discussed.

710. Dobson, J. (1992). Homeless and healthless. Nursing Times, 88, 18.

711. Drake, M.A. (1992). The nutritional status and dietary adequacy of single homeless women and their children in shelters. Public Health Reports, 107, 312-319.

712. Dube, B., & Meldrum-Bolf, P. (1991). Helping the homeless. Michigan Nurse, 64, 3-4.

713. Dubnik-Unruh, S., & See, V. (1989). Children of chaos: Planning for the emotional survival of dying children of dying families. Journal of Palliative Care, 5, 10-15.

714. Edwards, K.S. (1988). Does medical indigence exist in Ohio? Ohio Medicine, 84, 945-951.

715. English, A. (1991). Runaway and street youth at risk for HIV infection: legal and ethical issues in access to care. Journal of Adolescent Health, 12, 504-510.

716. Farrow, J.A., Deisher, R.W., & Brown, R. (1991). West Coast Scientific Symposium on Health Care of Runaway and Street Youth. Introduction. Journal of Adolescent Health, 12, 497-199.

717. Feldstein, A. (1986). Health care of the homeless: Portland Oregon. Paper presented at the 114th Annual Meeting of the American Public Health Association, September.

718. Ferenchick, G.S. (1991). Medical problems of homeless and nonhomeless persons attending an inner-city clinic: a comparative study. American Journal of Medical Science, 301, 379-382.
    Noting that research on homelessness over relies on descriptive methods and lacks comparisons to nonhomeless persons, this retrospective study of the medical needs of homeless and nonhomeless clients of an outpatient clinic for the medically indigent found there were no significant differences in occurrence of many of the illnesses considered to be prevalent in homeless populations. Among the few differences were a tendency for homeless clients to be identified as alcoholic and to be seen for cuts and gynecologic problems more often than nonhomeless controls.

719. Ferenchick, G.S. (1992). The medical problems of homeless clinic patients: a comparative study. Journal of General Internal Medicine, 7, 294-297.
    A comparison of homeless and non-homeless patients seeking care at an ambulatory clinic for the medically indigent found more similarities than differences in the prevalence of major health problems. Where differences were found, the homeless had a higher prevalence of illness than the non-homeless.

720. Fetter, M.S., & Larson, E. (1988). Preventing and treating human immunodeficiency virus infection in the homeless. Archives of Psychiatric Nursing, 4, 379-383.

721. Filardo, T. (1985). Chronic disease management in the homeless. In P.W. Brickner, L.K. Scharer, B., Conanan, A. Elvy, & M. Savarese (Eds.), Health care of homeless people. New York: Springer.

722. Foster, J.M. (1992). The nurse in a center for the homeless. Nursing Management., 23, 38-39.

723. Francis, M.B. (1987). Long-term approaches to end homelessness. Public Health Nursing, 4, 230-235.

724. Francis, M.B. (1992). Eight homeless mothers' tales. Image: Journal of Nursing Scholarship, 24, 111-114.
    A qualitative study of interviews with 8 homeless mothers describe their struggles to overcome violation and establish connection.

725. Froner, G. (1988). AIDS and homelessness. Journal of Psychoactive Drugs, 20, 197-202.

726. Gelberg, L., & Linn, L.S. (1988). Social and physical health of homeless adults previously treated for mental health problems. Hospital and Community Psychiatry, 39, 510-516.
    Surveyed homeless adults to explore the relationship between previous use of mental health services and various indices of physical health status. Respondents with a previous psychiatric hospitalization were more likely to report having serious physical symptoms in the last month than did either those who had previously used only outpatient services or no services at all. Further, these individuals were more likely to eat from garbage cans, have poorer overall

personal hygiene, and to report more reasons for not seeking adequate health care.

727. Gibson, D. (1990). The LP/VN as advocate for the homeless. Journal of Practical Nursing, 40, 12-13.

728. Gross, K.P., & Fitzpatrick, T. (1987). Bumming it over Christmas. Nebraska Medical Journal, 72, 282-283.

729. Hales, A., & Magnus, M.H. (1991). Feeding the homeless. Journal of Nursing Administration, 21, 36-41.
Discusses the unique role nurses have in addressing homelessness and the design and development of a community meal program for the homeless.

730. Hamblin, T.J. (1987). A shocking American report with lessons for all [editorial]. British Medical Journal of Clinical Research, 295, 73.

731. Hanzlick, R., & Lazarchick, J. (1989). Health care history and utilization for Atlantans who die homeless. Journal of the Medical Association of Georgia, 78, 205-208.

732. Hawkins, N.G. (1957). Skid road--a health challenge. Lancet, 77, 153-156.
Compares 72 alcoholic with 81 non-alcoholic tuberculosis patients from skid row. Fewer alcoholic patients than non-alcoholic patients left the hospital against advice.

733. Hempel, S. (1989). No fixed abode. Nursing Times, 85, 16-17.

734. Hikmat, J. (1987). Nursing care for the homeless. Pennsylvania Nurse, 42, 4, 10.

735. Hilfiker, D. (1989). Are we comfortable with homelessness. Journal of the American Medical Association, 262, 1375-1376.

736. Hodnicki, D.R. (1990). Homelessness: Health-care implications. Journal of Community Health Nursing, 7, 59-67.

737. Holden, C. (1988). Health problems of the homeless [news]. Science, 242, 188-189.

738. Hopper, K. (1987). Overview on the homeless. Paper presented at the Conference on Health Care for Homeless People, New York, June.

739. Hudson, R.M. (1963). A study of tuberculous Skid Row alcoholics. Master's thesis, University of Washington.

740. Hudson, R.M., & Rhodes, R.J. (1971). Follow-up study of tuberculous skid row alcoholics 2. Hospital and post-hospital attitudes and care. Quarterly Journal of Studies on Alcohol, 32, 116-122.

741. Hultman, C.I. (1989). The effects of cost containment and multi-hospital systems on indigent health care. Dissertation Abstracts International, 49, 2414 A.

742. Imperato,P.J. (1992). Tuberculosis, AIDS, and homelessness. Journal of Community Health, 17, 187-189.

743. Institute of Medicine, Committee on Health Care for Homeless People. (1988). Homelessness, health, and human needs. Washington, DC: National Academy Press.
Considers in detail the issues associated with homelessness and health care of homeless persons. The authors represent a broad range of disciplines and present numerous recommendations for improving the plight of the homeless. Findings from 10 studies commissioned by the committee are discussed.

744. Joseph, H., & Roman-Nay, H. (1990). The homeless intravenous drug abuser and the AIDS epidemic. National Institute on Drug Abuse Research Monograph Series, 93, 219-253.

745. Kelling, K. (1991). Homelessness--left out in the cold. Nursing Times, 87, 32.

746. Kinchen, K., & Wright, J.D. (1991). Hypertension management in health care for the homeless clinics: results from a survey. American Journal of Public Health, 81, 1164-1165.

747. Kinzer, D. (1991). Self-identified health concerns of two homeless groups...including commentary by Flagg JM and Vredevoe DL with author response. Western Journal of Nursing Research, 13, 181-194.

748. Klee, H., Faugier, J., Hayes, C., & Boulton, T. (1990). Factors associated with risk behavior among injecting drug users. AIDS Care, 2, 133-145.

749. Kozol, J. (1988). Heartbreak hotel. Journal of Christian Nursing, 5, 4-8.

750. Krueger, L.W., & Stretch, J.J. (1986). Health care for the homeless: The St. Louis experience. St. Louis, MO: Health Care for the homeless Coalition of Greater St. Louis.

751. LaKores, D., Jeffers, J., & Moss, E.J. (1991). Homelessness in America's heartland: health perceptions of the homeless. Part 1. Kansas Nurse, 66, 1-2.

752. Laws, D. (1992). Homelessness: exploding a modern myth. Nursing Standards, 6, 20-21.

753. Lawson, P. (1991). Homelessness--a home for Tom. Nursing Times, 87, 26-29.

754. Lewin and Associates. (1987). Primary care and the homeless: A guide for community health centers. Washington, DC: National Association of Community Health Centers.
Uses the experiences of leading-edge health care providers to address questions that community health centers have when attempting to incorporate primary care

for homeless persons into their broader mission and to health such centers implement effective health care programs for homeless persons.

755. Lindsey, A.M. (1989). Health care for the homeless. Nursing Outlook, 37, 78-81.

756. Lipsky, B.A. (1991). Pneumococcal pneumonia: Predispositions and prevention. Chest, 99, 2-3.

757. Lock, K. (1988). Homeless--out in the cold. Nursing Standards, 3, 30-1.

758. Luder, E., Boey, E., Buchalter, B., & Martinez-Weber, C. (1989). Assessment of the nutritional status of urban homeless adults. Public Health Reports, 104, 451-457.
Reports findings of an assessment of nutritional indicators of 55 urban homeless persons. Findings indicate that, although over 90% reported they obtained enough to eat, the quality of their diet was inadequate. Decreased levels of lean body mass and increased levels of body fat, coupled with elevated serum cholesterol levels and shortages of nutrients in the diets of homeless people may place them at risk for nutrition-related disorders.

759. Luder, E., Ceysens-Okada, E., Koren-Roth, A., & Martinez-Weber, C. (1990). Health and nutrition survey in a group of urban homeless adults. Journal of the American Dietetic Association, 90, 1387-1392.

760. Mallenby, M.L.D. (1989). A comprehensive evaluation of alternatives for the provision of health care to the medically indigent in Nebraska. Dissertation Abstracts International, 49, 1987 A.

761. Martell, J.V., Seitz, R.S., Harada, J.K., Kobayashi, J., Sasaki, V.K., & Wong, C. (1992). Hospitalization in an urban homeless population: the Honolulu Urban Homeless Project. Annals of Internal Medicine, 116, 299-303.

762. Martinez, W.C. (1987). The homeless person with diabetes. A diagnostic and therapeutic challenge [published erratum appears in Postgrad Med 1987 Mar;81(4):16]. Postgraduate Medicine, 81, 289-298.

763. Marwick, C. (1985). The sizable homeless population: A growing challenge for medicine. Journal of the American Medical Association, 253, 3217-3225.

764. McInnis, B. (1987). Bringing nursing care to homeless guests: Barbara McInnis and the Pine Street Inn's Nurses' Clinic. JEN, 13, 26A-30A.

765. McMillan, I. (1991). Homelessness--help for the outcasts. Nursing Times, 87, 30-31.

766. McMurray, D. (1991). Manufacturing homelessness: Producing street people in a small town in Tennessee. Journal of the Tennessee Medical Association, 84, 61-65.

767. Mercat, A., Nguyen, J., & Dautzenberg, B. (1991). An outbreak of pneumococcal pneumonia in two men's shelters. Chest, 99, 147-151.

768. Michael, M., & Brammer, S. (1988). Medical treatment of homeless hypertensives [letter]. American Journal of Public Health, 78, 94.

769. Moore, C. (1990). Homelessness: The hidden cost. Health Visitor, 63, 196-197.

770. Morris, J.T., & McAllister, C.K. (1992). Homeless individuals and drug-resistant tuberculosis in south Texas. Chest, 102, 802-804.

771. Morrow, R., Halbach, J.L., Hopkins, C., Wang, C., & Shortridge, L. (1992). A family practice model of health care for homeless people: collaboration with family nurse practitioners. Family Medicine, 24, 312-316.
Homeless children represent the majority of homeless persons in this study of homelessness in Weschester County, New York. Assessment of access to health care services for the homeless revealed numerous barriers to services, including: (1) the fragmentary lifestyles of the homeless, (2) lack of insurance, (3) insensitivity of care givers, (4) distance from services, and (5) inflexibility of traditional services. The development of a new model of health care services is described.

772. Moy, J.A., & Sanchez, M.R. (1992). The cutaneous manifestations of violence and poverty. Archives of Dermatology, 128, 829-839.

773. Mufson, M.A., Crown, C.W., Krause, H.E., & Castella, C. (1974). Epidemiology of pneumococcal carriage and disease in skid row inhabitants (meeting). American Journal of Epidemiology, 100, 518.

774. National Academy of Sciences, Institute of Medicine, Committee on Health Care for Homeless People. (1988). Homelessness, health, and human needs. Washington, DC: National Academy Press.

775. National Association of Community Health Centers. (1989). A national directory of homeless health care projects. Washington, DC: Author.

776. Nazar-Stewart, V., & Nolan, C.M. (1992). Results of a directly observed intermittent isoniazid preventive therapy program in a shelter for homeless men. American Review of Respiratory Diseases, 146, 57-60.

777. Nolan, C.M., Elarth, A.M., Barr, H., Saeed, A.M., & Risser, D.R. (1991). An outbreak of tuberculosis in a shelter for homeless men. A description of its evolution and control. American Review of Respiratory Diseases, 143, 257-261.

778. Nyamathi, A. (1992). Comparative study of factors relating to HIV risk level of black homeless women. Journal of Acquired Immune Deficiency Syndrome, 5, 222-228.
This comparison of black homeless women categorized as either high, moderate, or low risk for HIV infection found that high risk women were best differentiated from the other groups by greater use of emotion-focused coping, greater severity

of concerns, greater depression and less self-esteem. Suggestions for improving interventions with this populations are discussed.

779. Nyamathi, A., & Shuler, P. (1989). Factors affecting prescribed medication compliance of the urban homeless adult. Nurse Practitioner, 14, 47-54.
Report findings of a study of factors affecting compliance with prescribed medication in 61 residents of a shelter for the homeless. Over 60% reported their health status to be fair or poor and nearly one-third reported compliance rates of half of the time or less. Factors associated with low rates of compliance included: (1) availability of drugs, (2) lack of privacy, and (3) lack of storage space. Factors associated with high compliance included: (1) carrying medication, (2) close proximity to a health clinic, and (3) understanding the need for medication.

780. O'Bryant, H. (1990). President's page...work with the homeless. Journal of Practical Nursing, 40, 4.

781. O'Connell, J.J. (1991). Nontuberculous respiratory infections among the homeless. Seminar in Respiratory and Infectious Diseases, 6, 247-253.

782. Olin, J.S. (1986). Skid row syndrome: A medical profile of the chronic drunkenness offender. Canadian Medical Association Journal, 95, 205-214.

783. Packett, S., Oswald, N., Bronson, S., & Kraushar, T. (1991). A problem homeless patients may not mention. RN, 54, 53-55.

784. Padgett, D.K., & Struening, E.L. (1991). Influence of substance abuse and mental disorders on emergency room use by homeless adults. Hospital and Community Psychiatry, 42, 834-838.

785. Pohl, J.M. (1987). A nursing model for addressing the health needs of homeless families. Image Journal of Nursing Scholarship, 22, 263.

786. Pollio, D. (1990). The street person: An integrated service provision model. Psychosocial Rehabilitation Journal, 14, 57-68.
Examines service provision to "street persons" and describes the "street center," an integrated model that allows for consumer-initiated participation and provides a wide range of services. The services (e.g., assessment, information and referral, food, clothing, substance abuse services) are explored, and concepts for developing a treatment program are presented in the context of a philosophy of client empowerment.

787. Presley, A. (1983). Health problems of the homeless in the Denver metro area. Presented at the American Public Health Association Meeting, Dallas, Texas, November.

788. Rafferty, M. (1989). Standing up for America's homeless. American Journal of Nursing, 89, 1614-1617.

789. Rafferty, M., Hinzpeter, D.A., Colwin, L., & Knox, M. (1984). The shelter worker's handbook: A guide to identifying and meeting the health needs of homeless people. New York: Coalition for the Homeless.

790. Rasmusson, D.L., Jonas, C.M., & Mitchell, G.J. (1991). The eye of the beholder: Parse's theory with homeless individuals. Clinical Nurse Specialist, 5, 139-143.

791. Regna, J. (1987). Homelessness [letter]. American Journal of Public Health, 77, 239-40.

792. Reilly, F.E., Grier, M.R., & Blomquist, K. (1992). Living arrangements, visit patterns, and health problems in a nurse-managed clinic for the homeless. Journal of Community Health Nursing, 9, 111-121.
Studied residents of a nurse-managed health clinic for homeless persons over an 18 month period and found that living arrangements, health problems, and visit patterns varied by age and gender. Implications for planning nursing services for the homeless are discussed.

793. Reuler, J.B. (1989). Health care for the homeless in a national health program. American Journal of Public Health, 79, 1033-1035.
Based on an evaluation of the British National Health Service, the author argues that enactment of a national health program in the U.S. would not necessarily resolve all of the issues related to service delivery or quality of health care for the homeless. Problems with the British system include: (1) lack of central government control, (2) overlap of agency responsibilities, (3) mechanistic biases, (4) over reliance on delivery of services by emergency rooms, and (5) lack of advocacy outside of the non-profit sector. Failure to address these problems and the special needs of the homeless may lead to further marginalization of the homeless and continuation of a two-class health care system.

794. Rhodes, R.J., & Hudson, R.M. (1969). A follow-up study of tuberculous skid row alcoholics. Quarterly Journal of Studies on Alcohol, 30, 119-128.

795. Ritchey, F.J., LaGory, M. & Mullis, J. (1991). Gender differences in health risks and physical symptoms among the homeless. Journal of Health and Social Behavior, 32, 33-48.
Compared a sample of 100 homeless persons and the general population and found that homeless men appear to be at greater risk of exhibiting symptoms although homeless women generally report more symptoms. Although predisposing illness was the best predictor of symptoms, gender explained a significant amount of variation after health risks were controlled.

796. Robert Wood Johnson Foundation/Pew Memorial Trust. (1985). Health care for the homeless: Program announcement. Princeton, NJ.

797. Robertson, M.J., & Cousineau, M.R. (1986). Health status and access to health services among the urban homeless. American Journal of Public Health, 76, 561-563.
A study of 238 homeless adults revealed that one/third rated their health as only fair or poor. Further, women reported more health problems than men. Over half

reported having no regular source of health care while over three-fourths had no health insurance. The authors conclude that lack of income and health insurance are significant barriers to health care services for the homeless.

798. Ropers, R.H., & Boyer, R. (1987). Homelessness as a health risk. Alcohol Health and Research World, Spring, 38-41.
Report findings of interviews of homeless persons in Los Angeles County, California. The findings suggest that poor health among the homeless is precipitated by their poor financial situation.

799. Ropers, R.H., & Boyer, R. (1987). Perceived health status among the new urban homeless. Social Science and Medicine, 24, 669-678.
Conducted 269 interviews with homeless men and women in Los Angeles to uncover the correlates of physical and mental health status among the homeless. Compared to past homeless populations, the new homeless are younger, better educated, and more likely to be from a racial or ethnic minority. Half of the males were veterans, including 30% from the Vietnam War. The most common health problems were respiratory infections and hypertension. Mental health problems included high rates of depression and substance abuse disorders. Nearly 16% reported having previous psychiatric hospitalizations and another 13% reported previous hospitalizations for substance abuse. Multiple regression analyses suggested that the best predictors of poor health status were length of unemployment, education, gender, and number of nights spent in shelters. The authors conclude that the causes of homelessness are multiple and complex, resulting in numerous subgroups with differing problems requiring differing intervention strategies.

800. Rusness, B.A.R. (1992). Potential dietary risks and the food insecurity of the homeless. Dissertation Abstracts International, 51, 4785-B.
The homeless experience places individuals at dietary risk. Deficiencies in vitamin A, vitamin C, calcium and iron, along with excesses in total fat consumption were found in a survey of 560 homeless adults. Also, the homeless experienced food insecurity in a variety of ways including lack of sufficient food, eating fewer than 3 meals a day, going without food for extended periods, and frequent worry about food quantity or quality. Long-term homelessness, prior homelessness, non-usage of shelter resources, and poor health aggravated the dietary risks common to homeless adults.

801. Saunders, S.L. (1990). Continuity of care among the homeless. Dissertation Abstracts International, 51, 1020-A.

802. Schieffelbein, C.W., Jr., & Snider,D.E., Jr. (1988). Tuberculosis control among homeless populations. Archives of Internal Medicine, 148, 1843-1846.
The authors report recommendations for controlling tuberculosis among the homeless resulting from a meeting of consultants convened by the Center for Disease Control.

803. Schilling, R.F., el-Bassel, N., & Gilbert, L. (1992). Drug use and AIDS risks in a soup kitchen population. Social Work, 37, 353-358.
Conducted interviews with 148 drug users in an urban soup kitchen and found evidence of the need for community-based AIDS prevention strategies aimed at

high-risk populations that are beyond the reach of current drug treatment or AIDS prevention programs.

804. Schlosstein, E., St.Clair, R., & Connell, F. (1991). Referral keeping in homeless women. Journal of Community Health, 16, 279-185.
Studied 118 homeless women screened for health care needs and found that referral keeping for medical conditions was comparable with that found in low-income housed populations. However, homeless women were significantly less likely to keep referrals for preventive care. Severity of symptoms was positively associated with referral keeping.

805. Schutt, R.K., & Garrett, G.R. (1988). Social background, residential experience, and health problems of the homeless. Psychosocial Rehabilitation Journal, 12, 67-70.
Categorized 205 shelter users according to their health problems (alcohol abuse, psychiatric disorder, both, or neither). Health problems were related to several background characteristics and to residential experience. Women were more likely to have psychiatric disorders, while males were more likely to be alcoholic. Further, respondents with dual diagnoses (e.g., both alcohol abuse and psychiatric disorder) were found to be more frequent shelter users.

806. Scott, R.K., & Jeffers, J.M. (1991). Characteristics and health needs of homeless persons in and urban agency. Part 2. Kansas Nurse, 66, 4-5.

807. Seaver, J. (1992). Maggots took charge of this homeless patient's hygiene. RN, 55, 9-11.

808. Sergi, J.S., Murray, M., & Cotanch, P.H. (1989). An understudied population: The homeless. Oncological Nursing Forum, 16, 113-114.

809. Shader, R.I., & Greenblatt, D.J. (1987). Back to basics--diagnosis before treatment: homelessness, hypothyroidism, aging, and lithium [editorial]. Journal of Clinical Psychopharmacology, 7, 375-376.

810. Shanks, N.J. (1988). Medical morbidity of the homeless. Journal of Epidemiology and Community Health, 42, 183-186.

811. Shuler, P.A. (1991). Homeless women's holistic and family planning needs: An exposition and test of the nurse practitioner practice model. Dissertation Abstracts International, 52, 1959-B.

812. Skelly, A.H., Getty, C., Kemsley, M., Hunter, J., & Shipman, J. (1990). Journal of the New York State Nurses Association, 21, 20-24.

813. Slutkin, G. (1986). Management of tuberculosis in urban homeless indigents. Public Health Reports, 101, 481-485.
Discusses the difficulties in providing treatment to tuberculosis patients that are homeless and often alcoholic. Barriers to successful treatment include, (1) erratic schedules, (2) mistrust of authority, and (3) uncooperative or aggressive behavior. Techniques to better manage the problem of tuberculosis in homeless persons are discussed.

814. Smith, L.G. (1987). Teaching treatment of mild, acute diarrhea and secondary dehydration to homeless parents. Public Health Reports, 102, 539-542.
Discusses the importance of education in prevention of disease, especially among homeless children. Focussing on the prevalence of dehydration and diarrhea among homeless children, the authors argue that educating parents in homeless shelters may mean the difference between life and death for homeless children with these disorders. A description of an educational program developed to help homeless parents recognize and treat mild, acute diarrhea and secondary dehydration is provided.

815. Smith, L.G. (1988). Home treatment of mild, acute diarrhea and secondary dehydration of infants and small children: an educational program for parents in a shelter for the homeless. Journal of Professional Nursing, 4, 60-63.

816. Soffel, D. (1991). Health status, housing characteristics and homelessness. Dissertation Abstracts International, 52, 2288-A.
Compared public assistance families requesting emergency housing and housed public assistance families and explores a causal model of the relationship between health status and the use of emergency shelters. Findings indicate that poor health does not lead to homelessness, although persons who had experienced a shelter stay had more chronic health problems, suggesting that experiencing a shelter stay influenced health outcomes.

817. Solarz, A., & Mowbray, C. (1985). An examination of physical and mental health problems of the homeless. Paper presented at the 113th Annual Meeting of the American Public Health Association, Washington, DC.

818. Stead, W.W. (1989). Special problems in tuberculosis: Tuberculosis in the elderly and in residents of nursing homes, correctional facilities, long-term care hospitals, mental hospitals, shelters for the homeless, and jails. Clinics in Chest Medicine, 10, 397-405.

819. Stephens, D., Dennis, E., Toomer, M., & Holloway, J. (1991). The diversity of case management needs for the care of homeless persons. Public Health Reports, 106, 15-19.

820. Stern, G. (1989). Adolescents and HIV: Annotated bibliography. Special Issue: Incarcerated adolescents and AIDS. Journal of Prison and Jail Health, 8, 103-116.

821. Stern, R.G. (1991). Nutrition services for homeless persons. Journal of the American Dietetics Association, 91, 910.

822. Stoner, M.R. (1988). The voluntary sector leads the way in delivering health care to the homeless ill. Journal of Voluntary Action Research, 17, 24-35.

823. Strasser, J.A., Damrosch, S., & Gaines, J. (1991). Journal of Community Health Nursing, 8, 65-73.

824. Stricof, R.L., Kennedy, J.T., Nattell, T.C., Weisfuse, I.B., & Novick, L.F. (1991). HIV seroprevalence in a facility for runaway and homeless adolescents.

American Journal of Public Health, 81, 50-53.
This study of HIV-seroprevalence among 2,667 homeless adolescents found an overall 5.3% prevalence rate. Prevalence increased with age and was higher for Hispanic youth than with either non-Hispanic whites and non-Hispanic blacks. HIV seropositivity was related to intravenous drug use, male homosexual/bisexual activity, prostitution and history of other STD's.

825. Sullivan, M. (1992). Pittsburgh health care for the homeless: working toward self-sufficiency. Pennsylvania Nurse, 47, 13.

826. Thomison, J.B. (1991). Manufacturing a cultural subclass. Journal of the Tennessee Medical Association, 84, 88-90.

827. Thompson, A. (1991). Homelessness: Christmas in the open air. Nursing Standards, 6, 23-25.

828. Thompson, R., & Atkinson, J. (1989). Homelessness and health. Nursing Standards, 48, 30-32.

829. Torres, J. (1986). The health of the homeless: Strategies for empowerment. Paper presented at the New York Marxist School.

830. Torres, R.A., Lefkowitz, P., Kales, C., & Brickner, P.W. (1987). Homelessness among hospitalized patients with the acquired immunodeficiency syndrome in New York City [letter]. Journal of the American Medical Association, 258, 779-780.

831. Towber, R., & Ladner, S. (1985). Psychiatric indication and alcohol abuse among public shelter clients. Paper presented at MSIS Ninth Annual Users' Conference, November.

832. Towne, P. (1988). Health care for the homeless. Chart, 85, 6-9.

833. Tracy, R., & Sanders, G. (1991). Nursing directed health care with the homeless population. Kansas Nurse, 66, 12-13.

834. Truslow, G.Y. (1988). Providing medical care to the poor in rural India and in New York City [editorial]. Hospital Practice, 23, 13-16.

835. Turner, S.L., Bauer, G., McNair, E., McNutt, B., & Walker, W. (1989). The homeless experience: Clinic building in a community health discovery-learning project. Public Health Nursing, 6, 97-101.

836. U.S. Conference of Mayors. (1985). Health care for the homeless: A 40 city review. Washington, DC: Author.
Presents demographic characteristics of the homeless population, causes of homelessness, health care needs and services, and barriers to health care for the homeless in 40 cities. Recommendations for meeting the health care needs of the homeless are discussed.

837. U.S. House Committee on Energy and Commerce. (1987). Health Care for the Homeless. Hearing before the Subcommittee on Health and the Environment of the Committee on Energy and Commerce. House of Representatives, Ninety-Ninth Congress, Second Session (December 15, 1986). Washington, DC: U.S. Government Printing Office.

838. Valentine, P. (1990). PA students reach out to the homeless...physician assistants. Journal of the American Academy of Physician Assistants, 3, 504-510.

839. Visotsky, H.M. (1987). The great American roundup [editorial]. New England Journal of Medicine, 317, 1662-1663.

840. Vivic, W.J. (1991). Homelessness. Bulletin of the New York Academy of Medicine, 67, 49-54.

841. Wiecha, J.L., Dwyer, J.T., & Dunn-Stroehecker, M. (1991). Nutrition and health services needs among the homeless. Public Health Reports, 106, 364-374. Describes nutrition and related health problems among the homeless and identifies their nutritional and health service needs. Homeless persons are more likely to eat fewer meals per day, go without food for extended periods more often, and are more likely to have inadequate diets than the general population. Yet many homeless people eligible for food stamps do not receive them. Both public and private agencies often provide nutritious meals for homeless persons. However, availability of these services to homeless persons is often limited.

842. Witt, B.S. (1991). The homeless shelter: An ideal clinical setting for RN/BSN students. Nursing and Health Care, 12, 304-307.

843. Wlodarczyk, D., & Prentice, R. (1988). Health issues of homeless persons. Western Journal of Medicine, 148, 717-719.

844. Wolgemuth, J.C., Myers-Williams, C., Johnson, P., & Henseler, C. (1992). Wasting malnutrition and inadequate nutrient intakes identified in a multiethnic homeless population. Journal of the American Dietetics Association, 92, 834-839.
Studied a multiethnic sample of 277 homeless men and women and found wasting malnutrition in 20% of the men. Further, dietary intakes of calcium, zinc, and vitamin B-6, were significantly below recommended daily allowances for all ethnic groups. Intake of thiamin for whites and vitamin A and riboflavin for Hispanics were below recommended daily allowances.

845. Wood, D., & Valdez, R.B. (1991). Barriers to medical care for homeless families compared with housed poor families. American Journal of the Diseases of Childhood, 145, 1109-1115.

846. Wrenn, K. (1990). Foot problems in homeless persons. Annals of Internal Medicine, 113, 5567-5569.

847. Wrenn, K. (1991). Immersion foot. A problem of the homeless in the 1990s. Archives of Internal Medicine, 151, 785-788.

848. Wright, J.D. (1987). Homelessness and health: Effects of lifestyle on physical well-being among homeless people in New York City. In M. Lewis & J. Miller (Eds.), Research in social problems and Public Policy, Vol. 4., Greenwich, CT: JAI Press.
Information on the health status and health care histories of homeless people in New York was obtained through chart reviews of over 6,000 homeless who used medical services in New York City. Trends and prevalence rates for many health problems are presented.

849. Wright, J.D. (1987). The national health care for the homeless program. In R.D. Bingham, R.E. Green & S.B. White (Eds.), The homeless in contemporary society. Newbury Park, CA: Sage Publications.
The author describes the Health Care for the Homeless program and the evaluation being conducted by the author also provides preliminary data from the 19 program grantees from 1986, the first year of the project.

850. Wright, J.D. (1990). Poor people, poor health: The health status of the homeless. Journal of Social Issues, 46, 49-64.

851. Wright, J.D., Rossi, P.H., Knight, J.W., & Weber-Burdin, E. (1985). Health and homelessness in New York City: Research report to the Robert Wood Johnson Foundation. Amherst, MA: University of Massachusetts Social and Demographic Research Institute.

852. Wright, J.D., Weber-Burdin, E., Knight, J.W., & Lam, J.A. (1986). The National Health Care for the Homeless Program: The first year. Amherst, MA: University of Massachusetts Social and Demographic Research Institute.

853. Wright, J.D., & Weber-Burdin, E. (1987). Homelessness and health. Washington, DC: McGraw-Hill.

854. Zlotnick, C. (1987). Pediculosis corporis and the homeless. Journal of Community Health Nursing, 4, 43-48.

6

Families and Children

855. Abbott, M.L., & Blake, G.R. (1988). An intervention model for homeless youth. Clinical Sociology Review, 6, 148-158.
Describes a cooperative effort between a clinic and an urban university to develop an employment program for homeless street youth. An important element of the program was to provide immediate part-time employment rather than merely pre-job training. The authors conclude that linking meaningful employment with stable housing arrangements and health and mental health services was responsible for the success of the program.

856. Adams, G.R. (1980). Runaway youth projects: Comments on care programs for runaways and throwaways. Journal of Adolescence, 3, 321-324.

857. Adams, G.R., Gullotta, T., & Clancy, M.A. (1985). Homeless adolescents: A descriptive study of similarities and differences between runaways and throwaways. Adolescence, 20, 715-724.
Reports the findings of a study comparing 22 runaways (RAs), 19 throwaways (THAs), and 2 societal rejects. The results indicate that internal social control and psychopathological perspectives provide some understanding of differing types of runaway adolescents. Both RAs and THAs perceived extensive parent-child conflict in their homes. However, when compared with RAs, THAs perceived greater stress in their parents' interpersonal relationship and a greater desire by parents for them to leave home. Both groups perceived high levels of restrictive supervision by both parents and a tendency to be socially isolated. The authors argue for a greater emphasis on prevention, including training programs for working with problem adolescents and their families to reduce communication problems, parent-child conflict, and stress.

858. Alperstein, G., & Arnstein, E. (1988). Homeless children: A challenge for pediatricians. Pediatric Clinics of North America, 35, 1413-1425.
The health status of homeless children has become a major concern as the number of homeless families and children has increased in the United States over

the past few years. The authors cite some evidence that suggests that the health problems of homeless children are of greater frequency and of greater severity than those of non-homeless poor children. The authors feel that it is important for pediatricians to play a major role in solving the problem of sufficient health care for homeless children.

859. Alperstein, G., Rappaport, C., & Flanigan, J.M. (1988). Health problems of homeless children in New York City. American Journal of Public Health, 78, 1232-1233.
Compared the outpatient medical records of 265 homeless children less than 5 years of age in New York City with the records of non-homeless children of low socioeconomic status attending the same pediatric clinic. The frequency of health problems among the homeless children, including delayed immunizations, elevated blood lead levels, hospital admission rates, and the number of child abuse and neglect reports, exceeded those for the comparison group.

860. American Academy of Pediatrics. Committee on Community Health Services. (1988). Health needs of homeless children. Pediatrics, 82, 938-940.

861. American Medical Association, Council on Scientific Affairs. (1989). Health care needs of homeless and runaway youths. Journal of the American Medical Association, 262, 1358-1361.
Homeless youth are at risk for abuse and victimization due to their marginal existence which results from lack of help from social service agencies and lack of job skills. Further, homeless youth are at risk for numerous health problems and health care services for these youth are often inadequate. The recommendation is that reliable data on the extent of homelessness among adolescents and the nature of their needs be developed and that guidelines for health care of this population be generated.

862. Andrews, C. (1974). Reception of children into care because of homelessness. Social Work Today, 5, 333-334.

863. Armstrong, C.P. (1932). Six hundred runaway boys: Why boys desert their homes. Boston, MA: Richard C. Badger.
Compared 660 delinquent runaways with other groups of delinquent and non-delinquent boys and found that family maladjustment and an inflexible school system are seen as the primary causes of running away.

864. Axelson, L.J., & Dail, P.W. (1988). The changing character of homelessness in the United States. Family Relations, 37, 463-469.
Discusses the growing number of homeless persons and families who do not fit any of the traditional stereotypes of the homeless (e.g., hoboes, wanderers, or the mentally ill). The authors suggest recommendations for public policy responses.

865. Bach, V., & Steinhagen, R. (1987). Alternatives to the welfare hotel: Using emergency assistance to provide decent transitional shelter for the homeless families. New York: Community Service Society of New York.

866. Balanon, L.G. (1989) Street children: Strategies for action. Child Welfare, 68, 159-166.

867. Bass, J.L., Brennan, P., Mehta, K.A., & Kodzis, S. (1990). Pediatric problems in a suburban shelter for homeless families. Pediatrics, 85, 33-38.

868. Bassuk, E.L. (1986). Homeless families: Single mothers and their children in Boston shelters. New Directions for Mental Health Services, June, 45-53.
The author reports findings from interviews with 51 mothers and 78 children residing in 6 homeless shelters and 2 battered women's shelters. Findings indicate that the phenomenon of homeless families results from the combined effects of poverty, violence, and their effects on development and self-esteem and that many homeless children suffer from serious emotional problems.

869. Bassuk, E.L. (1987). The feminization of homelessness: Families in Boston shelters. American Journal of Social Psychiatry, 7, 19-23.
Reports findings of clinical interviews with 51 mothers and 78 children living in shelters in Boston. Mothers were characterized by chaotic developmental histories, patterns of long-term residential instability, few supportive relationships, a history of family violence, poor work histories, and lack of adequate involvement with service agencies. Children were characterized by severe developmental lags, anxiety and depression. The author makes recommendations for policy efforts.

870. Bassuk, E. (1990). Who are the homeless families? Characteristics of sheltered mothers and children. Special Issue: The homeless mentally ill. Community Mental Health Journal, 26, 425-434.

871. Bassuk, E.L. (1991). Homeless families. Scientific American, 265, 66-74.

872. Bassuk, E., & Gallagher, E. (1990). The impact of homelessness on children. Child and Youth Services, 14, 19-33.

873. Bassuk E.L., & Rosenberg, L. (1988). Why does family homelessness occur? A case-control study. American Journal of Public Health, 78, 783-788.
Reports findings of a study comparing homeless (N=49) and housed female-headed families (N=81). Homeless children were characterized by developmental lags and emotional difficulties. Homeless mothers had fewer supportive interpersonal relationships, perhaps due to their history of family violence, and more psychiatric, drug, and alcohol problems than non-homeless mothers. The recommendations include increasing: (1) the supply of decent affordable housing, (2) income maintenance, and (3) assistance from welfare agencies.

874. Bassuk, E.L., & Rubin, L. (1987). Homeless children: A neglected population. American Journal of Orthopsychiatry, 57, 279-286.
Studied 82 families with 156 children living in 14 shelters in Massachusetts and found that nearly half of the children were in need of psychiatric evaluation. Further, developmental delays, depression, anxiety, and learning difficulties were common among the children.

875. Bassuk, E.L., Rubin, L., & Lauriat, A.S. (1986). Characteristics of sheltered homeless families. American Journal of Public Health, 76, 1097-1101.
Interviews with 80 mothers and 151 children living in shelters were conducted to describe the characteristics of homeless families. Over 90% of the families were single-parent families and were receiving Aid to Families with Dependent Children, while nearly two-thirds lacked even minimal supportive relationships. Almost half of the children were found to have developmental lags, anxiety, depression and learning problems. The authors stress the need for comprehensive psychosocial and economic interventions for homeless families.

876. Beatty, J.W., & Carlson, H.M. (1985). Street kids: Children in danger. Paper presented at the 93rd Annual Convention of the American Psychological Association, Los Angeles, CA, August.
Describes the services provided by Project LUCK (Link Up the Community for Kids), a program designed to coordinate the efforts of several agencies serving homeless and runaway youth in Portland, Oregon. Services provided include: (1) shelter for runaways, (2) counseling services, (3) a youth advocacy program, (4) vocational training and job placement, (5) support groups for teenage mothers, (6) a walk-in emergency counseling center, and (7) street outreach.

877. Benalcazar, B. (1982). Study of fifteen runaway patients. Adolescence, 17, 553-566.
This paper attempts to uncover the causes of runaway behavior by studying a group of 15 adolescents in a long-term treatment setting over a one-year period.

878. Berne, A.S., Dato, C., Mason, D.J., & Rafferty, M. (1990). A nursing model for addressing the health needs of homeless families. Image Journal of Nursing Scholarship, 22, 8-13.
Reviews recent research concerning homeless families and the conditions in which they live and outline the significant health and mental health problems that these families experience. Effective nursing interventions for homeless families using Peszneckers' Model of Poverty are proposed.

879. Boxill, N.A., & Beaty, A.L. (1990). Mother/child interaction among homeless women and their children in a public night shelter in Atlanta, Georgia. Child and Youth Services, 14, 49-64.

880. Brantley, C. (1983). New York City's services to homeless families: A report to the mayor. New York: Health and Hospitals Corporation.

881. Brennan, T. (1980). Mapping the diversity among runaways. Journal of Family Issues, 1, 189-209.

882. Breton, M. (1978). The runaways. Boston, MA: Little Brown.

883. Brown, P.A. (1991). Educating homeless children and youth. Journal of Health Care for the Poor and Underserved, 2, 189-195.

884. Bullock, R., Hossie, K., Little, M. & Millham, S. (1990). Secure accommodation for very difficult adolescents: Some recent research findings. Journal of Adolescence, 13, 205-216.

885. Caro, F. (1981). Estimating numbers of homeless families. New York: Community Service Society of New York.

886. Caton, C.L. (1986). The homeless experience in adolescent years. New Directions for Mental Health Services, June, 63-70.
Describes social and clinical characteristics of homeless youth and factors associated with running away from home. Most runaway episodes take place in mid-adolescence and usually follow a family conflict (e.g., communication or relationship problems or allegations of physical and sexual abuse). Four major areas of social and behavior problems include: (1) school problems, (2) antisocial behavior, (3) depression, and (4) suicide attempts. Concludes with a discussion of the service needs of homeless youth.

887. Chauvin, V., Duncan, J., & Marcontel, M. (1990). Homeless students of the 1990s: A new school population. School Nurse, 6, 10-13.

888. Coalition for the Homeless (1984). Perchance to sleep: Homeless children without shelter in New York City. New York: Author.

889. Cohen, E., MacKensie, R.G., & Yates, G.L. (1991). HEADSS, a psychosocial risk assessment instrument: implications for designing effective intervention programs for runaway youth. Journal of Adolescent Health, 12, 539-544.
A comparison of homeless and non-homeless youths attending a high-risk youth clinic found that homeless teens were more likely than non-homeless youths to be depressed and actively suicidal, to have been victims of sexual abuse, to be at risk for HIV infection, to have engaged in prostitution, to abuse drugs, and to have dropped out of high school.

890. Collier, R. (1987). Focus Point--young people without homes. Caritas, 53, 5-13.

891. Commission on California State Government Organization and Economy. (1987). The Children's Services Delivery System in California: Preliminary Report--Phase I. Sacramento, CA: Author.
This is a criticism of the state of California's provision of children's services and a recommendation for viable solutions. Special emphasis is given to programs for abused and neglected children and runaway and homeless youth, and to the need for child care services. State programs and services for children are listed.

892. Council for Exceptional Children. (1991). Exceptional children at risk. Washington, DC: Council for Exceptional Children.

893. Crystal, S. (1986). Psychosocial rehabilitation and homeless youth. Psychosocial Rehabilitation Journal, 10, 15-21.
Reports findings of a study of homeless youth. Key factors leading to homeless include: (1) educational and vocational deficits, (2) family problems, (3) involvement in the criminal justice system, and (4) lack of adequate social services, outreach and entitlements. The author concludes that most of these youth wish to live independent of the shelter system but lack the skills and resources to do so.

894. Dail, P.W. (1989). Family poverty: The special case of homelessness. Paper presented at the Annual Meetings of the Society for the Study of Social Problems, Berkeley, CA, August.

895. Dail, P.W. (1990). The psychosocial context of homeless mothers and young children: Program and policy implications. Child Welfare, 69, 291-308.

896. Damrosch, S.P., Sullivan, P.A., Scholler, A, & Gaines, J. (1988). On behalf of homeless families. MCN, 13, 259-263.

897. Deisher, R.W., & Rogers, W.M. (1991). The medical care of street youth. Journal of Adolescent Health, 12, 500-503.
Based on clinical experience in providing medical care to homeless street youth, the authors contend that the numbers of youth on the street are increasing and that their health care needs are often neglected. Discussions of the street lifestyle and its impact on development are included.

898. Donahue, P.J. (1991). The role of fantasy in adaptation: A study of homeless children. Dissertation Abstracts International, 52, 2771-B.

899. Donough, R. (1985). Juvenile prostitution and street youth in Portland. Tri-County Youth Services Consortium.

900. Eddowes, E.A., & Hranitz, J.R. (1989). Educating children of the homeless. Childhood Education, 65, 197-200.

901. Edelman, M.W., & Mihaly, L. (1989). Homeless families and the housing crisis in the United States. Children and Youth Services Review, 11, 91-108.
The effect of homelessness on children's health, education, and emotional development are discussed. Lack of affordable housing and low income are seen as the primary causes of family homelessness. The authors argue for increasing the supply of affordable housing and implementing laws against discrimination in housing.

902. Ellwood, D.T. (1988). Poor support: Poverty in the American family. New York: Basic Books.

903. Ely, L. (1987). Broken lives: Denial of education to homeless children. Washington, DC: National Coalition for the Homeless.

904. Feitel, B., Margetson, N., Chama, J., & Lipman, C. (1992). Psychosocial background and behavioral and emotional disorders of homeless and runaway youth. Hospital and Community Psychiatry, 43(2), 155-159.
Of 140 adolescent residents of a shelter for homeless youths, most came from similar backgrounds characterized by emotional deprivation and physical or sexual abuse. Nine out of ten met DSM III-R criteria for emotional or behavior disorders, with nearly 60% having conduct disorder and 75% being depressed. Further, over 1/4 had attempted suicide.

905. Felsman, J.K. (1985). Abandoned Children Reconsidered: Prevention, Social Policy and the Trouble with Sympathy. Paper presented at the International Conference on Prevention, Montreal, Canada, April.

906. Felsman, J.K. (1989). Risk and resiliency in childhood: The lives of street children. In T.F. Dugan & R.Coles (Eds.), The child in our times: Studies in the development of resiliency. New York: Bruner/Mazel.

907. Ferran, E., & Sabatini, A. (1985). Homeless youth: The New York experience. International Journal of Family Psychiatry, 6, 117-128.
A review of the literature on homeless and runaway youths shows that academic failure, family problems, employment difficulties, and psychiatric disorders are common among this population. A discussion of the service needs of homeless and runaway youth is provided.

908. Fierman, A.H., Dreyer, B.P., Quinn, L., Shulman, S., Courtlandt, C.D., & Guzzo, R. (1991). Growth delay in homeless children. Pediatrics, 88, 918-925.

909. Fisher, E. (1980). Homeless families: A scheme of notification to ensure effective care. Nursing Times supplement 17, 76, 77-80.

910. Ford, C.B. (1991). Family influences on school adaptation and achievement among homeless children living in a transitional living center. Dissertation Abstracts International, 53, 991-A.
Studied the relationship between family environment, structure, and background and school adaptation and found no relationship between family variables and academic achievement. However, family organization, family conflict, and length of participation in a family support program predicted childrens' ability to adapt to the classroom environment.

911. Fors, S.W., & Rojeck, D.G. (1991). A comparison of drug involvement between runaways and school youths. Journal of Drug Education, 21, 13-25.
Comparisons of data collected from 253 youth in shelters for homeless/runaway youth and data from other studies of runaways and youths in school suggest that drug use and abuse is 2 to 3 times more prevalent among homeless youth than youth in school. Runaways' attitudes towards several illicit behaviors were found to be more tolerant than those of school youth.

912. Fox, S.J., Barnett, R.J., Davies, M., & Bird, H.R. (1990). Psychopathology and developmental delay in homeless children: A pilot study. Journal of the American Academy of Child and Adolescent Psychiatry, 29, 732-735.

913. Francis, M.B. (1991). Homeless families: rebuilding connections. Public Health Nursing, 8, 90-96.

914. Frawley, R., & Zafonte, S.M. (1984). Meeting the needs of homeless youth. A Report of the Homeless Youth Steering Committee. New York: State Council on Children and Families.

915.   Gallagher, E. (1986). No place like home: A report on the tragedy of homeless children and their families in Massachusetts.   Boston, MA: Massachusetts Committee for Children and Youth.

916.   Gewirtzman, R., & Fodor, I. (1987).   The homeless child at school: From welfare hotel to classroom. Child Welfare, 66, 237-245.
        Explores causes of homelessness among children and describe living conditions in emergency shelters and welfare hotels. The authors conclude by suggesting that a structured, non-threatening classroom environment is necessary to allow homeless children to express the fears and frustrations associated with the transition from welfare hotel to school.

917.   Goodman, L.A. (1992). Prevalence of lifetime abuse and level of social support in the lives of homeless and housed poor mothers: A comparative study. Dissertation Abstracts International, 52, 4466 B.

918.   Goodman, L.A. (1991). The prevalence of abuse among homeless and housed poor mothers: a comparison study. American Journal of Orthopsychiatry, 61, 489-500.
        Compared the physical and sexual abuse histories of homeless and non-homeless poor mothers and found few significant differences. However, nearly 90% of the total sample reported having experienced some sort of abuse at some time during their lives.

919.   Gore, T. (1991). A portrait of at-risk children. Journal of Health Care for the Poor and Underserved, 2, 95-105.

920.   Grams, V.G. (1991). Administering programs for children living in temporary housing: An investigation. Dissertation Abstracts International, 52, 2343 A.
        Evaluated a school districts policy of enrolling homeless children in regular schools and mainstreaming them in regular classes. Although implementation of the program involved substantial difficulties, evidence supported the effectiveness of the program in providing for homeless school-aged children.

921.   Grant, R. (1989). Assessing the damage: The impact of shelter experience on homeless young children. New York, NY: Association to Benefit Children.
        Examines the impact of welfare hotel placement on a sample of children who participated in a day care center located in a large welfare hotel in New York City. Data is primarily anecdotal and observational.

922.   Grant, R. (1991). The special needs of homeless children: Early intervention at a welfare hotel. Topics in Early Childhood Special Education, 10, 76-91.
        Studied the demographic characteristics of homeless families and of 87 homeless preschool children (aged 2-5 years) in day care at a large welfare hotel. Economic conditions most frequently led to loss of housing. Asthma and other chronic illnesses were prevalent. 75% of the children initially presented with developmental delays and deviations, primarily impulsivity and speech delay. Early intervention in the form of enriched day care restored age level functioning for most children. Disruptions in service for relocated families jeopardized gains for children under 4 years of age. In such cases, recidivism is an emerging problem.

923. Gutierres, S.E., & Reich, J.W. (1981). A developmental perspective on runaway behavior: Its relationship to child abuse. Child Welfare, 60, 89-94.

924. Hackman, T.G. (1977). Homeless youth in New York City: A field study. New York: Community Service Society.

925. Hancock, P.M. (1989). Education in the streets: An ethnographic study of homeless youth in New York City. Dissertation Abstracts International, 49, 2539 A.

926. Hall, J., & Maza, P. (1990). No fixed address: The effects of homelessness on families and children. Child and Youth Services, 14, 35-47.

927. Heard, D.R., & Boxill, N.A. (1988). Two steps back, one step forward: Homeless women and their children at a transition house. SAGE: A Scholarly Journal on Black Women, 5, 50-51.

928. Hermann, R.C. (1988). Center provides approach to major social ill: homeless urban runaways, 'throwaways' [news]. Journal of the American Medical Association, 260, 311-312.

929. Hersch, P. (1988). Coming of age on city streets. Psychology Today, 22, 28-37.
       Discusses characteristics and problems of runaway and homeless youth. Most runaways come from dysfunctional families and, because most obtain money through commercial sex, are at risk for AIDS. Further, runaways are characterized by emotional problems and depression.

930. Heusel, K.J. (1991). The experience of homelessness viewed through the eyes of homeless school-aged children. Dissertation Abstracts International, 51, 4777 B.
       Studied the childhood experiences of homelessness of 33 school-aged homeless children and found that children view homelessness in a variety of ways. Homeless children living in shelters perceived moving, leaving home, missing friends, changing schools, and being teased about living in shelters as the major stressors of the homeless experience. Homeless children not living in shelters did not consider themselves homeless. Half of the children interviewed said homeless was being sad, uncomfortable, poor, embarrassed or different, while nearly 1/4 did not verbalize feelings.

931. Hibbitt, E. (1990). Infant feeding in adversity: Health promotion with homeless families--extending the role of the midwife, Part 3. Midwives Chronicle, 103, 8-10.

932. Hier, S.J., Korboot, P.J., & Schweitzer, R.D. (1990). Social adjustment and symptomatology in two types of homeless adolescents: Runaways and throwaways. Adolescence, 25, 761-771.

933. Holloran, P.C. (1982). Boston's wayward children: Social services for homeless children, 1800-1930. Dissertation Abstracts International, 43, 1264 A.

934. Homelessness Information Exchange. (1988). Family and child homelessness.
      Washington, DC.: Author.
      This overview of the extent, causes, and effects of homelessness among families
      and children includes excerpts from a number of reports and case studies of
      emergency and transitional housing programs.

935. Horowitz, S.V., Springer, C.M., & Koze, G. (1988). Stress in hotel children:
      The effects of homelessness on attitudes towards school.   Children's
      Environments Quarterly, 5, 34-36.

936. Hu, D.J., Covell, R.M., Morgan, J., & Arcia, J. (1989). Health care needs
      for children of the recently homeless. Journal of Community Health, 14, 1-8.
      The authors report findings of a survey of the health care status and needs of
      homeless children. Thirty families residing in an emergency shelter who had
      been homeless less than six months were surveyed. Over half of those surveyed
      had no regular source of health care while 47% had no form of health care
      coverage. Families with a regular source of health care reported that their
      children were of better overall health and had more frequent checkups than
      families with no regular source of health care. Further, longer periods of
      homelessness were associated with poorer health among the children. The most
      frequently mentioned health care needs for children included: (1) general non-
      emergency clinics (76.7%), (2) emergency services (66.7%), and (3) dental
      services (66.7%). 43.3% of families expressed a need for dietary or nutritional
      counseling, while less than 7% felt their children needed social or psychological
      services.

937. Hui, E., & Knecht, R. (1991). Homeless teenagers on New York City streets.
      Imprint, 38, 55-57.

938. Ivers, K.J., & Carlson, H.M. (1987). Needs assessment of female street kids:
      Children in danger. Paper presented at the 95th Annual Convention of the
      American Psychological Association, New York, NY.

939. Johnson, R., & Carter, M.M. (1980). Flight of the young: Why children run
      away from their homes. Adolescence, 15, 483-489.

940. Jones, L.P. (1988). A typology of adolescent runaways. Child and Adolescent
      Social Work Journal, 5, 16-29.

941. Kassai, M. (1990). Caretaking environments. Clinical Issues in Perinatal and
      Women's Health Nursing, 1, 123-127.

942. Kates, G.L., Pennbridge, J., Swofford, A., & MacKensie, R.G. (1991). The
      Los Angeles system of care for runaway/homeless youth. Journal of Adolescent
      Health, 12, 555-560.

943. Kearon, W.G. (1987). Abuse of runaway and homeless children on the streets.
      Child Abuse and Neglect, 11, 587.

944. Kennedy, M.R. (1991). Homeless and runaway youth mental health issues: no
      access to the system. Journal of Adolescent Health, 12, 576-579.

Describes the major mental health problems of homeless and runaway youth and discusses behavioral and environmental variables which might help in developing preventive and treatment oriented interventions.

945. Knauss, J., & Nelson, K. (1986). Homeless in Chicago: The special case of pregnant teenagers and young parents. Paper presented at the Annual Children's Defense Fund National Conference, Washington, DC.

946. Knickman, J.R., & Weitzman, B.C. (1989). A study of homeless families in New York City: Risk assessment models and strategies for prevention (Final report: Volume I). New York: New York University.
This 22 month study of 1,228 New York City families of which 704 were homeless shelter residents and 524 were public assistance recipients who were not homeless attempted a comparison of these two groups in order to determine if it was possible to identify in advance families at high risk to seek shelter and what types of public initiatives might stabilize existing housing arrangements and reduce the use of the cities shelter system.

947. Konik, M.P. (1989). Homeless children living with their families in Florida emergency shelters: Their behavior problems, social competencies, and attitudes towards school. Dissertation Abstracts International, 49, 3270 A.

948. Kosof, A. (1977). Runaways. New York: Franklin Watts.

949. Kozol, J. (1989). Rachel and her children: Homeless families in America. Southbridge, MA: Crown.

950. Krueger, L.W., Stretch, J.J., & Johnson, A.K. (1988). Inequality and injustice among traumatized families: Differentials among black and white homeless. Paper presented at the National Association of Social Workers Annual Program Meeting, Philadelphia, PA., November.

951. Kruks, G. (1991). Gay and lesbian homeless/street youth: special issues and concerns. Journal of Adolescent Health, 12, 515-518.
Found that gay- lesbian- and bisexual- identified youth have an increased risk of both homelessness and suicide. Often gay and bisexual male youth are forced out of their homes because of their sexual orientation and are more likely to engage in prostitution than their non-gay counterparts.

952. Kufeldt, K., Durieux, M., Nimmo, M., & McDonald, M. (1992). Providing shelter for street youth: are we reaching those in need? Child Abuse and Neglect, 16, 187-199.

953. Kufeldt, K., & Nimmo, M. (1987). Kids on the street they have something to say: Survey of runaway and homeless youth. Journal of Child Care, 3, 53-61.
The authors report findings of interviews with 405 homeless and runaway youth and suggest making a distinction between sporadic runners and the truly homeless. The most frequent reasons for running away were poor communication at home (53%) and some form of physical or sexual abuse (33%).

954. Kufeldt, K., & Nimmo, M. (1987). Youth on the street: Abuse and neglect in the eighties. Child Abuse and Neglect, 11, 531-543.
Identified two groups of runaway youth based on interviews with 489 homeless and runaway youth. "Runners" are those who leave home and do not intend to return, and "in and outers" run away as an temporary coping mechanism and stayed away from home for short periods of time. The likelihood of engaging in criminal activity increased with greater distance and longer time away from home. The authors describe a safe house for runaways that was an outcome of the research.

955. Lauriat, A.S. (1986). Sheltering homeless families: Beyond an emergency response. New Directions for Mental Health Services, June, 87-94.
Uses the case of a single-parent female with 3 children to argue for shifting emphasis from emergency services to long-term services, including stable housing, for homeless families.

956. Layzer, J. (1986). Children in shelters. Children Today, 15, 6-11.

957. Lewis, M.R., & Meyers, A.F. (1989). The growth and development status of homeless children entering shelters in Boston. Public Health Reports, 104, 247-250.
Reports on the review of intake interviews conducted with 133 homeless families with 213 children who resided in 10 shelters and one hotel in Boston as a part of the Boston Health Care for the Homeless project. Each child was administered the Denver Developmental Screening Test (DDST).

958. Libertoff, K. (1980). The runaway child in America: A social history. Journal of Family Issues, 1, 151-164.

959. Liff, S.R. (1991). Homelessness: Perceptions and coping strategies of mothers and children living in one temporary urban shelter. Dissertation Abstracts International, 52, 3300-B.

960. Luna, G.C. (1987). Welcome to my nightmare: The graffiti of homeless youth. Society, 24, 73-78.
Describes the lives of homeless youth on the streets of American cities through the use of a photo essay on the use of graffiti to express the alienation and desperation of homeless youth.

961. Luna, G.C. (1991). Street youth: adaptation and survival in the AIDS decade. Journal of Adolescent Health, 12, 511-514.

962. Manov, A., & Lowther, L. (1983). A health care approach for hard-to-reach adolescent runaways. Nurse Clinicians of North America, 18, 333-342.

963. Mathieu, A. (1991). Parents on the Move: Families resist. Dissertation Abstracts International, 52, 2192 A.

964. Maxwell, B. (1992). Hostility, depression, and self-esteem among troubled and homeless adolescents in crisis. Journal of Youth and Adolescence, 21(2), 139-144.

In a study of 27 runaway and homeless adolescents, it was found that homeless youth exhibit higher levels of hostility and depression, and lower levels of self esteem than other adolescents.

965. McCarthy, W.A. (1990). Life on the street: Serious theft, drug selling and prostitution among homeless youth. Dissertation Abstracts International, 51, 1397 A.
Focussed on the experiences of living on the street and the incidence and prevalence of illegal activities of homeless youth. For each of the 3 illegal activities studied, homeless youth were more likely to violate the law after leaving home and typically were more likely to repeat offenses than offenders living at home. Sutherland's theory of differential association is used to explain the findings.

966. McChesney, K.Y. (1986). Families: The new homeless. Family Professional, 1, 13-14.

967. McChesney, K.Y. (1986). New findings on homeless families. Family Professional, 1, 15-17.

968. McChesney, K.Y. (1987). Paths to family homelessness. In M.J. Robertson & M Greenblatt (Eds.), Homelessness: The national perspective. New York: Plenum.

969. McChesney, K.Y. (1987). Women without: Homeless mothers and their children. Dissertation Abstracts International, 48, 1032 A.
Mental health programs that treat the individual without changing the overall low-income housing ratio will be ineffective in reducing homelessness. Three policy approaches to family homelessness are discussed: emergency shelters, service delivery, and transitional housing.

970. McChesney, K.Y. (1990). Family homelessness: A systemic problem. Journal of Social Issues, 46, 191-205.

971. McLarin, K.J. (1989). Giving families a fresh start. Public Welfare, 3, 37-41.

972. Miller, D.S., & Lin, E.H. (1988). Children in sheltered homeless families: reported health status and use of health services. Pediatrics, 81, 668-673.
Studied the health status of 158 children of 82 homeless families and found that nearly half the children (49%) reported numerous acute and chronic health problems. Less than 10% of the children measured were short for their age or underweight. When compared with the U.S. general pediatric population, the proportion of homeless children reported to be in "fair" or "poor" health was four times higher. Thirty-five percent of the children had no health insurance, and 59% of the children had no regular health care provider. Homeless children were found to use emergency rooms at a rate that was two to three times higher than the US general pediatric population.

973. Mills, C., & Ota, H. (1989). Homeless women with minor children in the Detroit metropolitan area. Social Work, 34, 485-489.
Reviews the admissions records of 87 homeless families residing in a Detroit

shelter. Most of the families were black and contained a single mother with one or two minor aged children. Most of the mothers were young, unemployed, and had not received a high school education. The authors argue that policies should address the prevention of homelessness through income support programs, provision of low income housing, basic living skills training and mental health services.

974. Molnar, J.M., Ruth, W.R., & Klein, T.P. (1990). Constantly compromised: The impact of homelessness on children. Journal of Social Issues, 46, 109-124. Summarizes the research and literature to date that focuses on the specific effects of homelessness on children. In each of the major areas surveyed (health, development, and education), studies reveal that homeless children are into simply at risk; most suffer specific physical, psychological, and emotional damage due to the circumstance that usually accompany episodes of homelessness for families and children. Research and policy implications are considered.

975. Morrissette, P.J., & McIntyre, S. (1989). Homeless young people in residential care. Social Casework, 70, 603-610.

976. Mundy, P., Robertson, M., Robertson, J., & Greenblatt, M. (1990). The prevalence of psychotic symptoms in homeless adolescents. Journal of the American Academy of Child and Adolescent Psychiatry, 29, 724-731.

977. Mundy, P., Robertson, J., Greenblatt, M., & Robertson, M. (1989). Residential instability in adolescent inpatients. Journal of the American Academy of Child and Adolescent Psychiatry, 28, 176-181. Reviewed the case records of 225 randomly selected adolescent psychiatric inpatients to examine the prevalence of residential instability in this population. Results indicate that residential instability was associated with variables such as caregiver neglect and/or abuse, parental separation, multiple hospitalizations, lower IQ, poor impulse control and antisocial behavior. The authors discuss the relationship of residential instability with treatment resistance and development of antisocial behavior.

978. Murata, J.E., Patrick-Mace, J., Strehlow, A., & Shuler, P. (1992). Disease patterns in homeless children: a comparison with national data. Journal of Pediatric Nursing, 7, 196-204. Comparisons of data from a group of uninsured homeless children and data from the National Ambulatory Medical Care Survey indicate that services to homeless children differed significantly from reimbursed services in the national sample for all categories except chronic disease.

979. National Coalition for the Homeless. (1988). Over the edge: Homeless families and the welfare system. Washington, DC. Explores the effects of inadequate levels of aid to families with dependent children on family homelessness. Many families are at risk for homelessness due to a combination of inadequate AFDC levels and a shortage of affordable housing. Specific policy recommendations include: (1) an increase in overall AFDC levels to the federal poverty level, (2) an increase in the shelter allowance

to at least the federally defined fair market rent, (3) an increase in federally funded housing programs to at least 1981 levels.

980. National Network of Runaway and Youth Services, Inc. (1985). To Whom Do They Belong? "A Profile of America's Runaway and Homeless Youth and the Programs That Help Them." Washington, DC.: Author.

981. Neill, P.P. (1990). The impact of homelessness on the academic achievement of children. Dissertation Abstracts International, 51, 2322 A.

982. Neiman, L. (1988). A critical review of resiliency literature and its relevance to homeless children. Children's Environments Quarterly, 5, 17-25.

983. Nerone, B.J. & Jarvis, V. (1983). Throwaway children: Runaway kids. Imprint, 30, 31-37.

984. New York State Legislative Commission on Expenditure Review. (1981). Runaway and homeless youth. Albany, NY.: Author.

985. Nye, F. I. (1980). A theoretical perspective on running away. Journal of Family Issues, 1, 274-299.

986. O'Connor, K. (1989). Homeless children. San Diego, CA: Lucent Books.

987. Parker, R.M., Rescorla, L.A., Finkelsteing, J.A., Barnes, N., Holmes, J.H., & Stolley, P.D. (1991). A survey of the health of homeless children in Philadelphia shelters. American Journal of the Diseases of Childhood, 145, 520-526.
This study of a random sample of homeless families with children found that children's most frequent health problems included numerous accidents and injuries, burns, and lead toxicity. Parents often suffered from depression, physical abuse, and substance abuse. School-aged children tended to have low tests scores on expressive vocabulary and word decoding, while preschoolers were below age level expectations for visual motor skills.

988. Pennbridge, J., MacKensie, R.G., Swofford, A. (1991). Risk profile of homeless pregnant adolescents and youth. Journal of Adolescent Health, 12, 534-538.
The special service needs of pregnant homeless young women are highlighted in this comparison of homeless and nonhomeless pregnant youth. The homeless sample tended to be younger than the nonhomeless sample, and were more likely to be depressed, to have attempted suicide, to have a history of sexual and physical abuse and to be diagnosed as drug abusing.

989. Pennbridge, J.N., Yates, G.L., David, T.G., & Mackenzie, R.G. (1990). Runaway and homeless youth in Los Angeles County, California. Journal of Adolescent Health Care, 11, 159-165.

990. Powers, J.L. (1988). Running away from home: A response to adolescent maltreatment. Paper presented at the Biennial Meeting of the Society for Research on Adolescence, Alexandria, Virginia.

991. Powers, J.L., Eckenrode, J., & Jaklitsch, B. (1990). Maltreatment among runaway and homeless youth. Child Abuse and Neglect, 14, 87-98.

992. Powers, J.L., & Jaklitsch, B.W. (1989). Understanding survivors of abuse: Stories of homeless and runaway adolescents. Lexington, MA: Lexington Books.

993. Price, V.A. (1989). Characteristics and needs of Boston street youth: One agency's response. Children and Youth Services Review, 11, 75-90.
Describes the activities of "Bridge Over Troubled Waters," an agency providing multiple services to homeless and runaway youth. Included is a discussion of causes of youth homelessness, survival strategies, the incidence of prostitution among street youth, and the psychological effects of homelessness on the young.

994. Pritchard, S. (1990). Safety of children in temporary accommodation. Health Visitor, 63, 194-195.

995. Radford, R.F. (1992). The identification of homeless school children. Dissertation Abstracts International, 53, 1803-A.

996. Rafferty, Y., & Rollins, N. (1989). Learning in limbo: The educational deprivation of homeless children. Long Island City, NY: Advocates for Children of New York, Inc.
Explores the effects of homelessness on the education of school-age children. Data from interviews with 227 homeless families as well as a comparison of New York City Board of Education data on homeless and non-homeless children are discussed.

997. Rafferty, Y., & Shinn, M. (1991). The impact of homelessness on children. American Psychologist, 46, 1170-1179.

998. Ravoira, L. (1990). Social bonds and teen pregnancy: A comparison of parenting teenagers, pregnant teenagers, and never pregnant teenagers who sought services at four homeless shelters. Dissertation Abstracts International, 51, 2341-A.
Developed and assessed the efficiency of psychological scales measuring social bonding in identifying young girls at risk of premarital pregnancy and motherhood. Strength of family bonds delayed initiation of sexual intercourse among homeless girls. The scales also predicted number of pregnancies and births experienced.

999. Raychaba, B. (1989). Canadian youth in care: Leaving care to be on our own with no direction from home. Children and Youth Services Review, 11, 61-73.
The author compares homeless children and adolescents with those receiving care from child welfare agencies. Similarities in transiency, alcohol and drug abuse, emotional problems, lack of employment, poor social skills, and little social support lead the authors to conclude that children leaving welfare agency care are at risk for homelessness.

1000. Rescorla, L., Parker, R., & Stolley, P. (1991). Ability, achievement, and adjustment in homeless children. American Journal of Orthopsychiatry, 61, 210-220.

This research compared the cognitive functioning and emotional and behavioral adjustment of 3 to 12 year old homeless children living in shelters with that of nonhomeless inner city children. Few significant differences were found between groups of school-aged children. However, homeless preschoolers tended to exhibit slower development and more emotional and behavioral problems than did nonhomeless controls.

1001. Ritter, B. (1989). Abuse of the adolescent. New York State Journal of Medicine, 89, 156-158.
The author describes the characteristics of adolescents in crisis centers for homeless and runaway youth. Typically, these youths are 17 to 18 years of age, are polydrug users, and engage in commercial sex practices. These youths are often from single-parent welfare families with histories of alcoholism, drug abuse, and physical or sexual abuse. Sexually transmitted diseases are also common.

1002. Rivlin, L. (1990). Home and homelessness in the lives of children. Child and Youth Services, 14, 5-17.

1003. Robbins, T. (1986). New York's homeless Families. In J. Erickson & C. Wilhelm (Eds.), Housing the homeless. New Brunswick, NJ: Center for Urban Policy Research, Rutgers University.

1004. Roberts, A.R. (1982). Adolescent runaways in suburbia: A new typology. Adolescence, 17, 387-396.

1005. Robertson, M.J. (1988). Homeless adolescents: a hidden crisis. Hospital and Community Psychiatry, 39, 475.

1006. Robertson, M.J. (1991). Homeless women with children: The role of alcohol and other drug abuse. American Psychologist, 46, 1198-1204.

1007. Rosenman, M., & Stein, M.L. (1990). Homeless children: A new vulnerability. Child and Youth Services, 14, 89-109.

1008. Rotheram-Borus, M.J., Koopman, C., & Ehrhardt, A.A. (1991). Homeless youths and HIV infection. American Psychologist, 46, 1188-1197.

1009. Rothman, J. (1989). Intervention research: Application to runaway and homeless youths. Social Work Research and Abstracts, 25, 13-18.
The collaboration of a university research group and a government agency in designing and establishing a community-based intervention for homeless and runaway youths is used to illustrate how research, practice, and policy interests can be merged through intervention research.

1010. Russell, S.C., & Williams, E.U. (1988). Homeless handicapped children: A special education perspective. Children's Environments Quarterly, 5, 3-7.

1011. Schumack, S. (1987). The Educational Rights of Homeless Children. Newsnotes, 38, 1-10.
This newsletter contains 4 articles addressing the education rights of homeless

children and the problems faced by educators and parents in providing schooling for homeless children. Of homeless children, nearly 43% do not attend school. The main reasons cited include: (1) inability to meet residency requirements, (2) inability to provide educational records, and (3) lack of transportation.

1012. Shaffer, D., & Caton, C. (1984). Runaway and homeless youth in New York City. New York: The Ittleson Foundation.
Reports findings of a two-week study of 175 children and adolescents in New York City shelters. Discusses the psychiatric and educational problems of runaway and homeless youth.

1013. Shane, P.G. (1989). Changing patterns among homeless and runaway youth. American Journal of Orthopsychiatry, 59, 208-214.
In this study of 536 clients of service agencies in New Jersey, only one-third of the sample were able to return home after treatment.

1014. Sherman, D.J. (1992). The neglected health care needs of street youth. Public Health Reports, 107, 433-440.

1015. Shinn, M. (1992). Homelessness: What is a psychologist to do? American Journal of Community Psychology, 20(1), 1-24.
Data collected from 700 families seeking shelter and 524 families on the public assistance roles in New York City found more evidence for a social-structural model of homelessness than for the individual deficit model. Implications of these findings for psychological research and intervention are discussed.

1016. Shinn, M., Knickman, J.R., Ward, D., & Petrovic, N.L. (1990). Alternative models for sheltering homeless families. Journal of Social Issues, 46, 175-190.

1017. Shinn, M., Knickman, J.R., & Weitzman, B.C. (1991). Social relationships and vulnerability to becoming homeless among poor families. American Psychologist, 46, 1180-1187.

1018. Shulsinger, E. (1990). Needs of sheltered homeless children. Journal of Pediatric Health Care, 4, 136-140.

1019. Simpson, J.H. (1988). Homeless black youth: A case of persistent unemployment. Journal of Voluntary Action Research, 17, 71-77.

1020. Smart, D.H. (1991). Homeless youth in Seattle. Planning and policy-making at the local government level. Journal of Adolescent Health, 12, 519-527.

1021. Smith, L.G. (1987). Teaching treatment of mild, acute diarrhea and secondary dehydration to homeless parents. Public Health Reports, 102, 539-542.
Discusses the importance of education in prevention of disease among homeless children. Focussing on the prevalence of dehydration and diarrhea among homeless children, the authors argue that educating parents in homeless shelters may mean the difference between life and death for homeless children with these disorders. The authors provide a description of an educational program developed to help homeless parents recognize and treat mild, acute diarrhea and secondary dehydration.

1022. Smith, L.G. (1988). Home treatment of mild, acute diarrhea and secondary dehydration of infants and small children: an educational program for parents in a shelter for the homeless. Journal of Professional Nursing, 4, 60-63.

1023. Smith, S. (1989). The Houston "Lighthouse" for unattended children. Educational Leadership, 46, 79.
Describes the efforts of a Houston, Texas, school superintendent's efforts to establish a shelter for homeless children. This program is funded primarily by community agencies.

1024. Stefanidis, N., Pennbridge, J., MacKensie, R.G., & Pottharst, K. (1992). Runaway and homeless youth: the effects of attachment history on stabilization. American Journal of Orthopsychiatry, 62, 442-446.

1025. Stiffman, A.R. (1989). Physical and sexual abuse in runaway youths. Child Abuse and Neglect, 13, 417-426.
Discusses the extent of physical and sexual abuse in a sample of 291 residents of shelters for runaway and homeless youths. Nearly 50% reported having been either physically or sexually abused. Multivariate analyses suggest that a history of physical or sexual abuse impacts self-esteem and overall behavior problems regardless of other family problems.

1026. Stretch, J.J. (1985). Children of the homeless. Paper presented at the Third National School of Social Work Conference, New Orleans, LA.

1027. Stretch, J.J., & Boyert, M. (1985). Children of the homeless. Paper presented at the Annual Program Meeting of the Missouri Association of Social Welfare, Columbia, MO.

1028. Stretch, J.J., Hutchinson, W.J., & Searight, P. (1985). Innovative networking for homeless families and children. Paper presented at the Biennial NASW Symposium, Chicago, IL.

1029. Sugarman, S.T., Hergenroeder, A.C., Chacko, M.R., & Parcel, G.S. (1991). Acquired immunodeficiency syndrome and adolescents. Knowledge, attitudes, and behaviors of runaway and homeless youths. American Journal of the Diseases of Childhood, 145, 431-436.

1030. Sullivan, P.A., & Damrosch, S.P. (1987). Homeless women and children. In R.D. Bingham, R.E. Green & S.B. White (Eds.), The homeless in contemporary society. Newbury Park, CA: Sage Publications.

1031. Teeter, R. (1988). Coming of age on the city streets in 19th century America. Adolescence, 23, 909-912.

1032. Templer, R.J. (1991). Homeless children: Perceived competence and social acceptance. Dissertation Abstracts International, 52, 1915 A.
Being homeless did not negatively affect how young homeless children perceived their competence and social acceptance. Direct observations showed that these children exhibited lower competence and social acceptance than self-reports indicated. Further, findings suggest that parents of homeless children view the

competence and social acceptance of their children significantly lower than do their children.

1033. Thorman, G. (1988). Homeless families. Springfield, IL: C.C. Thomas.

1034. Toelle, M.E., & Kerwin, S. (1988). Children in transition: The Salvation Army Playschool and Home Visiting Program. Child Today, 17, 7-31.

1035. Tyler, F.B. (1986). A preventive psychosocial approach for working with street children. Paper presented at the 94th Annual Convention of the American Psychological Association, Washington, DC., August.

1036. U.S. General Accounting Office, Division of Human Resources.   (1983). Federally Supported Centers Provide Needed Services for Runaways and Homeless Youths. Report to the Chairman, Subcommittee on Human Resources, Committee on Education and Labor, House of Representatives. Gaithersburg, MD: General Accounting Office.

1037. U.S. House Committee on Education and Labor. (1982). Oversight Hearing on Runaway and Homeless Youth Program. Hearing before the Subcommittee on Human Resources of the Committee on Education and Labor. House of Representatives, Ninety-Seventh Congress, Second Session. Washington, DC: U.S. Government Printing Office.

1038. U.S. House Committee on Education and Labor (1982). Oversight Hearing on Runaway and Homeless Youth Programs. Washington, DC: U.S. Government Printing Office.
These hearings concern the performance of 169 centers for runaway and homeless youth which are at least partially funded by the government through the Runaway and Homeless Youth Act. The report includes testimony, a review of 17 programs, and an overview of the National Program for Homeless and Runaway Youth.

1039. U.S. House Committee on Government Operations. (1986).   Homeless Families: A Neglected Crisis. Sixty-Third Report by the Committee on Government Operations together with Dissenting and Additional Views. Washington, DC: U.S. Government Printing Office.

1040. U.S. House Select Committee on Children, Youth, and Families. (1987). The Crisis in Homelessness: Effects on Children and Families. Hearing before the Select Committee on Children, Youth, and Families. House of Representatives, One Hundredth Congress, First Session. Washington, DC: U.S. Government Printing Office.

1041. U.S. Senate Committee on the Judiciary. (1980). Homeless youth: The saga of pushouts and throwaways in America. Washington, DC: U.S. Government Printing Office.

1042. U.S. Senate Committee on the Judiciary (1982). Problems of runaway youth. Washington, DC: U.S. Government Printing Office.
These hearings focus on financial support for community based programs for

dealing with the problem of runaway and homeless youth. Discussion centers on causes of homelessness, steps currently being taken, and future directions for dealing with the problem of homeless and runaway youths.

1043. Van der Ploeg, J.D. (1989). Homelessness: A multidimensional problem. Children and Youth Services Review, 11, 45-56.
Discusses prevention of youth homelessness based on data collected from 212 Dutch homeless youth. Five variables: (1) family conflicts, (2) length of contact with professionals, (3) school problems, (4) isolation from peers, and (5) low self-esteem were analyzed. The author concludes that a multidimensional approach is needed to prevent homelessness among adolescents.

1044. van Ry, M.J. (1990). Homeless families: Causes, effects and recommendations. Dissertation Abstracts International, 51, 1392 A.
A typology of homeless families with children based on interviews with 68 families found differences in the demographics and recommendations for preventing homelessness and helping those already homeless between groups. The typology derived was proposed as a tool to help develop improved programs for the homeless and preventive interventions.

1045. Vermund, S.H., Belmar, R., & Drucker, E. (1987). Homelessness in New York City: The youngest victims. New York State Journal of Medicine, 87, 3-5.
Studied the effects of homelessness on children who are born to homeless mothers and found that poor prenatal care, low birth-weight babies, high infant mortality, and socio-psychological stress exacerbate poor health among these children. The authors conclude that safe, low-cost housing is the ultimate cure for the plight of the homeless.

1046. Wagner, J.E., & Menke, E.M. (1991). The depression of homeless children: a focus for nursing intervention. Issues in Comprehensive Pediatric Nursing, 14, 17-29.
Findings of a descriptive study of depression among homeless children as measured by the Children's Depression Inventory are used in a discussion of the role of pediatric nursing and nursing interventions with homeless children.

1047. Wagner, J., & Menke, E.M. (1991). Stressors and coping behaviors of homeless, poor, and low-income mothers. Journal of Community Health Nursing, 8, 75-84.

1048. Wagner, J.D., & Menke, E.M. (1992). Case management of homeless families. Clinical Nurse Specialist, 6, 65-71.
The multiple health care needs of homeless families require individualized service delivery strategies such as case management. Clinical nurse specialists are urged to develop specialized skills in the areas of service stimulation and system advocacy in order to more effectively serve the growing number of homeless families.

1049. Walsh, M.E. (1992). Moving to nowhere: Children's stories of homelessness. Westport, CT: Auburn House.

1050. Waxman, L.D., & Reyes, L.M. (1987). <u>A Status Report on Homeless Families in America's Cities. A 29-City Survey</u>. Washington, DC: United States Conference of Mayors.

1051. Weitzman, B.C., Knickman, J.R., & Shinn, M. (1990).   Pathways to homelessness among New York City families. <u>Journal of Social Issues</u>, <u>46</u>, 125-140.

1052. Whitman, B.Y. (1985).   <u>Children of the homeless: A high risk population for developmental delay</u>. Paper presented at the second meeting of the American Public Health Association's Committee on Health Services Research Study Group on Homelessness, Washington, D.C., November.

1053. Whitman, B.Y, Accardo, P., Boyert, M., & Kendagor, R.   (1990). Homelessness and cognitive performance in children: A possible link. <u>Social Work</u>, <u>35</u>, 516-519.

1054. Whitman. B.Y., Accardo, P., & Sprankel, J. (1989). Families and children of the homeless. In R.I. Jahiel (Ed.), <u>Homelessness and its prevention</u>. Baltimore, MD: Johns Hopkins University Press.

1055. Whitman, B.Y., Accardo, P., Stretch, J., & Sprankel, J. (1986). <u>Families and children of the homeless</u>.   Paper presented at the   Annual Meeting of the American Public Health Association, Las Vegas, Nevada.

1056. Wimpfheimer, R.G. (1986).   Aging out: A child welfare dilemma of the 1980's (Homeless Youth). <u>Dissertation Abstracts International</u>, <u>47</u>, 1884 A.

1057. Wood, D. (1989). Homeless children: Their evaluation and treatment. <u>Journal of Pediatric Health Care</u>, <u>3</u>, 194-199.

1058. Wood, D., Schlossman, S., Hayashi, T., & Valdez, R. (1989). <u>Over the brink: Homeless families in Los Angeles</u>. Los Angeles, CA: Assembly Office of Research.
Explores similarities and differences between homeless and non-homeless poor families and the factors that might lead to homelessness for some families.

1059. Wood, D., Valdez, R.B., Hayashi, T., & Shen, A. (1990).   Homeless and housed families in Los Angeles: A study comparing demographic, economic, and family function characteristics. <u>American Journal of Public Health</u>, <u>80</u>, 1049-1052.

1060. Wright, J.D. (1991). Children in and of the streets: Health, social policy, and the homeless young. <u>American Journal of Diseases of Children</u>, <u>145</u>, 516-519.

1061. Yates, G.L., Mackensie, R.G., Pennbridge, J., & Swofford, A. (1991). A risk profile comparison of homeless youth involved in prostitution and homeless youth not involved. <u>Journal of Adolescent Health</u>, <u>12</u>, 545-548.
This comparison of homeless youth involved in prostitution and those who were not found that those involved in prostitution are at a greater risk for a wide variety of medical problems as well as drug abuse, suicide and depression.

1062. Ziefert, M., & Brown, K.S. (1991). Skill building for effective intervention with homeless families. <u>Families in Society</u>, <u>72</u>, 212-219.

7

Legal Issues

1063. Bach, J.P. (1989). Requiring due care in the process of patient deinstitutionalization: Toward a common law approach to mental health care reform. Yale Law Journal, 98, 1153-1172.
Discusses the use of the common law of torts to promote reform in the patient discharge process and in the provision of community care after discharge.

1064. Baker, P., & Ferrer, B. (1984). Down and out: A manual on basic rights and benefits for the homeless in Massachusetts. Boston, MA: Massachusetts Law Reform Institute and the Coalition for the Homeless.

1065. Belcher, J.R. (1988). Are jails replacing the mental health system for the homeless mentally ill? Community Mental Health Journal, 24, 185-195.
Explores the process of how homeless mentally ill persons become involved with the criminal justice system. The unique demands of homelessness and chronic mental illness were specifically examined in this naturalistically based study. The author concludes that a combination of severe mental illness, a tendency to decompensate in a non-structured environment, and an inability or unwillingness to follow through with aftercare contributed to involvement with the criminal justice system. Changes in the mental health system that would prevent the criminalization of the homeless mentally ill are suggested.

1066. Birkinshaw, P. (1982). Homelessness and the law: The effects and response to legislation. Urban Law and Policy, 5, 255-295.

1067. Bittner, E. (1967). The police on skid row: A study of peace keeping. American Sociological Review, 32, 699-715.
Findings from a year long field study of police activities in skid row areas of 2 cities are discussed. Skid row is seen as an area where peace keeping activities predominate, and law enforcement activities are minimal. The police perspective on skid row and its inhabitants are discussed as are the characteristics of skid row inhabitants and its social processes.

1068. Blasi, G.L. (1987).   Litigation on behalf of the homeless: Systematic approaches. Journal of Urban and Contemporary Law, 31, 137-142.

1069. Carty, L. (Ed.) (1987).   Federal and state rights and entitlements of people who are homeless in the District of Columbia. Washington, DC: Mental Health Law Project.

1070. Chackes, K.M. (1987).   Sheltering the homeless: Judicial enforcement of governmental duties to the poor. Journal of Urban and Contemporary Law, 31, 155-199.

1071. Chandler, S.M. (1992). Brown versus New York: the Rashomon of delivering mental health services in the 1990s. Health and Social Work, 17, 128-136.

1072. Collin, R.W. (1984). Homelessness: The policy and the law. Urban Lawyer, 16, 317-329.

1073. Fabricant, M., & Epstein, I. (1984).   Legal and welfare rights advocacy: Complementary approaches in organizing on behalf of the homeless. Urban and Social Change Review, 17, 15-19.
Discusses complementary aspects of legal and welfare rights advocacy on behalf of the homeless and present a case study of a welfare rights advocacy effort undertaken in New Jersey.

1074. Finn, P.E., & Sullivan, M. (1988).   Police response to special populations: Handling the mentally ill, public inebriate, and the homeless. National Institute of Justice Reports, 209, 2-8.

1075. Fischer, P.J. (1985).   Arrest of homeless people: A public health problem. Paper presented at the 113th annual meeting of the American Public Health Association, Washington, D.C., November.

1076. Fischer, P.J. (1987). Arrests of homeless people in Baltimore. Paper presented at the 113th Annual Meeting of the American Public Health Association, Washington, DC.

1077. Fischer, P.J. (1987). The criminalization of homelessness. In M.J. Robertson and M. Greenblatt (Eds.), Homelessness: The national perspective. New York: Plenum.

1078. Fischer, P.J. (1988). Criminal activity among the homeless: a study of arrests in Baltimore. Hospital and Community Psychiatry, 39, 46-51.
Compared the arrests of 634 homeless persons to 50,524 arrests in the general population in order to determine the extent of criminal activity among the homeless. Significant differences in demographics and type of offense were found. Homeless arrestees were more likely to be male, white and over 45 years of age. Further, homeless arrestees were arrested for far less severe offenses than other arrestees. The more serious offenses committed by the homeless arrestees were aimed at maintaining subsistence in the absence of housing.

1079. Fischer, P.J. (1989). Criminal behavior and victimization in the homeless: A review of the literature. In R. Jahiel (Ed.) Homelessness: A prevention-oriented approach. Baltimore: John Hopkins Press.

1080. Foote, C. (1956). Vagrancy-type law and its administration. University of Pennsylvania Law Review, 104, 603-650.
Describes the history of vagrancy law and its administration in Philadelphia. Interviews with convicted vagrants, official police and corrections records, and observations of trials provide the data for this article.

1081. Harring, S. (1977). Class conflict and suppression of tramps in Buffalo. Law and Social Review, 11, 879-911.

1082. Hombs, M.E. (1987). Social recognition of the homeless: Policies of indifference. Journal of Urban and Contemporary Law, 31, 143-149.

1083. Hopper, K., & Cox, S. (1986). Litigation in advocacy for the homeless: The case of New York City. In J. Erickson & C. Wilhelm (Eds.), Housing the homeless. New Brunswick, NJ: Center for Urban Policy Research.

1084. Kanter, A. (1989). Homeless but not helpless: Legal issues in the care of homeless people with mental illness. Journal of Social Issues, 45, 91-104.

1085. Keilitz, I., & Hall, T. (1985). State statutes governing involuntary outpatient civil commitment. Mental and Physical Disability Law Reporter, 9, 378-397.
Summarizes state laws providing for involuntary outpatient civil commitment (IOC) for alleged mentally disordered and dangerous persons who do not require full-time hospitalization, but who resist voluntary treatment in non-hospital settings. The authors discuss factors resulting in the increased interest in IOC including: (1) the failure of deinstitutionalization, (2) the plight of the homeless mentally ill, and (3) dissatisfaction with inflexible civil commitment laws, as well as, interstate differences in the provisions of these laws.

1086. Malone, M. (1981). Homelessness in a modern urban setting. Fordham Urban Law Journal, 10, 749-841.

1087. Morawetz, N. (1988). Welfare litigation to prevent homelessness. Review of Law and Social Change, 16, 565-590.
Reductions in real benefit levels of welfare assistance payments coupled with more restrictive eligibility requirements have caused many poor families to lose their homes and become trapped in a cycle of homelessness. The author argues for court involvement in determining how far the government can go with current welfare policies that deny even minimal subsistence to impoverished families with children.

1088. Mort, G. (1984). Establishing a right to shelter for the homeless. Brooklyn Law Review, 50, 939-994.

1089. Peele, R., Gross, B., Arons, B., & Jafri, M. (1984). The legal system and the homeless. In H.R. Lamb (Ed.), The homeless mentally ill: A task force report. Washington, DC: American Psychiatric Association.

1090. Pittman, D.J. (1974). Interaction between skid row people and law enforcement and health professionals. Addictive Diseases, 1, 369-388.

1091. Rice, L.W. (1987). A St. Louis solution to the homeless problem. Journal of Urban and Contemporary Law, 31, 151-153.

1092. Richman, B.J., Convit, A., & Martell, D. (1992). Homelessness and the mentally ill offender. Journal of Forensic Science, 37, 932-937.

1093. Rosenheim, M.K. (1966). Vagrancy concepts in welfare law. In J. TenBroeck (Ed.), The law of the poor. San Francisco, CA: Chandler.

1094. Schneider, N. (1990). Mental illness and homelessness as predictors of criminality: A secondary analysis of 728 male jail detainees. Dissertation Abstracts International, 52, 528 B.

1095. Smith, F. (1975). Church army and the homeless offender. International Journal of Offender Therapy, 19, 285-291.

1096. Solarz, A. (1985). An examination of criminal behavior among the homeless. Paper presented at the Annual Meeting of the American Society of Criminology, San Diego, California, November.

1097. Teplin, L.A., & Pruett, N.S. (1992). Police as streetcorner psychiatrist: managing the mentally ill. International Journal of Law and Psychiatry, 15, 139-156.

1098. Thornton, R. (1989). Homelessness through relationship breakdown: The local authorities' response. The Journal of Social Welfare Law, 2, 67-84.

1099. Trasler, G. (1972). Specialized hostels for homeless offenders 1. Types, numbers, and needs of the homeless offender. International Journal of Offender Therapy, 16, 224-249.

1100. Werner, F. (1983). On the streets: A look at homelessness and what is being done about it. Housing Law Bulletin, 13, 1-6.

1101. Werner, F. (1984). Homelessness: A litigation roundup. Housing Law Bulletin, 14, 1-14.

8

Social and Historical Perspectives

1102. Atkinson, J. (1987). I just exist. Community Outlook, 11, 12-15.

1103. Bahr, H.M. (1967). The gradual disappearance of skid row. Social Problems, 15, 41-45.
Findings from a survey of welfare commissioners in 40 cities indicate that the declining skid row population is a national rather than local or regional phenomenon. However, the decline in population is not apparently due to an absolute decline in the population of the homeless, but rather, reflects the operation of several factors (gentrification, etc.) that have contributed to the dispersal of these persons from traditional skid row areas to other areas of the city.

1104. Barak, G. (1991). Gimme shelter: A social history of homelessness in contemporary America: New York: Praeger.
Part 1 of this book examines the problem of homelessness, focussing on the changing nature of homelessness, politics, housing policy, and criminalization and victimization of the homeless. Part 2 evaluates government policies and the rights of the homeless and makes recommendations for confronting problems of injustice and redistribution.

1105. Baumann, D., & Grigsby, C. (1988). Understanding the Homeless: From Research to Action. Austin, TX: Texas University, Hogg Foundation for Mental Health.
Reports findings from a three year research study of the homeless in Austin, Texas and propose a model of homelessness that involves a progression from major loss to disaffiliation to entrenchment. The steps of this model are: (1) precipitating external circumstances, (2) weakening of resources, (3) disaffiliation, and (4) entrenchment in chronic homelessness. The authors suggest action strategies based on the proposed model.

1106. Beard, R. (Ed.) (1989). <u>On being homeless: historical perspectives</u>. New Brunswick, NJ: Rutgers University Press.

1107. Belcher, J.R., & Singer, J. (1988). Homelessness: A cost of capitalism. <u>Social Policy</u>, <u>18</u>, 48-53.

1108. Beller, J. (1980). <u>Street people.</u> New York: Macmillan.

1109. Benda, B.B. (1987). Crime, drug abuse, mental illness and homelessness. <u>Deviant Behavior</u>, <u>8</u>, 361-375.
       The author describes the results of an interview study of 345 homeless persons conducted between May, 1985, and May, 1986, in Richmond, Virginia. Findings suggest that "current afflictions" (e.g., hallucinations) were related to major life events (i.e., psychiatric hospitalizations), and further, that childhood drug use predicted major life events. The author proposes a general "drift down" hypothesis to explain homelessness.

1110. Benda, B. (1990). Crime, drug abuse, and mental illness: A comparison of homeless men and women. <u>Journal of Social Service Research</u>, <u>13</u>, 39-60.

1111. Benedict, A., Shaw, J.S., & Rivlin, L.G. (1988). Attitudes toward the homeless in two New York City Metropolitan samples. <u>Journal of Voluntary Action Research</u>, <u>17</u>, 3-4.

1112. Bingham, R.D., Green, R.E., & White, S.B. (Eds.) (1987). <u>The homeless in contemporary society</u>. Newbury Park, CA: Sage Publications.
       This book is divided into two sections. The first seven chapters describe the "new" homeless population. The final eight chapters discuss policy and program options used in attempting to resolve the problems of the homeless.

1113. Blasi, G.L. (1990). Social policy and social science research on homelessness. <u>Journal of Social Issues</u>, <u>46</u>, 207-219.
       If research is to inform efforts to end mass homelessness, the focus of current research must be broadened and research questions must be redefined. Epidemiological studies can indicate only who is likely to lose in the competition to find housing. Much useful research remains to be done on such things as ways in which images of homelessness are communicated through the mass media, the determinants of attitudes toward the poor and homeless, and the success or failure of organized advocacy on these issues.

1114. Blau, J. (1988). On the uses of homelessness: A literature review. <u>Catalyst</u>, <u>6</u>, 5-25.

1115. Blau, J. (1992). <u>The visible poor: Homelessness in the United States</u>. New York: Oxford University Press.

1116. Bogue, D.J. (1967). A theory of why skid row exists. In R.A. Decritler (Ed.), <u>Major American social problems</u>. Chicago, IL: Rand-McNally.

1117. Brandon, P. (1974). Homeless. <u>New Society</u>, <u>30</u>, 635-637.

1118. Breakey, W.R., Fischer, P.J., & Cowan, C.D. (1986). Homeless people in Baltimore: Demographic profile and enumeration. Paper presented at the Annual Meeting of the American Public Health Association, Las Vegas, NV.

1119. Brown, C.E., MacFarlane, S., Paredes, R., & Stark, L.(1983). The homeless of Phoenix: Who are they? and what do they want? Phoenix, AZ: Phoenix South Community Mental Health Center.

1120. Brown, C.E., Paredes, R., & Stark, L. (1983). The homeless of Phoenix: A profile. In, Homelessness in America. Washington, DC: U.S. Government Printing Office.

1121. Brown, J.L. (1989). When violence has a benevolent face: The paradox of hunger in the world's wealthiest democracy. International Journal of Health Services, 19, 257-277.

1122. Brown, M.E., & Krivo, L.J. (1989). Structural determinants of homelessness in the United States. Paper presented at the Annual Meetings of the American Sociological Association.

1123. Buckrop, J.J. (1992). Homelessness in America: An analysis of the rhetorical relationship between legitimacy and guilt. Dissertation Abstracts International, 53, 1322 A.

1124. Burnam, M.A., & Koegel, P. (1988). Methodology for obtaining a representative sample of homeless persons: The Los Angeles Skid Row study. Evaluation Review, 12, 52.
In order to obtain a probability sample of homeless adults, data were collected from meal centers, bed counts, and outdoor congregations of the homeless. The sampling design allows for longer interview protocols and data collection periods than some other methods and allows for unbiased estimates of the prevalence of mental disorders.

1125. Burns, L.S. (1987). Third world solutions to the homelessness problem. In R.D. Bingham, R.E. Green & S.B. White (Eds.), The homeless in contemporary society. Newbury Park, CA: Sage Publications.

1126. Burt, M.R., & Cohen, B.E. (1989). Differences among homeless single women, women with children, and single men. Social Problems, 36, 508-524. Demographic variables, psychiatric history, homeless history, psychiatric and substance abuse indicators and patterns of shelter and soup kitchen usage were used to differentiate 3 groups of homeless persons.

1127. California Department of Housing and Community Development. (1985). A study of the issues and characteristics of the homeless population in California. Sacramento, CA: Author.

1128. Campbell, J.L., III. (1988). "All men are created equal": Waiting for godot in the culture of inequality. Communication Monographs, 55, 143-161.

1129. Campbell, K.E. (1987). Work experiences of the homeless. Paper presented at the Annual Meetings of the Society for the Study of Social Problems, Chicago, August.

1130. Caton, C.L. (1989). Without dreams: The homeless of America. Fairlawn, N.J.: Oxford University Press.

1131. City of Chicago. (1983). Homelessness in Chicago. Chicago: Social Services Task Force.

1132. Cleghorn, J.S. (1983). Residents without residences: A study of homelessness in Birmingham, Alabama. Unpublished Master's Thesis, University of Alabama at Birmingham.

1133. Clement, P.F. (1984). The transformation of the wandering poor in nineteenth century Philadelphia. In E. Monkonnen (Ed.), Walking to work: Tramps in America 1790-1935. Lincoln, NE: University of Nebraska Press.

1134. Coalition for the Homeless. (1982). Cruel brinkmanship: Planning for the homeless - 1983. New York. Author.

1135. Cook, T. (Ed.) (1979). Vagrancy: Some new perspectives. New York: Academic Press.

1136. Cooper, M.A. (1987) The role of religious and nonprofit organizations in combating homelessness. In R.D. Bingham, R.E. Green & S.B. White (Eds.), The homeless in contemporary society. Newbury Park, CA: Sage Publications.

1137. Couto, R.A. (1987). Participatory research: Methodology and critique. Clinical Sociology Review, 5, 83-90.
   Describes a research effort combining survey research and methodological tenets from participatory observation. The cases presented raise questions to ask about research in relation to the participatory model.

1138. Crystal, S. (1984). Homeless men and homeless women: The gender gap. The Urban and Social Change Review, 17, 4-11.
   Compares homeless men and women seeking lodging in emergency shelters. The findings suggest that women were more likely than men to have been previously married, to have previous psychiatric hospitalizations or treatment, and to have grown up in stressful situations. Homeless women were also more likely to maintain some ongoing parental relationships with their children.

1139. Crystal, S., & Goldstein, M. (1984). The homeless in New York City Shelters. New York: Human Resources Administration.

1140. Culhane, D.P. (1990). On becoming homeless: The structural and experiential dynamics of residential instability. Dissertation Abstracts International, 51, 4100 B.
   Studied 43 shelter residents and non-residents and found that neither reductionistic models of homelessness which stress the causal influence of deviant behavior nor deterministic models which consider structural factors

independent of biographical mediation were sufficient to explain the complex relationships that result in homelessness episodes.

1141. Dahl, S., Harris, H., & Gladden, J. (1992). Homelessness: a rural perspective. Prairie Rose, 61, 1-6.

1142. David, A.S. (1988). On the street in America. British Medical Journal of Clinical Research, 296, 1016.

1143. Davis, M. (1984). Forced to tramp: The perspective of the labor press. In E. Monkonnen (Ed.), Walking to work: Tramps in America 1790-1935. Lincoln, NE: University of Nebraska Press.

1144. Dear, M.J., & Gleeson, B. (1989). Community attitudes toward the homeless. Los Angeles, CA: University of Southern California, Department of Geography, Los Angeles Homelessness Project.
Discusses community attitudes towards the homeless based on a content analysis of over 200 newspaper articles from 1985 to 1988.

1145. Dennis, D. (1987). Research methodologies concerning homeless persons with serious mental illness and/or substance abuse disorders. Albany, NY: New York State Office on Mental Health.
The author reports the proceedings of an ADAMHA sponsored conference of researchers in the areas of homelessness, mental illness and substance abuse. The report includes papers presented at the conference, reports of the general discussions on methodological issues, and results of work on specific research design issues.

1146. Devine, D.J. (1989). Homelessness and the social safety net. Dissertation Abstracts International, 49, 2832 A.

1147. Dresser, I. (1985). Psychological homelessness: A clinical example. Journal of Social Work Practice, 1, 67-76.

1148. Emmelman, D.S. (1989). Defense alliance: An odyssey of indigent defense reform. Paper presented at the Annual Meetings of the Society for the Study of Social Problems, Berkeley, CA, August.

1149. Evans, M.A. (Ed.) (1988). Homeless in America. Washington, DC: Acropolis.

1150. Fangmeier, R.A. (1990). The hidden homeless: An exploratory study of the formerly doubled up. Dissertation Abstracts International, 52, 682 A.

1151. Farnsworth, P.S., & Baker, V.G. (1988). Under the bridge. New Britain, CT: Farnsworth and Baker.

1152. Fischer, P.J., Breakey, W.R., Shapiro, S., & Kramer, M. (1986). Baltimore mission users: Social networks, morbidity, and employment. Psychosocial Rehabilitation Journal, 9, 51-63.
The authors compared the health and social characteristics of 51 randomly selected male mission users to those of 1,338 non-homeless males from eastern

Baltimore. No significant differences between the groups were found for age, race, education or military service. However, homeless men were found to have poorer mental health, greater social dysfunction and less employment. Implications for psychosocial rehabilitation are discussed.

1153. Foscarinis, M. (1991). The politics of homelessness. A call to action. American Psychologist, 46, 1232-1238.

1154. Fowler, T. (1988). Out of the rain. San Francisco, CA: Strawberry Hill.

1155. Freeman, R.B., & Hall, B. (1987). Permanent homelessness in America? Cambridge, MA: National Bureau of Economic Research.
Relying primarily on findings from a survey of 500 homeless people in New York City, the authors attempt to determine whether or not homeless is a transitory or permanent problem. The findings indicate that the number of homeless people has been on the rise since 1983 despite signs of economic recovery, with the number of homeless families rising especially fast. Periods of homelessness lasting from 6 to 8 years for homeless individuals were common, and most homeless persons surveyed did not receive any public assistance. The authors conclude that economic recovery alone will not solve the homelessness problem, but rather, increases in low-income housing and improvements in the economic position of the very poor are necessary to reduce the numbers of homeless.

1156. Freeman, R.B., & Hall, B. (1987).   Permanent homeless in America. Population Research and Policy Review, 6, 3-27.

1157. Giamo, B.F. (1989). On the bowery: Confronting homelessness in American society. Iowa City, IA: University of Iowa Press.

1158. Giamo, B., & Grunberg, J. (1992).   Beyond Homelessness: Frames of reference. Iowa City, IA: University of Iowa Press.

1159. Gioglio, G.R., & Jacobsen, R.J. (1986). Homelessness in New Jersey: A study of shelters, Agencies and the Clients they serve. New Jersey Department of Youth and Family Services, New Jersey Department of Human Services.

1160. Gist, R.M. & Welch, Q.B. (1986).   Estimates of period prevalence of homelessness in Kansas City, Missouri - 1985. (Report # 27). Kansas City, MO: Missouri Health Department, Office of Health Research and Analysis.

1161. Gorder, C. (1988). Homeless: Without addresses in America. Bedford, NY: Bluebird Press.

1162. Grigsby, C., Baumann, D., Gregorich, S.E., & Roberts-Gray, C. (1990). Disaffiliation to entrenchment: A model for understanding homelessness. Journal of Social Issues, 46, 141-156.

1163. Hagen, J.L. (1987). Gender and homelessness. Social Work, 32, 312-316.
The author discusses gender differences in a sample of 227 homeless adults seeking social services. The findings indicate that men and women experience

homelessness differently, with the women more likely to become homeless because of domestic violence or eviction than the men. The men, on the other hand, were more likely to become homeless as a result of unemployment, alcohol abuse or release from jail.

1164. Hagen, J.L. (1987). The homeless of the capital district. Albany, NY: State University of New York-Albany, School of Social Welfare.

1165. Hamilton, Rabinowitz and Alschuler, Inc. (1986). Los Angeles skid row demographic survey. Beverly Hills, CA.

1166. Harrington, M. (1984). The new American poverty. New York: Holt, Rinehart and Winston.

1167. Harvey, A. (1974). April and homeless. New Society, 27, 707-708.

1168. Hayes, C. (1988). Homeless sweet homeless. The Socialist Republic, 31, 3-4.

1169. Health and Welfare Council of Central Maryland. (1983). A report to the Greater Baltimore Shelter Network on homelessness in central Maryland. Baltimore: HWC.

1170. Health and Welfare Council of Central Maryland. (1986). Where do you go from Nowhere? A study of the homeless in Maryland commissioned by the Maryland Department of Human Resources. Baltimore, MD: Author.

1171. Henniss, A.G. (1987). Chattanooga survey of the homeless. Chattanooga, TN: Metropolitan Council for Community Services.

1172. Hertzberg, E.L. (1988). Homelessness: From the clients' perspectives. Paper presented at the 4th National Symposium on Doctoral Research and Social Work Practice, Columbus, Ohio.

1173. Hertzberg, E.L. (1988). Homelessness in Hennepin County: From the clients' perspectives. Dissertation Abstracts International, 49, 967 A.

1174. Hilfiker, D. (1989). Are we comfortable with homelessness? Journal of American Medical Association, 262, 1375-1376.

1175. Hill, R.P., & Stamey, M. (1990). The homeless in America: An examination of possessions and consumption behaviors. Journal of Consumer Research, 17, 303-321.

1176. Hoch, C. (1987). A brief history of the homeless problem in the United States. In R.D. Bingham, R.E. Green & S.B. White (Eds.), The homeless in contemporary society. Newbury Park, CA: Sage Publications.

1177. Hoch, C. (1988). A pragmatic inquiry. Society, 26, 27-35.

1178. Holden, C. (1986). Homelessness: Experts differ on root causes. Science, 232, 569-570.

Discusses varying explanations of homelessness in America and suggests that housing would be the answer to the homelessness problem if the problem is primarily socio-economic. However, if most of the homeless are psychological disabled, then the issue becomes more complex, because such a population would require comprehensive health services and, since a great number would never be able to live independently; residential alternatives other than independent living arrangements would be necessary.

1179. Hombs, M.E., & Snyder, M. (1982). Homeless in America: A forced march to nowhere. Washington, DC: Community for Creative Non-violence.

1180. Hombs, M.E., & Snyder, M. (1983). Homelessness in America: One year later. Washington, DC: Community for Creative Non-violence.

1181. Hope, M., & Young, J. (1986). The faces of the homeless. Lexington, MA: Lexington Books.

1182. Hopper, K. (1983). Homelessness: Reducing the distance. New England Journal of Human Services, Fall, 30-47.

1183. Hopper, K. (1990). Public shelter as "a hybrid institution": Homeless men in historical perspective. Journal of Social Issues, 46, 13-29.
Homelessness among single men has typically been viewed as a problem of troubled (and troublesome) individuals. Shelters historically have been "hybrid institutions," plugging gaps in the formal institutional supports and serving as dwellings of last resort for usually-working men who have exhausted informal resources. A coherent unemployment relief policy is still lacking, despite the centrality of labor market dynamics in the homelessness of these men.

1184. Hopper, K., Baxter, E., & Cox, S. (1982). One year later: The homeless poor in New York City. New York: Community Service Society.
In a 1 year follow-up study of New York City's homeless, changes noted include: (1) an expansion of the public shelter system, (2) a dramatic increase in the number of homeless people requesting public shelter, (3) a growing recognition of the mental health dimensions of homelessness, (4) increasingly sympathetic media coverage of the homeless, (5) more positive public attitudes towards the homeless, and (6) the emergence of several groups as vocal advocates for the homeless. The authors discuss implications of the findings and make policy recommendations.

1185. Hopper, K., & Hamburg, J. (1984). The making of America's homeless: From skid row to new poor. New York: Community Service Society of New York.
Discusses homelessness in America since World War II and suggest that the homeless population is growing and becoming younger and more heterogeneous. The causes of contemporary homelessness are discussed, with particular attention paid to the role of deinstitutionalization and the housing crisis in creating a large population of mentally ill homeless, and the Reagan administration's cuts in welfare and benefit payments.

1186. Hopper, K., Susser, E., & Conover, S. (1985). Economics of makeshift: Deindustrialization and homelessness in New York City. Urban Anthropology,

14, 183-236.
Changes in the economic restructuring of cities like New York, rather than individual deficits of the homeless themselves, are the root causes of homelessness. The most important of these changes are gentrification of urban neighborhoods coupled with increasing numbers of low-paying jobs in the service sector replacing higher paying jobs in industry that have been lost in the past decade. These changes have led to the depletion of affordable housing, leaving vulnerable populations, such as the mentally ill, without housing. Emergency food and shelter have become a routine element of survival strategies for those made homeless by economic changes.

1187. Hubbard, J. (1991). American refugees. Minneapolis, MN: University of Minnesota Press.

1188. Hudson, C.G. (1988). The development of policy for the homeless: The role of research. Social Thought, 14, 3-15.

1189. Hudson, C.G. (1988). The social class and mental illness correlation: Implications of the research for policy and practice. Journal of Sociology and Social Welfare, 15, 27-54.

1190. Huelsman, M. (1983). Violence on Anchorage's 4th Avenue from the perspective of street people. Alaska Medicine, 25, 39-44.

1191. Huth, M.J. (1987). Homelessness in America: Its nature and extent. Paper presented at the Annual Meeting of the American Sociological Association, Chicago, IL.

1192. Hyde, M.O. (1989). The homeless: Profiling the problem. Hillside, NJ: Enslow Publishers.

1193. Ille, M. (1980). Burnside: A study of hotel residents in Portland's skid row. Portland, OR: Burnside Consortium, Inc.

1194. Jahiel, R. I. (1987) The situation of homelessness. In R.D. Bingham, R.E. Green & S.B. White (Eds.), The homeless in contemporary society. Newbury Park, CA: Sage Publications.

1195. Jewell, J.R. (1986). Searching for the city of light: Homelessness in Thomas Hardy's modern novels. Dissertation Abstracts International, 47, 188-A.

1196. Johnson, A.K. (1988). Homelessness in America: A historical and contemporary assessment. St. Louis, MO: Washington University, George Warren Brown School of Social Work.

1197. Johnson, A.K. (1989). Measurement and methodology: Problems and issues in research on homelessness. Social Work Research and Abstracts, 25, 12-20.

1198. Jones, D.L. (1984). The beginning of industrial tramping. In E. Monkonnen (Ed.), Walking to work: Tramps in America 1790-1935. Lincoln, NE: University of Nebraska Press.

1199. Joseph, S.C. (1987). Making the most of crises. Journal of Public Health Policy, 8, 309-314.

1200. Kaufman, N., & Harris, J. (1983). Profile of the homeless in Massachusetts. Boston: Governor's Office of Human Resources.

1201. Kiesler, C.A. (1991). Homelessness and public policy priorities. American Psychologist, 46, 1245-1252.

1202. Killian, T. & Killian, L. (1990). Sociological investigations of mental illness: A review. Special Issue: Clozapine. Hospital and Community Psychiatry, 41, 902-911.

1203. King, C.E. (1989). Homelessness in America. The Humanist, 49, 8-32.

1204. King County Department of Planning and Community Development. (1986). Homelessness revisited. Seattle, WA. Author.

1205. King, L. (1982). Skid row: A geographical perspective. Unpublished doctoral dissertation, University of Oregon.

1206. Kline, M.V., Bacon, J.D., Chinkin, M., & Manov, W.F. (1987). The client tracking system: A tool for studying the homeless. Alcohol Health and Research World, 11, 66-67.

1207. Knight, R.H. (1987). Homelessness: An American problem. In R.D. Bingham, R.E. Green & S.B. White (Eds.), The homeless in contemporary society. Newbury Park, CA: Sage Publications.

1208. Koch, J.Q. (1987). The federal role in aiding the homeless. In R.D. Bingham, R.E. Green & S.B. White (Eds.), The homeless in contemporary society. Newbury Park, CA: Sage Publications.

1209. Koegel, P. (1987). Subsistence patterns among homeless adults in the inner-city of Los Angeles. Paper presented at the Annual Meeting of the American Public Health Association.

1210. Koegel, P. (1989). Understanding homelessness: An ethnographic approach. In R. Jahiel (Ed.), Homelessness: A prevention-oriented approach. Baltimore, MD: John Hopkins University Press.
Reviews ethnographic research on homelessness and discusses how reliance on cross-sectional, quantitative research methods has limited our understanding of homelessness.

1211. Koegel, P., Burnam, M.A., & Farr, R.K. (1990). Subsistence adaptation among homeless adults in the inner city of Los Angeles. Journal of Social Issues, 46, 83-107.

1212. Koegel, P., Farr, R.K., & Burnam, M. A. (1986). Heterogeneity in an inner-city homeless population: A comparison between individuals surveyed in traditional skid row locations and in voucher hotel rooms. Psychosocial

Rehabilitation Journal, 10, 31-45.
The authors compared 111 homeless adults in an inexpensive hotel to 379 homeless adults in other skid row settings. Significant differences were found on several demographic characteristics, subsistence patterns, and level of psychological distress. However, few differences in rates of mental disorder were found. Implications for both the homeless and homeless mentally ill populations are discussed.

1213. Koenig, A. (1983). Street people survey. Richmond, VA: Department of Public Welfare and Virginia Commonwealth University of Social Work.

1214. Kondratas, A. (1991). Ending homelessness. Policy challenges. American Psychologist, 46, 1226-1231.
Discusses the formulation of federal government policy to address the multifaceted nature of homelessness. Increasing cooperation at federal, state, and local levels and a long-term, broad spectrum attack on poverty in general, are urged in order to more effectively address the problem.

1215. Kooi, R.V. (1973). Main stem: Skid row revisited. Society, 10, 64-71.

1216. Kosof, A. (1988). Homeless in America. New York: Watts.

1217. Kroll, J., Carey, K., Hagedorn, D., Fire Dog, P., & Benavides, E. (1986). A survey of homeless adults in urban emergency shelters. Hospital and Community Psychiatry, 37, 283-286.
The findings of this survey of 68 homeless adults revealed high rates of mental illness, alcoholism, minor criminality, and chronic medical conditions. Further, most were socially isolated and did not use social or health care services for which they were eligible. The results are compared with those from other studies.

1218. Kusmer, K.L. (1981). The underclass: Tramps and vagrants in American Society, 1865-1930. Dissertation Abstracts International, 41, 4130 A.

1219. LaGory, M., Ritchey, F., & Mullis, J. (1989). Homelessness and affiliation. Paper presented at the Annual Meeting of the American Sociological Association.

1220. Landau, E. (1987). The homeless. Englewood Cliffs, NJ: Messner.

1221. Lee, B.A. (1978). Residential mobility on skid row: Disaffiliation, powerlessness, and decision making. Demography, 15, 285-300.

1222. Lee, B.A. (1980). The disappearance of skid row: Some ecological evidence. Urban Affairs Quarterly, 16, 81-107.

1223. Lee, B.A. (1987). Homelessness and community. Paper presented at the Annual Meetings of the American Sociological Association, Chicago, IL.

1224. Lee, B.A., Jones, S., & Lewis, D. (1990). Public beliefs about the causes of homelessness. Social Forces, 69, 253-265.

1225. Leepson, M. (1982). The homeless: Growing national problem. Editorial Research Reports, 2, 801-802.

1226. Leland, P.J. (1992). Homelessness in post-industrial society: A case of Economic Darwinism. Dissertation Abstracts International, 53, 1803-A.
Related contemporary homelessness to the broken relationship between capital- and place-based communities resulting from post industrial restructuring of society. The political and economic dynamics of contemporary homelessness at the local level are described for Atlanta, Georgia.

1227. Levinson, B.M. (1966). A comparative study of northern and southern negro homeless men. The Journal of Negro Education, 35, 144-150.
Reports findings of a study of WAIS I.Q. test scores for 12 northern born and 12 southern born homeless black males residing in New York. The author finds states that educational experiences have been over emphasized and life experiences under emphasized in the scoring and interpretation of I.Q. tests.

1228. Levinson, B.M. (1966). Subcultural studies of homeless men. Transactions of the New York Academy of Sciences, 29, 165-182.
Summarizes studies of homeless men on assistance from the New York City Department of Welfare, the city operated Men's Shelter, and private shelters. The author concludes from reviewing these studies that regardless of the subcultural context of the homeless person, it is necessary to address the personality traits and patterns of personality disorders among homeless men.

1229. Levinson, D. (1974). The etiology of skid rows in the United States. International Journal of Social Psychiatry, 20, 25-33.

1230. Levinson, D. (1974). Skid row in transition. Urban Anthropology, 3, 79-93.

1231. Levy, A. (1991). The effects of peer counseling training on homeless individuals self-esteem, world assumptions, and social networks. Dissertation Abstracts International, 52, 1041 B.

1232. Linn, L.S., & Gelberg, L. (1989). Priority of basic needs among homeless adults. Social Psychiatry and Psychiatric Epidemiology, 24, 23-29.
Based on the responses of 529 homeless adults, the homeless are depicted as a heterogeneous group with differing needs, habits, and priorities which should be considered when developing and providing services for the homeless.

1233. Lipsky, M., & Smith, S.R. (1989). When social problems are treated as emergencies. The Social Service Review, 63, 5-25.

1234. Lovell, A.M. (1984). Marginality without isolation: Social networks and the new homeless. Paper presented at the 83rd annual meeting of the American Anthropology Association, Denver, Colorado.

1235. Lovell, A.M. (1992). Marginal arrangements: Homelessness, mental illness, and social relations. Dissertation Abstracts International, 53, 1986 A.

1236. Lovell, A.M., Barrow, S.M., & Struening, E.L. (1989). Between relevance and rigor: Methodological issues in studying mental health and homelessness. In R.I. Jahiel (Ed.), Homelessness: A prevention oriented approach. Baltimore, MD: John Hopkins Press.

1237. Luke, J. (1986). A preliminary study of the homeless in Omaha-Douglas County. Omaha, NE: University of Nebraska Center for Applied Urban Research.

1238. Malloy, C, Christ, M.A., & Hohloch, F.J. (1990). The homeless: Social isolates. Journal of Community Health Nursing, 7, 25-36.

1239. Marcuse, P. (1988). Isolating the homeless. Shelterforce, 11, 12-15.

1240. Marcuse, P. (1988). Neutralizing homelessness. Socialist Review, 18, 69-96. Homelessness is viewed as a systemic problem resulting from the prevailing economic and political forces in American society. In particular, the profit structure of housing, distribution of income, and government policies are viewed as the primary causative factors. The author argues that sweeping changes in national housing and economic policies hold the most promise in resolving homelessness problem.

1241. Masi, E.L. (1988). The homeless of New York: A case study in social welfare policy. Dissertation Abstracts International, 48, 2160 A.

1242. Maurer, H. (1979). Not working. New York: Holt, Rinehart & Winston.

1243. Maurin, J.T. (1990). Research utilization in the social-political arena. Applied Nursing Research, 3, 48-51.
Many of the health problems of populations at greater risk for ill health require action at the social-political level for intervention. The researcher must protect the integrity of the research process so that the results will be meaningful. The formation of the research questions and reporting of results also must take into account the social-political aims of the research.

1244. Maurin, J.T., Russell, L., & Hitchcox, M. (1989). Obstacles to research analysis. Journal of Psychosocial Nursing and Mental Health Services, 27, 19-23.
Care must be taken when drawing conclusions from research studies on the homeless. Because the homeless are made up of a number of distinct subgroups with different mental health status and needs, poor sampling methods may lead to under-representation or over-representation of some groups. Further, differing psychosocial abilities and skills of respondents may also bias studies that do not address these differences.

1245. Maynard, C., Gross, J., & Kent, C. (1989). Debunking myths about the homeless: A survey of the homeless population of Providence, Rhode Island. Administration and Policy in Mental Health, 16, 215-226.

1246. Maz, V. (1988). How to help the hungry & homeless. Journal of Christian Nursing, 5, 10-15.

1247. McChesney, K.Y. (1989). Growth of homelessness: An aggregate rather than an individual problem. In R. Jahiel (Ed.), Homelessness: A prevention oriented approach. Baltimore, MD: Johns Hopkins Press.

1248. McNulty, J.J. (1992). Homelessness and hopelessness: Resignation in news media constructions of homelessness as a social problem. Dissertation Abstracts International, 53, 2146 A.
Analyzed 92 news magazine articles and 111 television news broadcasts on homelessness, and found that news stories used the term homelessness to describe multiple and diverse populations. In general, news stories portrayed homelessness as a vague, incomprehensible, and intractable problem, and are plagued by imprecise language and lack of clarity in terms of the relationship between homelessness and other social problems.

1249. McSheehy, W. (1979). Skid Row. Cambridge, MA: Shenkman.

1250. Michigan Human Services Task Force on the Homeless. (1986). Life in transit: Homelessness in Michigan. Lansing, MI: Department of Mental Health.

1251. Milburn, N.G., & Watts, R.J. (1984). A Neglected Special Population: The Homeless. Paper presented at the Annual Convention of the American Psychological Association, Toronto, Ontario, Canada, August.

1252. Milburn, N.G., & Watts, R.J. (1985-1986). Methodological issues in research on the homeless and the homeless mentally ill. International Journal of Mental Health, 14, 42-60.
Conceptual frameworks underlying research of homeless populations are inadequate. Although many studies appear sound in design, they differ greatly in sophistication, content, and rigor.

1253. Milburn, N.G., Watts, R.J., & Anderson, S.L. (1984). An analysis of current research methods for studying the homeless. Washington, DC: Howard University.
Reviews and critiques research methods used in 75 research studies of the homeless over the 20 year period of 1964-1984.

1254. Miller, R. (1982). The demolition of skid row. Lexington, MA: Lexington Books.

1255. Missouri Association for Social Welfare. (1985). Homelessness in Missouri. Jefferson City, MO.

1256. Missouri Department of Mental Health. (1984). The homeless. In, Progress Notes, Jefferson City, MO: Missouri Department of Mental Health, Spring, pp. 3-6.

1257. Momeni, J.A. (Ed.) (1989). Homeless in the United States. Westport, CT: Greenwood Press.

1258. Morrissey, J.P., Dennis, D.L., & Gounis, K. (1985). The development and utilization of the Queens Mens's Shelter. Albany, NY: New York State Office

of Mental Health.
Reports findings of a study of a shelter for men who need mental health services. Extensive data on the demographics and psychiatric treatment history of residents was collected through participant observation, interviews with staff and residents, and reviews of shelter records.

1259. Morse, G.A. (1985). Homeless people: A typological analysis and gender comparisons. Dissertation Abstracts International, 45, 3626 B.

1260. Morse, G.A. (1986). A contemporary assessment of urban homelessness: Implications for social change. St. Louis, MO: University of Missouri-St. Louis. Describes a multilevel systems approach to homelessness and discusses characteristics, causes, and problems of homelessness as they relate to levels of social organization. The model further distinguishes between causal factors and forces that maintain homelessness. The author concludes with recommendations for social change interventions in three areas: (1) immediate assistance, (2) status change, and (3) prevention.

1261. Morton, J. (1971). Varieties of homelessness. New Society, 18, 18-23.

1262. Mowbray, C.T. (1985). Homelessness in America: Myths and realities. American Journal of Orthopsychiatry, 55, 4-8.
Describes the four most common myths about the homeless in America, which are: (1) most homeless are homeless because they choose to be, (2) many mentally ill are homeless because of deinstitutionalization, (3) homelessness is a "new" problem, and (4) homelessness can be solved by providing more money for emergency shelter beds.

1263. Multnomah County Social Services Division. (1984). The homeless poor. Portland, OR: Department of Social Services.

1264. Nanko, C.M. (1991). The use of contemporary catholic social teaching as a catalyst for praxis and reflection by adolescents on an issue of economic justice: An internship in homelessness. Dissertation Abstracts International, 52, 868-A.

1265. Nash, G., & Nash, P. (1966). The non-demanding society: An analysis of the social structure of skid row. Paper presented at the annual meeting of the Eastern Psychological Association, New York, April.

1266. National Coalition for the Homeless. (1983). Downward spiral: The homeless in New Jersey. New York: Author.

1267. National Coalition for the Homeless. (1983). The homeless and the economic recovery. New York.

1268. National Coalition for the Homeless. (1984). The homeless and the economic recovery: One year later. New York.

1269. New York State Department of Social Services. (1984). Homelessness in New York State: A report to the Governor and legislature. Albany, NY: New York State Department of Social Services.

1270. New York State Legislature. Senate Mental Hygiene and Addiction Control Committee. (1980). Single room occupancy hotels: A dead end in the human services delivery system. Albany, NY: Author.

1271. New York State Office of Mental Health. (1983). Who are the homeless? In, Homelessness in America. Washington, DC: U.S. Government Printing Office.

1272. Nooe, R.M. & Lynch, M. (1986). Homeless in Knox county: Report of the Knoxville Coalition for the Homeless. Knoxville, TN: Knoxville Coalition for the Homeless.

1273. Parsons, L. (1986). Bibliographic review on studies estimating the size of homeless populations. Amherst, MA: Social and Demographic Research Institute.

1274. Passero, J.M., Zax, M., & Zozus, R.T. (1991). Social network utilization as related to family history among the homeless. Journal of Community Psychology, 19, 70-78.

1275. Patton, L.T. (1987). The rural homeless. Washington, DC: U.S. Department of Health and Human Services.
Examines the nature and causes of homelessness in rural areas based on a review of available research, a survey of community health center grantees, and from two site visits.

1276. Peroff, K. (1987). Who are the homeless and how many are there. In R.D. Bingham, R.E. Green & S.B. White (Eds.), The homeless in contemporary society. Newbury Park, CA: Sage Publications.

1277. Power, J.G. (1991). Mass communication of otherness and identification: An examination of the portrayal of homeless people in network television news. Dissertation Abstracts International, 52, 1557 A.

1278. Proch, K., & Taber, M.A. (1987). Helping the homeless: Why people are on the streets is irrelevant to their need for shelter. Journal of the American Public Welfare Association, 45, 5-9.

1279. Quigley, G.H. (1988). Homeless and street people: Index of modern information. New York: ABBE Publishers Association.

1280. Redburn, F.S., & Buss, T.F. (1986). Beyond shelter: The homeless and public policy. New York: Praeger.

1281. Redburn, F.S., & Buss, T.F. (1986). Responding to America's homeless: Public policy alternatives. New York: Praeger.

1282. Resener, C.R. (1988). Crisis in the streets. Nashville, TN: Broadman.

1283. Reyes, L.M., Waxman, L.D. (1987). The Continuing Growth of Hunger, Homelessness, and Poverty in America's Cities: 1987. A 26-City Survey. Washington, DC: United States Conference of Mayors.

1284. Ringenbach, P.T. (1973). Tramps and reformers, 1873-1916: The discovery of unemployment in New York. Westport, CT: Greenwood Press.

1285. Ringheim, K.E. (1989). Estimating a population at risk of homelessness: The roles of income and rent in four metropolitan areas. Dissertation Abstracts International, 51, 301 A.

1286. Ringheim, K.E. (1990). At risk of homelessness: The roles of income and rent. Westport, CT: Praeger Publications.
Developed a vulnerability index to measure the size of the populations facing a high risk of becoming homeless in order to explain the relationship between economic inequality and homelessness in terms of changing relationships between economic vulnerability, housing affordability, and social composition of tenant households.

1287. Rivlin, L.G. (1986). New look at the homeless. Social Policy, 16, 3-11.
Discusses causes of homelessness and the problems homeless people encounter in their daily lives. The author also reviews the public's attitudes toward the homeless, and the socio-psychological impact upon children and adults of losing the social identity and security that having a home provides.

1288. Rivlin, L.G. (1990). Paths toward environmental consciousness. Human Behavior and Environment Advances in Theory and Research, 11, 169-185.

1289. Rivlin, L.G. (1990). The significance of home and homelessness. Marriage and Family Review, 15, 39-56.

1290. Rivlin, L.G., & Imbimbo, J. (1990). Self-help efforts in a squatter community: Implications for addressing contemporary homelessness. American Journal of Community Psychology, 17, 705-728.

1291. Roanoke Valley Council of Community Services. (1984). Demonstration project client tracking of non-medical emergency services: February-March, 1984. Roanoke, VA: Author.

1292. Roberts, R.E., & Keefe, T. (1986). Homelessness: Residual, institutional and communal solutions. Journal of Sociology and Social Welfare, 13, 400-417.
Presents a typology of homeless persons which includes: (1) the homeless mentally ill, (2) the "new poor," (3) alcoholics, (4) low income persons who have been recently evicted, and (5) single-parent women.

1293. Robertson, M.J., Ropers, R.H., & Boyer, R. (1985). The homeless of Los Angeles County: An empirical assessment. Los Angeles, CA: University of California School of Public Health Psychiatric Epidemiology Program.
Explores demographic, economic and health characteristics of a sample of 238 homeless persons surveyed in Los Angeles County, California. Included are discussions of differences by race, gender, length of homelessness, and geographic location.

1294. Robinson, F.G. (1985). Homeless people in the nation's capital: A census. Papers in the Social Sciences, 5, 1-12.

1295. Rooney, J.F. (1976).   Friendship and disaffiliation among the skid row population. Journal of Gerontology, 31, 82-88.

1296. Rooney, J.F. (1980). Organizational success through program failure: Skid row rescue mission. Social Forces, 58, 904-924.

1297. Ropers, R.H. (1988).   The invisible homeless: A new urban ecology.   New York: Human Sciences Press.

1298. Ropers, R.H., & Robertson, M.J. (1984).   The inner-city homeless of Los Angeles: An empirical assessment. Los Angeles: Los Angeles Basic Shelter Project.

1299. Rosenberg, A.A., Solarz, A.L., & Bailey, W.A. (1991).   Psychology and homelessness. A public policy and advocacy agenda.   American Psychologist, 46, 1239-1244.

1300. Rosenthal, R. (1988). Homeless in paradise: A map of the terrain. Dissertation Abstracts International, 49, 153 A.

1301. Rosenthal, R. (1989).   Worlds within worlds: Interactions of homeless people in context.   Paper presented at the Annual Meetings of the American Sociological Association.

1302. Rossi, P.H. (1988).   First out: Last in: Extreme poverty and homelessness. Amherst, MA: University of Massachusetts, Social and Demographic Research Institute.
The three sections of this report address: (1) describing the homeless population both now and in the past, (2) exploring causal factors on both institutional and individual levels of analysis, and (3) offering policy alternatives based on the current state of knowledge about homelessness.

1303. Rossi, P.H. (1989).   Down and out in America: The origins of homelessness. Chicago, IL: University of Chicago Press.

1304. Rossi, P.H. (1990).   The old homeless and the new homelessness in historical perspective. American Psychologist, 45, 954-959.

1305. Rossi, P.H., Fischer, G.A., & Willis, G. (1986). The condition of the homeless of Chicago. Amherst, MA: Social and Demographic Research Institute.
Used observations and interviews with homeless persons in shelters, on the streets, and in public places to provide a description of the living conditions of homeless persons and to estimate the size of the Chicago homeless population.

1306. Rossi, P.H., & Wright, J.D. (1987). The determinants of homelessness. Health Affairs, 6, 19-32.
Based on findings from surveys of a probability sample of shelter users and of homeless persons on the street, the authors argue that homelessness is an interaction of the effects of extreme poverty and disability and isolation.   The shortage of low-income housing, coupled with the inadequacy of income maintenance and lack of low-skill jobs, is seen as the major contributor to the

rising numbers of homeless, many of whom report poor physical health and previous psychiatric hospitalizations.

1307. Rossi, P.H., & Wright, J.D. (1989). The urban homeless: A portrait of urban dislocation. Annals of the American Academy of Political and Social Science, 501, 132-142.

1308. Rossi, P.H., Wright, J.D., Fisher, G.A. & Willis, G. (1987). The urban homeless: Estimating composition and size. Science, 235, 1336-1341.
Although homelessness has been recognized as a significant social problem, reliable and valid methods for estimating the size and composition of the homeless population have been lacking. This article presents the results of an extensive survey of the homeless in Chicago using modern sampling methods. The authors argue that their findings are the first scientifically defensible estimates of the size and composition of the homeless population in any city.

1309. Roth, D., & Bean, G.J. (1986). New perspectives on homelessness: Findings from a statewide epidemiological study. Hospital and Community Psychiatry, 37, 712-719.
Interviews with 979 homeless people in both urban and rural areas of Ohio suggest that economic factors (e.g., unemployment, inability to pay rent, etc.) are the major reasons for homelessness. Further, nearly 30% reported previous psychiatric hospitalizations and 31% exhibited symptoms serious enough to warrant mental health services. The authors conclude that homelessness is a multidimensional problem requiring intervention strategies that reflect the multiple needs and varying characteristics of the homeless population.

1310. Roth, D., & Bean, J. (1986). The Ohio study: A comprehensive look at homelessness. Psychosocial Rehabilitation Journal, 9, 31-39.
Findings from a statewide study of nearly 1,000 homeless persons in Ohio suggest that typical stereotypes of the homeless are incorrect. Statewide, economic problems were common among the homeless, as was a lack of geographic mobility among the homeless. Rates of mental illness and alcohol abuse varied across the state. Three subtypes of homeless were identified, each requiring differing interventions.

1311. Roth, D., Bean, J., Lust, N., & Saveanu, T. (1985). Homelessness in Ohio: A study of people in need. Columbus, OH: Ohio Department of Mental Health.
The results of a statewide study of homeless persons suggest that the primary causes of homelessness are economic and family problems. Further, 31% of those surveyed had serious mental health problems, although few had become homeless because of deinstitutionalization. Recommendations for interventions are presented.

1312. Royse, D. (1987). Homelessness among trash pickers. Psychological Reports, 60, 808-810.
Interviews with 50 "aluminum can pickers" found that most were unable to find another job because of age or disability. Nearly 60% were judged to be alcoholic, psychotic, or mentally retarded; and 18% were found to be homeless.

1313. Rubington, E. (1968).   The bottle gang.   Quarterly Journal of Studies on Alcohol, 29, 943-955.
Bottle gangs are groups of men who meet for the purpose of buying and drinking alcoholic beverages.   The author studied the social structure and control among bottle gangs through direct observation, participation, and use of key informants.

1314. Rubington, E. (1971).   The changing skid row scene.   Quarterly Journal of Studies on Alcohol, 32, 123-135.

1315. Rubington, E. (1973).   Variations in bottle-gang controls.   In E. Rubington & M.S. Weinberg (Eds.), Deviance: The interactionist perspective (2nd Ed.).   New York: The Macmillan Company.

1316. Salerno, D., Hopper, K., & Bassuk, E. (1984).   Hardship in the heartland: Homelessness in eight American cities. New York: Community Service Society of New York.

1317. Sawyer, C. (1985).   From Whitechapel to Old Town: The life and death of the skid row district Portland, Oregon. Unpublished doctoral dissertation, Portland State University.

1318. Schmaltz, D.A. (1992).   Nobodies: Homeless in paradise.   Dissertation Abstracts International, 53, 2124-A.
Explored social psychological circumstance and coping strategies of homeless persons.   Specific policy recommendations include developing social support systems in order to rehabilitate both the new homeless and chronic alcoholic subpopulations.

1319. Schneider, J.C. (1984).   Tramping workers, 1890-1920: A sub-cultural view.   In E. Monkonnen (Ed.), Walking to work: Tramps in America 1790-1935. Lincoln, NE: University of Nebraska Press.

1320. Schupf, H.W. (1971).   The perishing and dangerous classes: Efforts to deal with the neglected vagrant and delinquent juvenile in England, 1840-1875. Dissertation Abstracts International, 32, 1455 A.

1321. Schussheim, M.J. (1986).   The Reagan 1987 budget and the homeless. Washington, DC: Congressional Research Service, Library of Congress.

1322. Schutt, R.K. (1985).   Boston's homeless: Their backgrounds, problems and needs. Boston, MA: University of Massachusetts.

1323. Schutt, R.K. (1987).   Boston's homeless, 1986-1987: Change and continuity. Boston, MA: University of Massachusetts.
Describes the characteristics of the homeless in a Boston shelter and their changing characteristics over a 2 year period. Supplemental reports on the shelter and homeless veterans are included.

1324. Sebastian, J.G. (1985).   Homelessness: A state of vulnerability.   Family and Community Health, 8, 11-24.
Discusses the history of homelessness in the United States and the characteristics

of the homeless population today, with emphasis on the health and mental health problems faced by the homeless. Social problems, including disconnectedness, lack of continuity of care, and lack of resources tend to contribute to the health and mental health problems of the homeless. Discusses special needs of women, children and the elderly.

1325. Segal, S.P., & Specht, H. (1983). A poorhouse in California, 1983: Oddity or prelude? Social Work, 28, 319-323.

1326. Sexton, P.C. (1986). The epidemic of homelessness. Dissent, 33, 137-140.

1327. Sexton, P.C. (1986). The life of the homeless. In J. Erickson & C. Wilhelm (Eds.), Housing the homeless. New Brunswick, NJ: Center for Urban Policy Research, Rutgers University.

1328. Seyo, P. (1975). Shelter: The national campaign for the homeless. Political Quarterly, 46(4), 418-431.

1329. Shaffer, M. (1988). Homelessness results from lack of jobs. Hospitals, 62, 72.

1330. Shapiro, J. (1966). Single room occupancy: Community of the alone. Social Work, 11, 24-33.

1331. Shinn, M., & Weitzman, B.C. (1990). Research on homelessness: An introduction. Journal of Social Issues, 46, 1-11.
Research on homelessness has tended to focus on problems of the homeless individuals, sometimes diverting attention from underlying causes and reinforcing stereotypes about the population. The authors suggest a more comprehensive model would include factors at the levels of individuals, social groups, and the socioeconomic context that contribute to homelessness.

1332. Siegal, H.A. (1978). Outposts of the forgotten. New Brunswick, NJ: Transaction Books.

1333. Siegal, H.A., & Inciardi, J.A. (1982). The demise of skid row. Society, 19, 39-45.

1334. Silverman, C.J., Segal, S.P., & Anello, E. (1989). Community and the homeless and mentally ill: The structure of self-help groups. Paper presented at the annual meetings of the American Sociological Association.

1335. Simmons, R.C. (1985). The Homeless in the Public Library: Implications for Access to Libraries. RQ, 25, 110-120.

1336. Simpson, J.H., Kilduff, M., & Blewett, C.D. (1984). Struggling to survive in a welfare hotel. New York City: Community Service Society.

1337. Slayton, R. (1987). SRO hotels and the homeless in Chicago. Paper presented at the Annual Meeting of the Midwest Sociological Society, Chicago, IL. April.

1338. Sloss, M. (1984). The crisis of homelessness: Its dimensions and solutions. Urban and Social Change Review, 17, 18-20.
One of the most salient problems in addressing urban homelessness lies in integrating the efforts to eliminate its structural causes and in drawing the lines of responsibility between government, private welfare groups and individuals for the shelter and rehabilitative needs of the homeless.

1339. Snow, D.A., & Anderson, L. (1987). Identity work among the homeless: The verbal construction and avowal of personal identities. American Journal of Sociology, 92, 1336-1371.
A field study of 168 homeless persons was conducted to understand how homeless persons construct personal identities that provide them with a measure of self-worth and dignity. Three distinct patterns of "identity talk" (e.g., distancing from other homeless, embracing street role identity, and fictive storytelling) were identified. The latter two patterns were most common among those on the streets for 2 or more years. The authors conclude that personal identities appear to change with length of time spent on the streets.

1340. Snow, D., Baker, S., & Anderson, L. (1989). Criminality and homeless men: An empirical assessment. Social Problems, 36, 532-549.

1341. Snyder, N., & Penner, S.J. (1989). Images of the urban street homeless. Paper presented at the Annual Meetings of the Society for the Study of Social Problems, Berkeley, CA, August.

1342. Solarz, A. (1985). Social supports among the homeless. Paper presented at the 113th Annual Meeting of the American Public Health Association, Washington, DC., November.

1343. Sosin, M.R. (1989). Homelessness in Chicago: A study sheds new light on an old problem. Public Welfare, 47, 22-28, 46.

1344. Sosin, M.R., Colson, P., & Grossman, S. (1988). Homelessness in Chicago: Poverty and pathology, social institutions and social change. Chicago, IL: University of Chicago, School of Social Service Administration.
The results of a survey of 535 individuals selected at random from persons at soup kitchens, free meal programs, shelters, and a residential treatment program for the indigent are discussed. Homeless persons are compared to non-homeless poor in an effort to determine whether the homeless have unique traits compared to others surveyed. Finally, the authors discuss the social institutions of Chicago as well as general social and economic conditions and the impact of these forces upon the homeless population.

1345. Sosin, R., Piliavin, I., & Westerfelt, H. (1990). Toward a longitudinal analysis of homelessness. Journal of Social Issues, 46, 157-174.

1346. Speigelman, R. (1984). Comment on "Dysfunctional side-effects..." Evaluation and Program Planning, 7, 17-18.
Social dysfunctionality follows from the attempt to distribute scarce resources in a manner that appears politically legitimate. Two examples to support this argument (e.g., prisoners on psychotropic drugs and homeless individuals who

are likely to find shelter if judged to be suffering from alcohol-related problems) are cited.

1347. Spradley, J.P. (1970). You owe yourself a drunk: An ethnography of urban nomads. Boston, MA: Little, Brown.

1348. Spradley, J.P. (1972). Adaptive strategies of urban nomads: The ethnoscience of tramp culture. In T. Weaver & D. White (Eds.), The anthropology of urban environments (Monograph 11). Boulder, CO: Society for Applied Anthropology.

1349. Stark, L.R. (1985). From winos to crazies: Demographics and stereotypes of the homeless. Paper presented at the second meeting of the American Public Health Association's Committee on Health Services Research Study Group on Homelessness, Washington, D.C.

1350. Stefl, M.E. (1987). The new homeless: A national perspective. In R.D. Bingham, R.E. Green & S.B. White (Eds.), The homeless in contemporary society. Newbury Park, CA: Sage Publications.

1351. Stern, M.J. (1984). The emergence of homelessness as a social problem. Social Service Review, 58, 290-300.

1352. Stoner, M.R. (1984). An analysis of public and private sector provisions for homeless people. Urban and Social Change Review, 17, 3-8.
Discusses the causes and demographics of homelessness. Based on a review of existing programs and services for the homeless, the author argues for a comprehensive service system for the homeless that includes: (1) emergency shelter, (2) crisis intervention, (3) transitional living accommodations, and (4) long-term residence.

1353. Stoner, M.R. (1989). Inventing a non-homeless future: A public policy agenda for preventing homelessness. New York: P. Lang Publishers.

1354. Streeter, C.L., & Frank, R. (1985). Bitter Harvest: The question of homelessness in rural America. Homelessness in Missouri. Jefferson City, MO: Missouri Association for Social Welfare.

1355. Struening, E.L. (1986). A study of residents of the New York City shelter system. New York: New York State Psychiatric Research Institute, Epidemiology of Mental Disorders Research Department.
Reports findings of study of a representative sample of 832 homeless men and women in New York City. The purpose of the study is to provide reliable information on the needs of the homeless, particularly their housing and service needs.

1356. Sudman, S., Sirken, M.G., & Cowan, C.D. (1988). Sampling rare and illusive populations. Science, 240, 991-996.

1357. Susko, M.A. (ed.) (1991). Cry of the invisible: Writings from the homeless and survivors of psychiatric hospitals. New York: The Conservatory Press.

1358. Susser, E., Conover, S., & Struening, E.L. (1989). Problems of epidemiologic method in assessing the type and extent of mental illness among homeless adults. Hospital and Community Psychiatry, 40, 261-265.
The authors criticize surveys on homelessness made during the 1980's in terms of weakness in sampling and measurement of mental disorder. Because the homeless problem has received much attention, the authors feel that poorly designed studies receive undue attention and that poorly designed interventions follow. The authors suggest using alternative sampling methods and measurement strategies within studies to combat the problem.

1359. Swanson, C.R. (1973). Alcoholism, skid row and the police. Crime and Delinquency, 19, 94-95.

1360. Task Force on Emergency Shelter. (1983). Homelessness in Chicago. Chicago, IL: Department of Human Services.

1361. Tennessee Department of Human Services. (1986). Problems of the homeless in 91 rural counties. Nashville, TN.

1362. Texas Health and Human Service Coordinating Council. (1985). Final report on the homeless in Texas. Austin, TX.

1363. Timmer, D.A. (1988). Homelessness as deviance: The ideology of the shelter. Free Inquiry in Creative Sociology, 16, 163-170.

1364. Toro, P.A., & McDonell, D.M. (1992). Beliefs, attitudes, and knowledge about homelessness: A survey of the general public. American Journal of Community Psychology, 20(1), 53-80.
A telephone survey conducted in a medium sized metropolitan area found that 58% of respondents were willing to pay more taxes to help homeless persons, and that respondents were accurate in estimating the extent of mental illness among the area's homeless persons. Women and younger respondents viewed homelessness as a more serious problem, saw fewer personal deficits among the homeless, and viewed employment as more critical in solving the homeless problems than did other respondents.

1365. Toro, P.A., Trickett, E.J., Wall, D.D., & Salem, D.A. (1991). Homelessness in the United States: An ecological perspective. American Psychologist, 46, 1208-1218.

1366. U.S. Conference of Mayors. (1984). Homelessness in America's cities: Ten case studies. Washington, DC.

1367. U.S. Conference of Mayors. (1986). The growth of hunger, homelessness and poverty in American cities in 1985. Washington, DC.
Findings of surveys concerning the status of homelessness and hunger in 25 American cities are reported. Increases in the number of homeless mentally ill persons are reported in over 1/4 of the cities responding. The most frequently reported reasons for homelessness include: (1) shortages of affordable housing, (2) inadequate services for the chronically mentally ill, and (3) unemployment.

1368. U.S. Conference of Mayors. (1989). A status report on hunger and homelessness in America's cities: 1989. Washington, DC.
Summarizes surveys conducted in 27 cities concerning the demographic characteristics of shelter users, the demand for emergency food and shelter, the status of affordable housing, and the overall outlook for hunger and homelessness for 1990.

1369. U.S. Department of Housing and Urban Development. (1984). Report to the secretary on the homeless and emergency shelters. Washington, DC: Department of Housing and Urban Development.

1370. U.S. Department of Housing and Urban Development. (1989). The 1988 national survey of shelters for the homeless. Washington, DC.
Findings of a survey of a probability sample of 205 shelter managers and administrators of voucher programs for the homeless are reported. The findings will be used in administering homeless assistance under the Stewart B. McKinney Act.

1371. Usherwood, T.P. (1987). Crisis at Christmas [letter]. Lancet, 1, 811.

1372. Volkman, N. (1991). Belonging, a study of home and homelessness; A contribution to a theory of personality. Dissertation Abstracts International, 52, 2343-B.

1373. Vosburgh, M.L. (1982). An ethnological study of Philadelphia street people. Philadelphia, PA: University of Pennsylvania School of Social Work.

1374. Vosburgh, W.W. (1988). Voluntary associations, the homeless and hard-to-serve populations: Perspectives from organizational theory. Journal of Voluntary Action Research, 17, 10-23.

1375. Wallace, S.E. (1965). Skid row as a way of life. Totowa, NJ: Bedminster Press.
Skid row should be viewed as a unique and distinctive subculture with its own values, rules of interaction and status system. The argument includes a history of skid rows in America. Successful socialization into the skid row subculture depends on employment history, personality makeup, financial background and manner of exposure to the skid row way of life.

1376. Wallace, S.E. (1968). The road to skid row. Social Problems, 16, 92-105.
Explores definitions of skid row and the inconsistencies among research findings associated with variations in definitions employed. A description of 4 phases of recruitment into the skid row lifestyle is provided.

1377. Weiner, S., & Weaver, L. (1974). Begging and social deviance on skid row. Quarterly Journal of Studies on Alcohol, 35, 1307-1315.

1378. Wellington Group. (1984). A study of the homeless population in Erie County, New York. Buffalo, NY: Adult Residential Care Advocates, Inc.

1379. Wenzel, S.L. (1991). Psychological and social resources, self-efficacy, and employment preparation: Their relationship to employment experiences for the homeless and nonhomeless disadvantaged. <u>Dissertation Abstracts International,</u> <u>51</u>, 5077 B.
In a study of 115 homeless and nonhomeless persons attending job training programs, participants related psychological and social resources to post-program self-efficacy. Persons with higher levels of psychological and social resources had higher levels of confidence in their ability to find employment. Employment outcomes were also influenced by levels of psychological and social resources. Comprehensive approaches to job training that consider a person's resources and organizational and economic contexts appears necessary to achieve successful employment-related outcomes.

1380. Wenzel, S.L. (1992). Length of time spent homeless: Implications for employment of homeless persons. <u>Journal of Community Psychology, 20(1)</u>, 57-71.
Studied the relationship of length of time spent homeless and employment outcomes for participants in a job training program for the homeless. Psychological resources and social support were found to buffer the negative effects of longer periods of homelessness on subsequent employment.

1381. Westerfelt, H. (1990). The ins and outs of homelessness: Exit patterns and predictions. <u>Dissertation Abstracts International, 51</u>, 3223 A.

1382. Whitley, M.P. (1983). On liberty and paternalism: An investigation of the dilemma of citizenship and obligation to schizophrenic vagrants in a liberal state. <u>Dissertation Abstracts International, 44</u>, 1202 A.

1383. Wiegard. B. (1985). Counting the homeless. <u>American Demographics,</u> December, 34-47.

1384. Winograd, K. (1983). <u>Street people and other homeless: A Pittsburgh study</u>. Pittsburgh, PA: Emergency Shelter Task Force.

1385. Wiseman, J.P. (1974). Control of the socially undesirable: The skid row bum. <u>American Journal of Orthopsychiatry, 44</u>, 198-199.

1386. Wray, L.B. (1984). On skid row: Just who are the bowery boys of the 1980's. <u>University of Maryland Chronicle, 18</u>, 3-6.

1387. Wright, J.D. (1988). The worthy and unworthy homeless. <u>Society, 25</u>, 64-69.

1388. Wright, J.D. (1989). <u>Address unknown: The homeless in America</u>. Hawthorne, NY: Aldine de Gruyter.

1389. Zettler, M.D. (1975). <u>The Bowery</u>. New York: Drake.

9

Special Populations: Elderly, Minorities, & Veterans

1390. Anonymous. (1991). Characteristics and risk behaviors of homeless black men seeking services from the Community Homeless Assistance Plan--Dade County, Florida, August 1991. <u>Morbidity and Mortality Weekly Report</u>, <u>40</u>, 865-868.

1391. Aging Health Policy Center. (1985). <u>The homeless mentally ill elderly (Working Paper)</u>. San Francisco: University of California.

1392. Barrow, S.M., & Lovell, A.M. (1987). Homelessness and the limited options of older women. <u>Association for Anthropology and Gerontology Newsletter</u>, <u>8</u>, 3-6.

1393. Boondas, J. (1985). The despair of the homeless aged. <u>Journal of Gerontological Nursing</u>, <u>11</u>, 8-13, 36.
Discusses factors contributing to the increase in the homeless aged population, including: (1) deinstitutionalization, (2) a shortage of affordable housing, and (3) an increase in poverty among the aged. Recommendations for serving this population are presented.

1394. Carboni, J. (1990). Homelessness among the institutionalized elderly. <u>Journal of Gerontological Nursing</u>, <u>16</u>, 32-37.

1395. City of New York, Office of the Comptroller, Research and Liaison Unit. (1982). <u>Soldiers of misfortune: Homeless veterans in New York City</u>. New York: Office of the Comptroller.

1396. Coalition for the Homeless. (1984). <u>Crowded out: Homelessness and the elderly poor in New York City</u>. New York.

1397. Cohen, C.I. (1984). <u>The aging men of Skid Row: A target for research and service intervention</u>. Portions of this paper were presented at the 37th Annual

Scientific Meeting of the Gerontological Society, San Antonio, November. Reports findings of a study comparing 281 aged homeless men (Mean age=61.5 years) to a national community sample of the elderly. The findings suggest high rates of psychiatric illness and alcohol abuse. Further, many had insufficient money for food and few received public assistance or medicaid. A description of Project Rescue, a program developed as an outgrowth of the research which provides several services for aging homeless men is also provided.

1398. Cohen, C.I. (1989). Social ties and friendship patterns of old homeless men. In R.G. Adams & R. Blieszner (Eds.), Older adult friendship: Structure and process. Newberry Park, CA: Sage Publications.

1399. Cohen, C.I., & Sokolovsky, J. (1983). Toward a concept of homelessness among aged men. Journal of Gerontology, 38, 81-89.
Compared a group of homeless aged men to a group of Bowery men living in SRO hotels. Three of Donald Bogue's (1963) criteria for skid row social formation differentiated the two groups, with socioeconomic status being the most powerful set of predictors. Differences on sociability were also found between the two groups.

1400. Cohen, C.I., Teresi, J.A., & Holmes, D. (1988). The mental health of old homeless men. Journal of the American Geriatric Society, 36, 492-501.
Although 23% of a group of homeless men over 50 years old evidenced psychosis or had previous psychiatric hospitalizations, depression was more prevalent, with 33% of subjects categorized as clinically depressed. Only 5% evidenced organic brain disease.

1401. Cohen, C.I., Teresi, J.A., & Holmes, D. (1988). The physical well-being of old homeless men. Journal of Gerontology, 43, 121-128.
Assessed the physical health status of 281 aged homeless men living either on the street or in Bowery flophouses. Compared to age-matched community controls, the Bowery men scored worse on all physical health scales. Predictors of poor health were stress, unfulfilled needs, being relatively younger, and lack of contacts with service agencies.

1402. Cohen, C.I., Teresi, J.A., Holmes, D., & Roth, E. (1988). Survival strategies of older homeless men. The Gerontologist, 28, 58-65.
Report findings of interviews with 281 homeless males (aged 50 to 80) living on the streets or in flophouses in New York City's Bowery area. Factors linked to inability to fulfill basic needs included: (1) physical health problems, (2) depression, (3) few contacts with service agencies, and (4) stress. The findings suggest that health care and housing were the most pressing needs of this population.

1403. Coppin, V.E.H. (1974). Life styles and social services on skid row: A study of aging homeless men. Dissertation Abstracts International, 35, 3877 A.

1404. Coston, C. (1989). The original designer label: Prototypes of New York City's shopping-bag ladies. Deviant Behavior, 10, 157-172.

1405. Damrosch, S.P., & Strasser, J.A. (1988). The homeless elderly in America. Journal of Gerontological Nursing, 14, 26-29.

1406. Doolin, J. (1986). Planning for the special needs of the homeless elderly. The Gerontologist, 26, 229-231.
The special needs of the homeless elderly are discussed, followed by the presentation of a program designed to augment the work of public shelters by coordinating medical, nutrition, and social services in a day center format that is structurally integrated within the local aging service infrastructure, utilizing existing resource patterns.

1407. El-Bassel, N., & Schilling, R.F. (1991). Drug use and sexual behavior of indigent African-American men. Public Health Reports, 106, 586-590.

1408. Elston, L., & Slavin, L. (1985). Safe shelter for homeless elders. Generations, 9, 48-49.
Describes two programs in New York City, the Educational Alliance-Respite House program and the Homelessness Prevention program of Project DOROT, both of which aid in relocation of homeless elderly through use of small transitional shelters.

1409. First, R.J., Roth, D. & Arewa, B.D. (1988). Homelessness: Understanding the dimensions of the problem for minorities. Archives of General Psychiatry, 28, 633-635.
Little attention has been paid to the characteristics and services needs of the minority homeless in either the literature or in service delivery efforts. In this article, the authors review available research on this population, report differences between white and black respondents from a large epidemiological study of homeless persons, and discuss the implications of these differences for service delivery and policy development.

1410. Harris, J.L., Williams, L.K. (1991). Universal self-care requisites as identified by homeless elderly men. Journal of Gerontological Nursing, 17, 39-43.

1411. Hudson, B., Rauch, B., Dawson, G., & Santos, F. (1987). Homelessness: Special problems related to training, research, and the elderly. Gerontology and Geriatrics Education, 10, 31-69.

1412. Keigher, S.M. (1992). A preliminary study of elderly emergency service clients in Chicago and their housing-related problems. Journal of Applied Gerontology, 11(1), 4-21.
A review of case records of elderly clients of the Chicago Department of Human Services Emergency Services program revealed a broad range of service needs for the elderly who are at risk for homelessness. Suggestions for improving client services, stressing the need for ongoing services rather than emergency services are provided.

1413. Kerson, T.S. (1989). Community-based mental health program: Outreach and rehabilitation center for homeless veterans. Health and Social Work, 14, 140-141.

1414. Leda, C., & Rosenheck, R. (1992).   Mental health status and community adjustment after treatment in a residential treatment program for homeless veterans.   American Journal of Psychiatry, 149, 1219-1224.
This study of 255 veterans admitted to the VA Domiciliary Care for Homeless Veterans Program found that program participation was associated with improvement in all areas of mental health and community adjustment. Further improvement in alcohol related problems was associated with improvement in employment status.   Weaker links between program participation and areas outside of mental health status suggest that treatment programs should focus separately on the multiple life domains of homeless veterans.

1415. Martin, M. (1987).   The implications of NIMH-supported research for homeless mentally ill racial and ethnic minority persons.   Rockville, MD: NIMH.
Discusses findings from NIMH-supported research concerning what is known about the ethnic minority homeless mentally ill sub-population.

1416. Mellinger, J.C. (1989).   Emergency housing for frail older adults.   The Gerontologist, 29, 401-404.
Describes an innovative emergency housing program for homeless older adults that places clients in private homes for 2 to 4 weeks while permanent housing arrangements are made.   The findings indicate that the program was more cost efficient than traditional emergency housing programs and provided more social support for clients.   A 1 year follow-up investigation of 63 clients found a significantly lower rate of institutionalization for program participants than comparable non-participants.

1417. New York City Office of the Comptroller. (1982).   Soldiers of misfortune: Homeless veterans in New York City.   New York: Office of the Comptroller.

1418. Nyamathi, A.M. (1991).   Relationship of resources to emotional distress, somatic complaints, and high-risk behaviors in drug recovery and homeless minority women.   Research in Nursing and Health, 14, 269-277.

1419. Peterson, M.L. (1987).   Homeless veterans, continued.   Hospital and Community Psychiatry, 38, 774-775.

1420. Pottieger, A.E., & Inciardi, J.A. (1981).   Aging on the street: Drug use and crime among older men.   Journal of Psychoactive Drugs, 13, 199-211.

1421. Raiford, G.L. (1987).   The vanishing black American family or: What's happening with the manchild?   Journal of Intergroup Relations, 14, 29-37.
Discusses the causes and effects of changes in the family of American Blacks. Persistent, institutional racism is seen as the primary cause for the plight of Black male youths. The author classifies black males youth into three groups: (1) those who attain a career, (2) those who steadily seek work and rarely succeed, and (3) the displaced and homeless.

1422. Reilly, F.E. (1991).   Health, space use, and time use by homeless elderly people.   Dissertation Abstracts International, 52, 2996 B.

1423. Robertson, M.J. (1987). Homeless veterans: An emerging problem. In R.D. Bingham, R.E. Green & S.B. White (Eds.), The homeless in contemporary society. Newbury Park, CA: Sage Publications.

1424. Robertson, M.J., & Abel, E. (1985). Homeless veterans in Los Angeles County. Paper presented at the annual meeting of the American Public Health Association, Washington, D.C.

1425. Rosenheck, R., & Gallup, P. (1991). Involvement in an outreach and residential treatment program for homeless mentally ill veterans. Journal of Nervous and Mental Disorders, 179, 750-754.
Levels of involvement in a national VA outreach program for homeless, chronically ill veterans was modest, with only about 24% of those admitted still involved after 90 days. Demographic and clinical characteristics were only mildly related to involvement. However, those admitted to residential treatment programs were more than 5 times more likely to participate in the program than those not admitted.

1426. Rosenheck, R., Gallup, P., & Leda, C.A. (1991). Vietnam era and Vietnam combat veterans among the homeless. American Journal of Public Health, 81, 643-646.
A study of homeless veterans in VA programs (N > 10,000) found that nearly half were Vietnam era veterans, while Vietnam era veterans make up only 29% of veterans in the general population. This does not reflect a greater likelihood of homelessness for Vietnam veterans, but reflects the increased risk of homelessness for men between the ages of 30 and 45. Non-white homeless combat veterans were more likely to have psychiatric, alcohol and medical related problems than non-white non-combat veterans.

1427. Rosenheck, R., Gallup, P., Leda, C., Gorchov, L., & Errera, P. (1989). Reaching out across America: The third progress report on the Department of Veterans Affairs homeless chronically mentally ill veterans program. West Haven, CT: Northeast Program Evaluation Center, West Haven Veterans Administration Medical Center.
The authors report findings of evaluations of treatment outcomes from veterans in 9 of the 43 V.A. programs for homeless mentally ill veterans.

1428. Rosenheck, R., Gallup, P., Leda, C., Thompson, D., & Errera, P. (1988). Reaching out: The second progress report on the Veterans Administration homeless chronically mental ill veterans program (Volume I: Text). West Haven, CT: Northeast Program Evaluation Center, West Haven Veterans Administration Medical Center.
Reports preliminary findings from an evaluation of the first 14 months of the Homeless Chronically Mentally Ill Veterans Program which provides a number of health care and rehabilitative services to homeless veterans in 41 cities.

1429. Rosenheck, R., & Leda, C. (1991). Who is served by programs for the homeless? Admission to a domiciliary care program for homeless veterans. Hospital and Community Psychiatry, 42, 176-181.
This study found that more than 2/3 of the veterans (N=4138) who were screened for admission into the Department of Veterans Affairs Domiciliary

Care for Homeless Veterans program had been hospitalized in the VA system in the previous year, and over 1/3 were hospitalized at the time of their screening assessment. Veterans who were admitted to the program were more likely to have previous mental heath treatment, without public financial support, and to be homeless at the time of their admission than were those who were not admitted.

1430. Rosenheck, R., Leda, C., & Gallup, P. (1992). Combat stress, psychosocial adjustment, and service use among homeless Vietnam veterans. Hospital and Community Psychiatry, 43(2), 145-149.
More than 40% of the veterans studied show signs of combat-related stress which was associated with high levels of substance abuse and psychiatric disorder. Compared to Vietnam veterans assessed in a national epidemiological study, homeless veterans were more socially and vocationally dysfunctional. Further, homeless mentally ill veterans with combat stress used VA mental health services more often than homeless mentally ill veterans with other disorders.

1431. Rosenheck, R., Leda, C., Gallup, P., & Astrachan, B.M. (1989). Initial assessment data from a 43-site program for homeless chronic mentally ill veterans. Hospital and Community Psychiatry, 40, 937-942.
The authors report findings of intake assessments of 10,529 homeless veterans conducted at the 43 sites of the Veterans Administration Homeless Chronically Mentally Ill Veterans Program during the first 11 months of its operation. Homeless veterans are younger than veterans in the general population and more had served in the Vietnam era than in any other military eras. Nearly half manifested at least one severe psychiatric symptom at screening and nearly two-thirds had a previous hospitalization for either a psychiatric or substance abuse disorder.

1432. Sanford, E.K. (1991). Patterns of adjustment among the homeless elderly: An investigation into their personal histories and characteristics. Dissertation Abstracts International, 52, 2278 A.
Based on indepth interviews with 20 homeless men over 50 years of age, a 6-stage theoretical model of adjustment to homelessness involving psychological factors, informal support systems, formal support systems, and personal resources is presented and tested.

1433. Schutt, R.K. (1986). A short report on homeless veterans: A supplement to Homeless in Boston, 1985. Boston, MA: University of Massachusetts.

1434. Smith, J.P. (1992). Are the needs of older homeless people being ignored? Journal of Advances in Nursing, 17, 763.

1435. Struening, E.L., Pittman, J., & Rosenblatt, A. (1988). Characteristics of homeless veterans in the New York City shelter system. New York: New York State Psychiatric Institute.
The authors compare 202 homeless veterans with a control group of non-veteran shelter residents. With the exception that the veterans had a significantly higher educational level, the two groups exhibited few differences. Both groups rated housing, income, and employment as their greatest needs. Further, 26.4% of

the veterans were found to be in need of psychiatric treatment for a serious mental disorder, while an additional 14.6% show moderate symptoms of mental disorder.

1436. Sullivan, M.A. (1991). A family systems-oriented approach to the treatment of the homeless mentally ill older woman. <u>Dissertation Abstracts International</u>, <u>52</u>, 3434 A.
Using clinical observation, this study of 10 chronically mentally ill women living in a residence program for elderly homeless women derives 5 principles for applying a family systems approach to assessment and treatment of homeless mentally ill older women.

1437. Sweet, M. (1987). Homeless veterans. <u>Hospital and Community Psychiatry</u>, <u>38</u>, 78-79.

1438. U.S. House Committee on Veterans' Affairs. (1986).   <u>Homeless and Unemployed Veterans</u>.   Hearing before the Subcommittee on Education, Training and Employment of the Committee on Veterans' Affairs. House of Representatives, Ninety-Ninth Congress, Second Session. Washington, DC: U. S. Government Printing Office.

1439. U.S. House of Representatives Select Committee on Aging, Subcommittee on Housing and Consumer Interest. (1984).   <u>Homeless older Americans</u>. Washington, DC: U.S. Government Printing Office.

1440. Welch, W.M., & Toff, G.E. (1987). <u>Service needs of minority persons who are homeless and homeless mentally ill</u>. Washington, DC: Intergovernmental Health Policy Project.

10

Programs, Services, & Training

1441. Advisory Commission on Intergovernmental Relations. (1988). <u>Assisting the homeless: State and local responses in an era of limited resources</u>. Washington, DC.

1442. Anello, R. (1984). <u>A guide for non-profit shelter operators in New York: Negotiating the public assistance system on behalf of homeless adults</u>. New York: Community Service Society of New York.

1443. Anello, R., & Shuster, T. (1985). <u>Community relations strategies: A handbook for sponsors of community-based programs for the homeless</u>. New York: Community Service Society of New York.

1444. Axelroad, S., & Toff, G. (1987). <u>Outreach services for homeless mentally ill people</u>. Washington, DC: George Washington University.

1445. Baltimore, D.A. (1991). The impact of the Stewart B. McKinney Homeless Assistance Act on the administration of state programs for the homeless. <u>Dissertation Abstracts International, 52</u>, 1953 A.
Surveyed state coordinators of homeless programs across the U.S. and found that the impact of the McKinney Act depends largely upon how state coordinators direct and administer state programs. The McKinney Act's impact on education of homeless children, the difficulties state coordinators had in meeting the mandates of the act, the number and kind of programs operating in different states, and the common elements of successful programs were examined.

1446. Barrow, S.M. (1988). <u>Delivery of services to homeless mentally ill clients: Engagement, direct service and intensive case management at five CSS programs</u>. New York: New York State Psychiatric Institute.
Describes innovative services (e.g., mobile outreach, drop-in services, etc.) provided by five programs for the homeless mentally ill administered by

community social service agencies. Clients are recruited from the streets, parks, bus and train terminals, and meal programs, as well as from emergency shelters.

1447. Barrow, S.M. (1988). Linking mentally ill homeless clients to psychiatric treatment services. New York: New York State Psychiatric Institute.
Reports findings of a six month study of changes in psychiatric treatment status of homeless mentally ill clients who participated in Community Support System programs in New York City. Among the services provided by CSS programs that were most associated with linkage to psychiatric treatment services were: (1) referral to stable housing, (2) psychiatric referrals, and (3) case management.

1448. Barrow, S.M., Hellman, F., Lovell, A., Plapinger, J., & Struening, E.L. (1989). Effectiveness of programs for the mentally ill homeless: Final report. New York: New York State Psychiatric Institute.
Examined the services provided by five programs for the homeless mentally ill in New York and compares the impact of these services on the housing and mental health status of the programs' clients.

1449. Barrow, S.M., Hellman, F., Lovell, A.M., Plapinger, J.D., & Struening, E.L. (1991). Evaluating outreach services: lessons from a study of five programs. New Directions in Mental Health Services, Winter, 29-45.

1450. Barrow, S.M., Hellman, F., Plapinger, J., Lovell, A.M., & Struening, E.L. (1986). Residence outcomes, preliminary findings from an evaluation of programs for the mentally ill homeless, 1986. Executive Summary. New York: New York State Psychiatric Institute.

1451. Barrow, S.M., & Lovell, A. (1982). Evaluation of Project Reach Out, 1981-1982. New York: Community Support System Evaluation Program, New York State Psychiatric Institute.

1452. Barrow, S.M., & Lovell, A. (1983). Evaluation of the referral of outreach clients to mental health services. New York: New York State Psychiatric Research Institute.

1453. Barrow, S.M., Lovell, A, & Struening, E.L. (1985). Serving the mentally ill homeless: Client and Program characteristics. New York: New York Psychiatric Research Institute.

1454. Baumohl, J. (1992). Hope needs work: Picking up from Hopper and Hawks. British Journal of Addiction, 87(1), 15-16.
Massive public employment programs, similar to those during the great depression, are necessary as a major aspect of the overall solution of the homeless problem.

1455. Benda, B.B. (1991). Undomiciled: A study of drifters, other homeless persons, their problems, and service utilization. Psychosocial Rehabilitation Journal, 14, 39-67.
Interviewed 446 homeless persons over 19 months to assess geographic mobility, prior problems, and present afflictions. Data reveal that the prevalence and incidence of problems were high for the geographically mobile as well as for

subjects who remained in one locality, and that a small percentage of both groups received professional services. A three pronged approach to homelessness is advocated, which involves institutionalization, an array of living arrangements with different intensities of services linked to other community services, and the establishment of support networks in the community.

1456. Billig, N.S., & Levinson, C. (1987). Homelessness and case management in Montgomery County, Maryland: A focus on chronic mental illness. Psychosocial Rehabilitation Journal, 11, 59-66.
Discusses the use of case management (e.g., assessment, goal setting, linkage, monitoring, and advocacy) with homeless mentally ill residing in shelters. Relationship building was found to be important in getting clients to accept services.

1457. Boaz, T., & Kunkel, M. (1989). Working with the homeless mentally ill: A manual for caregivers. Tampa, FL: University of South Florida.
Intended to serve as a resource for persons working in various treatment or service settings, this manual discusses case management services, outreach, entitlements, and mental illness.

1458. Brantley, C. (1983). New York City's services to homeless families: A report to the mayor. New York: Health and Hospitals Corporation.

1459. Breton, M. (1984). A drop-in program for transient women: Promoting competence through the environment. Social Work, 29, 542-546.
Describes the services and resources provided by a drop-in program designed to help homeless women, especially those with chronic mental illness, develop social competencies.

1460. Brickner, P.W., Greenbaum, D., Kaufman, A., O'Donnell, F., O'Brian, J.T., Scalice, R., Scandizzi, J., & Sullivan, T. (1972). Clinic for male derelicts: Welfare hotel project. Annals of Internal Medicine, 77, 565-569.

1461. Brookdale Center on Aging of Hunter College of the City of New York. (1986). New York City shelter care curriculum outline on homeless youth, adult and elderly. New York: Hunter College.
Outlines the curriculum of a training program for shelter caseworkers and managers. This manual emphasizes working with homeless mentally ill single adults with particular emphasis placed on crisis intervention and conflict resolution.

1462. Broughton, J. (1987). Foodservice for the homeless: An innovative approach. Journal of the American Dietetics Association, 87, 1684-1685.

1463. Brown, K.S. & Fellin, P. (1988). Practice models for serving the homeless mentally ill in community shelter programs. In J. Bowker (Ed.), Services for the chronically mentally ill: New approaches for mental health professionals. Washington, DC: Council on Social Work Education.
Emphasizes developing practice frameworks for social workers working in community based programs serving the homeless mentally ill.

1464. Burt, M.R., & Burbridge, L.C. (1985). Evaluation of the emergency food and shelter program: Summary, conclusions and recommendations. Washington, DC: Urban Institute.

1465. Chaiklin, H. (1985). The service needs of shelter residents. Baltimore: University of Maryland School of Social Work and Community Planning.

1466. Chaiklin, H. (1985). The service needs of soup kitchen users. Baltimore: University of Maryland School of Social Work and Community Planning.

1467. Cohen, N.L., & Marcos, L.R. (1986). Psychiatric care of the homeless mentally ill. Psychiatric Annals, 16, 729-732.
The authors describe the services of Project HELP, a mobile outreach program that is designed to permit transport of psychiatrically impaired homeless persons to emergency rooms for psychiatric evaluations. A description of the project operations over the first three years of the program's operation is provided. The authors also discuss the legal and ethical issues involved with involuntary transport and treatment of the homeless mentally ill.

1468. Cohen, N.L., Putnam, J.F., & Sullivan, A.M. (1984). The mentally ill homeless: Isolation and adaptation. Hospital and Community Psychiatry, 35, 922-924.
The authors describe the activities of Project HELP, a mobile outreach unit providing crisis medical and psychiatric services to homeless persons. Demographic characteristics of the population served are presented and problems in serving the homeless population, many of whom distrust authority, are discussed.

1469. Cohen, N.L., & Tsemberis, S. (1991). Emergency psychiatric intervention on the street. New Directions in Mental Health Services, Winter, 3-16.

1470. Columbia University Community Services. (1986). Building skills for work with the homeless. New York: Columbia University.
Provides information to enable shelter coordinators and volunteers to develop and lead skills-building training groups in their shelters. Part 1 focuses on organizational, administrative and advocacy skills for shelter coordinators. Part 2 provides information on 10 particular content areas with sample curriculum designs, knowledge overviews, case histories and references for each area.

1471. Comer, R.C. (1989). Homelessness and the mentally disabled: A study of specialized services in Philadelphia and residential stability. Dissertation Abstracts International, 49, 2808 A.

1472. Crystal, S., Ladner, S., Towber, R., Callendar, B., & Calhoun, J. (1986). Project Future: Final report. New York: Human Resources Administration.

1473. Culbertson, N.B. (1991). A descriptive policy study of the impact of the Stewart B. McKinney Homeless Assistance Act on rural homelessness in ten southwest Missouri counties utilizing a continuum of service model. Dissertation Abstracts International, 52, 1894 A.

1474. Dobra, J.L., & Jones, M.P. (1973). Feasibility study for a skid row security facility. The Gerontologist, 13, 93.

1475. Dowell, D.A., & Farmer, G. (1992). Community response to homelessness: Social change and constraint in local intervention. Journal of Community Psychology, 20(1), 72-83.
Describes an action-research project developed to promote mobilization of community response to homelessness in a large city. The program involved collaboration between a city-sponsored task force, a grassroots coalition, and a university. Results suggest a need to link local efforts with regional, state, and national organizations and agencies to be effective.

1476. Fabricant, M. (1986). Creating survival services. Administration in Social Work, 10, 71-84.
Argues for the creation of new, survival-oriented social services for the homeless, documentation of need to increase public awareness, and organization of resources to serve the contemporary homeless population. The role of community organizations in providing such services is discussed.

1477. Fabricant, M. (1988). Beyond bed and board: Teaching about homelessness. Journal of Teaching in Social Work, 2, 113-130.

1478. Fabricant, M. (1988). Empowering the homeless. Social Policy, 18, 49-55.

1479. Fagan, R.W. (1986). Modern rescue missions: A survey of the International Union of Gospel Missions. Journal of Drug Issues, 16, 495-509.
Surveyed directors (N=208) of missions associated with the International Union of Gospel Missions. Funding for missions surveyed was obtained primarily from private, individual contributions. Services offered included: (1) medical care, (2) psychological counseling, (3) vocational training, (4) benefits counseling, and (5) alcoholism treatment.

1480. Federal Task Force on the Homeless. (1987). Summary of Federal programs available to help the homeless. Washington, DC: U.S. Government Printing Office.
This report reviews programs in 12 federal departments and agencies that may be used to assist homeless persons. Although many of these programs were not designed specifically for the homeless, they may be possible sources of funds to provide emergency food, shelter and support services to the homeless.

1481. Fellin, P., & Brown, K.S. (1989). Application of homelessness to teaching social work foundation content. Journal of Teaching Social Work, 3, 17-33.

1482. Garrett, G., & Knight, B. (1989). Alcohol, drugs and the homeless: A training program for working with homeless clients. Boston, MA: University of Massachusetts.
Provides the agenda and supporting information for a 3 session service training program for mental health professionals working with substance abusing homeless persons. Session 1 concentrates on the substance abuse field in general, with some emphasis placed on the drug and alcohol problems of homeless persons. Section 2 emphasizes substance abuse patterns and how the homeless

subculture helps maintain substance abuse pathology. Section 3 focuses on the dually diagnosed homeless person.

1483. Garrett, G.R., & Schutt, R.K. (1986). <u>Homeless in the 1980's: Social services for a changing population</u>. Paper presented at the Annual Meeting of the Eastern Sociological Society, New York City.

1484. Garrett, G., Walker, F., & Bellew, S. (1988). <u>The homeless with alcohol problems</u>. Boston, MA: University of Massachusetts.
Consists of a list of in-service training topics, an outline of a training session on homeless persons with alcohol problems and numerous references on homelessness and substance abuse.

1485. Gasper, G. (1991). "Parents on the Move": A qualitative study of a self-help organization of homeless parents. <u>Dissertation Abstracts International</u>, <u>52</u>, 3448 A.
Constituents of Parents on the Move (POM), a self-help organization for homeless persons in temporary lodgings, were found to fall into 2 categories. The first group was more politically committed and willing to engage in social action to better their lives. The second group was less politically active and more concerned with assuring they received social services. Findings indicate the POM was most successful with persons in the first category.

1486. Ginsberg, L. (1988). Shelter issues in the 1990's: The potential roles of adult foster care and community residential facilities. <u>Adult Foster Care Journal</u>, <u>2</u>, 260-272.

1487. Glasser, I., & Suroviak, J. (1988). Social group work in a soup kitchen: Mobilizing the strengths of the guests. <u>Social Work With Groups</u>, <u>11</u>, 95-109.
Three projects involving teaching sociability, acceptance, affiliation, and use of community resources to 21 soup kitchen patrons are described.

1488. Goldfinger, S.M., & Chafetz, L. (1984). Developing a better service delivery system for the homeless mentally ill. In H.R. Lamb (Ed.), <u>The homeless mentally ill: A task force report</u>. Washington, DC: American Psychiatric Association.

1489. Gore, A. (1990). Public policy and the homeless. <u>American Psychologist</u>, <u>45</u>, 960-962.

1490. Goulart, M., & Madover, S. (1991). An AIDS prevention program for homeless youth. <u>Journal of Adolescent Health</u>, <u>12</u>, 573-575.

1491. Hagen, J.L. (1987). The heterogeneity of homelessness. <u>Social Casework</u>, <u>68</u>, 451-458.
Most studies of homeless persons are limited by their focus on emergency shelter clients in large metropolitan areas. This article focuses on homeless individuals and families requesting social services from an centralized intake agency in a moderately sized city.

1492. Hagen, J.L. (1989). Participants in a day program for the homeless: A survey of characteristics and service needs. Psychosocial Rehabilitation Journal, 12, 29-37.
Presents findings of in-depth interviews focussing on employment conducted with 47 homeless adults. The findings suggest that several barriers (e.g., lack of education, substance abuse problems, health and mental health problems, being on probation or parole) to employment exist for this population. The authors conclude that independence through employment may not be a reasonable short-term goal for the homeless.

1493. Hagen, J.L., & Hutchison, E. (1988). Who's serving the homeless? Social Casework, 69, 491-497.

1494. Hamburg, J. (1984). Building and zoning regulations: A guide to sponsors of shelters and housing for the homeless in New York City. New York: Community Service Society of New York.

1495. Haus, A. (Ed.). (1988). Working with homeless people: A guide for staff and volunteers. New York: Columbia University Community Services.
Aimed at volunteers and paraprofessionals, this book provides basic information for working with homeless persons in shelters or meal programs. (ABS)

1496. Henry, E.M. (1987). Voluntary shelters for the homeless as a population of organizations: A study of classical charity as an alternative to bureaucratic-professional models. Dissertation Abstracts International, 48, 1016 A.

1497. Henry Street Settlement. (1987). Training program for shelter managers, staff and volunteers. New York: Henry Street Settlement.
Developed to train managers, staff, and volunteers, this 2 part manual emphasizes skills in family shelter administration, relating effectively with homeless persons, social services interventions, advocacy and entitlements.

1498. Henry Street Settlement. (1990). Homeless family shelter management training project. New York: Henry Street Settlement.
Primarily directed at administrators, staff, and volunteers of family shelters, this training curriculum consists of 7 manuals for training workshops on family shelter management and services, each of which include lectures, group discussion topics, written exercises, and handouts.

1499. Henshaw, S.K. (1968). Camp LaGuardia: A voluntary total institution for homeless men. New York: Bureau of Applied Social Research, Columbia University.

1500. Hoch, C., & Cibulskis, A. (1985). Planning for the homeless. Paper presented at the Annual Conference of the American Planning Association, Montreal, Canada.

1501. Holt, R. (1986). Report of the Baltimore Rescue Mission. Baltimore, MD: Baltimore Rescue Mission.

1502. Homelessness Information Exchange. (1987).   Comprehensive planning to address homelessness: City initiatives. Washington, DC.
This guide for state and city officials, local planners, and service providers focuses, addresses six major areas of services for the homeless: (1) task forces, (2) assessment, (3) emergency services, (4) transitional housing and support services, (5) permanent housing, and (6) prevention. The efforts of 18 cities on behalf of the homeless is presented.

1503. Human Resource Administration. (1987).   Comprehensive homeless assistance plan. Washington, DC.: Author.

1504. Hunter, J.K., Crosby, F.E., Ventura, M.R., & Warkentin, L. (1991).   A national survey to identify evaluation criteria for programs of health care for homeless. Nursing and Health Care, 12, 536-542.

1505. Hutchison, W.J., Searight, P., & Stretch, J.J. (1986).   Multi-dimensional networking: A response to the needs of homeless families. Social Work, 31, 427-430.
Discusses the techniques used by the Salvation Army Emergency Lodge in St. Louis to place homeless families in permanent housing in terms of a 4 stage model of intervention (crisis intervention, stabilization, relocation, and follow-up).

1506. Hutchison, W.J., Stretch, J.J., Anderman, S.J., & Searight, P.R. (1982).   The Salvation Army Emergency Lodge in the City of St. Louis: An impact study. St. Louis, MO: The Salvation Army.

1507. Hutchison, W.J., Stretch, J.J., Anderman, S.J., Searight, P.R., & Triegaardt, J. (1981).   A profile of the emergency housing program in the City of St. Louis. St. Louis, MO: A Joint Demonstration Project of the Community Development Agency and the Salvation Army.

1508. Hutchison, W.J., Stretch, J.J., & Searight, P.R. (1983).   An evaluative study of The Salvation Army Emergency Lodge in the City of St. Louis. St. Louis, MO: The Salvation Army.

1509. Johnson, A.K. (1988).   Community services to the homeless: Winter 1930-31 & winter 1987-88: Has anything changed? Paper presented at the Annual Meeting of the Missouri Association for Social Welfare. Columbia, MO.

1510. Johnson, A.K. (1988).   Homeless shelters as a system: Services, budgets, and community coordination. Paper presented at the 7th Annual Meeting of the Homelessness Study Group, Medical Care Section, American Public Health Association. Boston, MA, November.

1511. Johnson, A.K., Krueger, L.W., & Stretch, J.J. (1987).   A court ordered consent decree: Process, conflicts and control. Paper presented at the 6th Annual Meeting of the Homelessness Study Group, Medical Care Section, American Public Health Association. New Orleans, LA.

1512. Johnson, A.K., Kreuger, L.W., & Stretch, J.J. (1989). A court-ordered consent decree for the homeless: Process, conflict and control. <u>Journal of Sociology and Social Welfare</u>, <u>16</u>, 29-42.
Discusses the linking of the legal system, city government, and human service providers resulting from a 1985 class action suit on behalf of the homeless of St. Louis that mandates both short- and long-term services for homeless persons. Issues discussed relate to service provision, advocacy, privatization, and the ethics of public disclosure from conflict and control perspectives.

1513. Johnson, A.K., & Taylor, S. (1988). <u>Homeless shelters: New poor-houses and asylums</u>. St. Louis, MO: Washington University, George Warren Brown School of Social Work.

1514. Kaufman, N. (1984). Homelessness: A Comprehensive Policy Approach. <u>Urban and Social Change Review</u>, <u>17</u>, 21-26.
Reviews the problem of homelessness and its causes and describes the comprehensive policy approach implemented in Massachusetts.

1515. Knight, L. (1980). Homeless centre: An alternative way of caring. <u>Nursing Mirror</u>, <u>150</u>, 16-18.

1516. Krueger, L.W. (1987). <u>Tracking health services for the homeless: Issues in information management</u>. Paper presented at the Annual Program Meeting of the National Institute for Information Technology, Health Related Services. Murtle Beach, NC.

1517. Krueger, L.W., Stretch, J.J., & Johnson, A.K. (1988). <u>The human service needs of homeless children: Practice and policy implications</u>. Paper presented at the 6th National Conference on Research, Demonstration, and Evaluation in Public Human Services. Washington, DC.

1518. Krueger, L.W., Stretch, J.J., & Johnson, A.K. (1988). <u>Implementing information systems for services to homeless populations</u>. Paper presented at the Annual Program Meeting of the Missouri Association for Social Welfare. Columbia, MO.

1519. Larew, B.I. (1980). Strange strangers: Serving transients. <u>Social Casework</u>, <u>63</u>, 107-113.
The author argues that transients and the homeless have traditionally been viewed as hopeless cases and undesirables. This article discusses issues related to providing casework and treatment services to this population and concludes that active outreach may be necessary to effectively help these persons.

1520. Lauriat, A.S., & McGerigle, P. (1983). <u>More than a shelter: A community response to homelessness</u>. Boston, MA: United Community Planning Corporation and Massachusetts Association of Mental Health.

1521. Leaf, A., & Cohen, M.B. (1982). <u>Providing services for the homeless: The New York City Program</u>. New York: City of New York Human Resources Administration.

1522. Levine, I.S. (1984). Service programs for the homeless mentally ill. In H.R. Lamb (Ed.), The homeless mentally ill. Washington, DC: American Psychiatric Association.
This chapter discusses the failure of both the mental health system and the shelter network to provide adequate services for the homeless mentally ill. A typology of services required by this population is presented and several "best practice" programs are described. The author argues that the service needs of the homeless mentally ill include: (1) decent emergency shelter, (2) outreach programs, (3) drop-in centers, (4) transitional housing and (5) long-term housing.

1523. Lezak, A.D. (1985). Synopses of NIMH-funded research projects on the homeless mentally ill. Rockville, MD: NIMH.
Summarizes ten NIMH-funded research projects addressing demographics, mental health problems, and service needs of the mentally ill homeless.

1524. Lezak, A.D. (1986). Synopses of National Institute of Mental Health Community Support Program Service Demonstration Grants for homeless mentally ill persons. Rockville, MD: NIMH.
Summarizes 20 NIMH-supported demonstration programs for homeless mentally ill persons. Each project provides at least one of the following services: (1) outreach to shelters and streets, (2) case management, or (3) transitional housing. Other innovative services provided are described.

1525. Lipostad, D. (1989). Mentally ill homeless training project. Ames, IA: Iowa State University, Department of Child Development, Child Welfare Research and Training Project.
Divided into 2 sections, this guide provides introductory material focussing on the service needs of homeless mentally ill persons, descriptions of major mental illnesses, and relevant legal issues, as well as, a resource guide listing a wide range of agencies in Iowa which serve homeless mentally ill persons.

1526. Lomas, E., & Honnard, R. (1987). Development of a model community mental health program to serve the homeless mentally ill. Los Angeles, CA: Los Angeles Department of Mental Health.
Reviews the development and major components of Los Angeles' Skid Row Mental Health Services, which provides comprehensive services for the homeless mentally ill including: outreach, case management, SSI assistance, and mail/check pick-up services.

1527. Long, L. (1988). Helping homeless families: A training curriculum. Long Island City, NY: LaGuardia Community College.
Aimed primarily at training of paraprofessionals, this curriculum is divided into 5 sections covering causes of family homelessness, unique problems of homeless families, relating to homeless families, working in community organizations and programs for homeless families.

1528. Long, L., & Jacobs, E.L. (1986). A curriculum for working with the homeless mentally ill. Long Island City, NY: LaGuardia Community College.
Divided into 5 sections, each with an instructors guide, study materials, and

cases examples, this manual is intended for training paraprofessionals or volunteers new to working with the homeless mentally ill.

1529. Long, L., & Van Tosh, L. (1988). <u>An annotated bibliography on self-help and homeless people with a mental illness (Volume I)</u>. Rockville, MD: NIMH.

1530. Long, L., & Van Tosh, L. (1988). <u>Program descriptions of consumer-run programs for homeless people with a mental illness (Volume II)</u>. Rockville, MD: NIMH.

1531. Long, L., & Van Tosh, L. (1988). <u>Consumer-run self-help programs serving homeless people with a mental illness (Volume III)</u>. Rockville, MD: NIMH.

1532. MacFarlane, D.C. (1991). The design and development of an employment training program for homeless men and women. <u>Dissertation Abstracts International</u>, <u>52</u>, 2371 A.
The author's experiences, observations and insights about homelessness and the realities of developing programs are discussed in the context of the author's work designing and developing an employment preparation program for homeless persons.

1533. Massachusetts Department of Mental Health. (1988). <u>Shelter services policy: Background and summary</u>. Boston, MA: Author.
Discusses the planning and implementation of the Massachusetts Shelter Service Policy to provide state funded mental health services to all shelters in the state.

1534. Mauch, D. (Ed.). (1985). <u>Homelessness: An integrated approach</u>. Boston, MA: Association for Mental Health.
Prepared for policymakers and service providers, this report reviews the approach to the homelessness problem taken by the state of Massachusetts. Included are background data on homelessness, characteristics of homeless persons, descriptions of methods and models used in Massachusetts, and recommendations focusing on developing an integrated approach to the homelessness problem.

1535. Mayer, R., & Shuster, T. (1985). <u>Developing shelter models for the homeless: Three program design options</u>. New York: Community Service Society of New York.

1536. McGergle, P., & Lauriat, A. (1983). <u>More than shelter: A community response to homelessness</u>. Boston: United Community Planning Corporation and Massachusetts Association for Mental Health.

1537. McManus, J., Monajem, S., & Dincer, E. (1992). Mobile mission. <u>New York State Dental Journal</u>, <u>58</u>, 51-52.

1538. Milburn, N.G. (1987) Homelessness: An overview. <u>Urban Research Review</u>, <u>11</u>, 9-14.
Reviews the major elements of the Stewart B. McKinney Homeless Assistance Act and briefly discusses NIMH efforts on behalf of the homeless.

1539. Morrissey, J.P., Gounis, K., Barrow, S, Struening, E., & Katz, S. (1985). Organizational barriers to serving the mentally ill homeless. In B.E. Jones (Ed.), Treating the homeless: Urban psychiatry's challenge. Washington, DC: American Psychiatric Association.
Describes the Creedmoor initiative, an innovative effort to serve the homeless population with serious psychiatric disabilities. In contrast to many psychiatric services for the homeless, this initiative attempts to provide both emergency and long-term housing and treatment services.

1540. Morse, G.A. (1982). A conceptual paper to develop a comprehensive system of care for chronically mentally disturbed homeless persons in St. Louis, Missouri. St Louis, Community Support Program.

1541. Morse, G.A. (1987). Community Advocacy and Support Alliance (CASA) Project: Program description. St. Louis, MO: Malcolm Bliss Mental Health Center.
Describes a 3 year NIMH-funded demonstration project that provides case management, assistance with daily living tasks, medication, and money management to homeless mentally ill persons.

1542. Morse, G.A., Calsyn, R.J., Dannelet, M., Muether, R.O., & Harmann, L. (1988). Community Services for the homeless: Preliminary experimental results. St. Louis, MO: Malcolm Bliss Mental Health Center.
Reports preliminary findings of the Community Advocacy and Support Alliance (CASA) project which provides case management and direct services to the homeless mentally ill. Data from a sample of 60 clients show they had higher rates of social stability and satisfaction than other mental health center clients, and spent less time homeless than day program clients.

1543. Morse, G.A., Shields, N.M., Hanneke, C.R., Calsyn, R.J., Burger, G.K., & Nelson, B. (1985). Homeless people in St. Louis: A mental health program evaluation, field study and follow-up investigation. Jefferson City, MO: Missouri Department of Mental Health.
Reports findings from: (1) an evaluation of existing Missouri Department of Mental Health services for the homeless, (2) a field study of 248 shelter users, and (3) a 60 day follow-up of subjects in the field study. Nearly 1/4 of the participants had previous psychiatric hospitalizations, 56% had serious mental health problems, but only 15% were currently receiving mental health services. Recommendations for improved mental health and human services for the homeless are made.

1544. Mulkern, V., & Bradley, V.J. (1986). Service utilization and service preferences of homeless persons. Psychosocial Rehabilitation Journal, 10, 23-29.
Among the services that 155 homeless adults generally wanted and sought were: (1) adequate food, (2) adequate clothing, (3) housing, and (4) employment. Mentally ill homeless tended to have low interest in mental health services and failed to maintain contact with service providers.

1545. National Association of Community Health Centers. (1989). A national directory of homeless health care projects. Washington, DC.: Author.

1546. National Coalition for the Homeless. (1988). The Stewart B. McKinney Homeless Assistance Act: Revised summary of programs, 1989 and 1990. Washington, DC.: Author.
Summarizes the grant programs available to develop services under the Stewart B. McKinney Homeless Assistance Act. Programs include funding for emergency food and shelter services, housing assistance, identification and use of surplus government property, provision of health care, education, job training, and services for veterans.

1547. National Governors' Association. (1989). Status of programs under the Stewart B. McKinney Homeless Assistance Act and related legislation. Washington, DC. Presents summaries of the grant programs provided under the Stewart B. McKinney Homeless Assistance Act which includes names of contact persons for each of the grant programs.

1548. National Institute of Alcohol Abuse and Alcoholism. (1988). Synopses of community demonstration projects for alcohol and drug abuse treatment of homeless individuals. Rockville, MD.

1549. National Institute of Mental Health. (1988). Synopses of NIMH- funded mental health services demonstration projects for the homeless mentally ill. Rockville, MD.

1550. National Mental Health Association. (1987). Urgent relief for homeless: A summary of the Stewart B. McKinney Homeless Assistance Act of 1987 (PL 100-77). Alexandria, VA.
Provides both a general description of Stewart B. McKinney Act programs and a "check list for action" that describes the ways in which mental health agencies can become more involved and successful in accessing funds for services to aid the homeless.

1551. New York City Human Resources Administration. (1984). New York City plan for homeless adults. New York.: Author

1552. New York City Human Resources Administration (1983). Project future: Focusing, understanding, targeting, and utilizing resources for homeless mentally ill, older persons, youth and employables. New York.: Author.

1553. New York City Office of the Comptroller. (1982). Report on the problems of and services available to the homeless in New York City. New York: Office of the Comptroller.

1554. New York State Office of Mental Health. (1981). Shelter outreach project: Statistical Report, February to June, 1981. New York City, Regional Office of Mental Health.

1555. O'Connor, J. (1983). Sheltering the homeless in the nation's capital. Hospital and Community Psychiatry, 34, 863-879.

1556. Ohio Coalition for the Homeless. (1988). Lives in the balance: Establishing programs for the homeless. Columbus, OH: Author.

This manual was compiled as an orientation for service providers new to the development of shelter services for the homeless. Issues discussed include: (1) steps in providing emergency shelter, (2) special issues in serving the homeless mentally ill and substance abusers, (3) employment programs for the homeless, (4) transitional housing, (5) basics of coalition building, and (6) resources and funding for programs. Also included are descriptions of innovative programs from many areas of the country.

1557. O'Loughlin, K. (1991). The Lazarus House Ministries Medical-Dental Clinic. Journal of the Massachusetts Dental Society, 40, 186.

1558. Phillips. M.H., Kronenfeld, D., & Jeter, V. (1986). A model of services to homeless families in shelters. In J. Erickson & C. Wilhelm (Eds.). Housing the homeless. New Brunswick, NJ: Center for Urban Policy Research, Rutgers University.

1559. Plapinger, J.D. (1988). Program service goals: Service needs, service feasibility, and obstacles to providing services to the mentally ill homeless. New York: New York State Psychiatric Institute.
The author surveyed case managers and outreach workers in 5 Community Support System programs for the homeless mentally ill to study goals and obstacles in linking homeless mentally ill clients to mental health services. Factors associated with accessibility of services included having adequate community resources and whether their was agreement between programs and their clients on the type of service needed.

1560. Putnam, J.F. (1985-1986). Innovative outreach services for the homeless mentally ill. International Journal of Mental Health, 14, 112-124.
Describes the activities of a mobile psychiatric outreach project providing emergency psychiatric services to homeless persons in New York City. Discussion of the funding sources for the program and its specific service aims is also provided.

1561. Rafferty, M., Hinzpeter, D., Cowlin, L., & Knox, M. (1984). The shelter workers handbook. New York: Coalition for the Homeless.
Provides practical information on the basic health and mental health problems common among homeless persons and strategies for dealing with these conditions and the broader problems shelter staff workers may encounter.

1562. Reuler, J.B. (1991). Outreach health services for street youth. Journal of Adolescent Health, 12, 561-566.

1563. Ridgway, R., Spaniol, L., & Zipple, A. (1986). Case management services for persons who are homeless and mentally ill. Boston, MA: Boston University Center for Psychiatric Rehabilitation.

1564. Ritzdorf, M., & Sharpe, S.M. (1987). Portland, Oregon: A comprehensive approach. In R.D. Bingham, R.E. Green & S.B. White (Eds.), The homeless in contemporary society. Newbury Park, CA: Sage Publications.
Discusses homelessness in Portland, Oregon, emphasizing the unusually high numbers of mentally ill among Portland's homeless. Findings of a survey of

community-based residential facilities are reported which provide descriptions of local programs for the homeless.

1565. Rog, D., Andranovich, G., & Rosenblum, S. (1987).   Intensive case management for persons who are homeless and mentally ill: A review of Community Support Program and Human Resource Development Program efforts. Rockville, MD: NIMH.

1566. Roth, D., & Hyde, P.S. (1988). Translating research into public policy: Ohio's coordinated response to the problems of homelessness. Columbus, OH: Ohio Department of Mental Health.

1567. Salem, D.A., & Levine, I.S. (1989).   Enhancing mental health services for homeless persons: State proposals under the MHSH block grant program. Public Health Reports, 104, 241-246.
Reviews state proposals to the Mental Health Services for the Homeless Block Grant program during the 3 year period of 1987-1989. More than $57 million dollars was made available to the states during this period for developing and improving community based services for the homeless mentally ill. Funds were made available for 5 categories of services including: (1) outreach services, (2) case management, (3) mental health treatment, (4) residential support services, and (5) training for service providers. The authors report considerable diversity among services proposed by the states.

1568. Sargent, M. (1989).   Update on programs for the homeless mentally ill. Hospital and Community Psychiatry, 40, 1015-1016.
Presents a brief discussion of NIMH funded research on homelessness and mental health. Three of the major issues addressed by researchers are: (1) variations in definitions of homelessness, (2) problems in locating the homeless population, and (3) determining mental health status of homeless persons. The major provisions of the McKinney Homeless Assistance Act and implications for future research are also briefly discussed.

1569. Schram, D.D., Giovengo, M.A. (1991).   Evaluation of Threshold: an independent living program for homeless adolescents. Journal of Adolescent Health, 12, 567-572.

1570. Segal, S.P., & Baumohl, J. (1985).   The community living room.   Social Casework, 66, 111-116.
Describes a day program for the homeless. poor, and chronically mentally ill whose major goals are to address the basics of survival, social connection and trust. The program also provides food and shelter as well as being a point for case finding and case management.

1571. Seven Counties Services, Inc. (1988). Community support to high risk and/or homeless persons. Louisville, KY: Author.
Describes the philosophy, goals, and population served by an intensive case management program for homeless mentally ill persons in operation in Louisville, Kentucky since 1985.

1572. Shandler, I.W., & Shipley, T.E. (1987). New focus for an old problem: Philadelphia's response to homelessness. Alcohol Health and Research World, 11, 54-57.
The authors discuss the history and components of the Diagnostic and Rehabilitation Center of Philadelphia which provides a variety of alcohol related services to the homeless.

1573. Share Your Bounty. (1988). Program description. New York: Author.
Describes a consumer-directed program to distribute food to agencies providing meals for the homeless which has recently received NIMH funding.

1574. Skid Row Mental Health Service, Los Angeles County Department of Mental Health. (1986). Gold award: A network of services for the homeless chronic mentally ill. Hospital and Community Psychiatry, 37, 1148-1151.
Describes an inner-city program that provides case-management, medication, and crisis intervention for the homeless mentally ill.

1575. Solarz, A., & Bogat, G. (1990). When social support fails: The homeless. Journal of Community Psychology, 18, 79-96.

1576. Solomon, P. (1988). Services to severely mentally disabled homeless persons and to emergency food and shelter providers. Psychosocial Rehabilitation Journal, 12, 3-13.
Describes a demonstration project designed to provide services to mentally disabled homeless persons and to emergency food and shelter providers. While providing such services as outreach, case management, and drop-in centers for the homeless mentally ill, the program also provided service providers with training, consultation services, support, and crisis back up.

1577. St. Martin's Hospitality Center. (1988). Project Care: Final report for the first contract year. Albuquerque, NM.
Reviews the first year of a NIMH-funded intensive case management demonstration for the homeless mentally ill. Discussions of program activities, interactions with other agencies, and methods of program evaluation are presented. Successes included providing basic needs such as temporary and permanent shelter and medical care. Most of the problems experienced by the program were with providing daily living skills such as hygiene and control of alcohol and drug abuse.

1578. Stefl, M. (Ed.). (1989). Helping mentally ill homeless people: A manual for shelter workers. Washington, DC: American Public Health Association.
Describes and explains the unique problems facing the homeless mentally ill and suggests ways that shelter workers can attempt to reach and help these persons. This manual is intended for shelter workers who have direct, daily or regular contact with the homeless mentally ill, rather than volunteers.

1579. Stein, L.I. (1990). The Robert Wood Johnson Foundation Mental Health Services Development Program. New Directions for Mental Health Services, 45, 75-89.
Describes a $10 million competitive program that funds 18 mental health projects. These include 4 systems change projects, 4 projects for the homeless,

2 housing projects, 2 vocational programs, 2 rural projects, and 4 specialized projects, dealing with such topics as delivering services to chronically mentally ill older adults and training nurses who work with the mentally ill. The process used to select grantees is also described.

1580. Stewart, R.E. (1991).   The homeless-gold within the garbage: A process oriented approach to working with the homeless.   Dissertation Abstracts International, 53, 1285 A.

1581. Stoner, M.   (1989).   Beyond shelter: Policy directions for the prevention of homelessness.   Social Work Research and Abstracts, 25, 7-11.

1582. Stoner, M.R. (1989).   Money management services for the homeless mentally ill.   Hospital and Community Psychiatry, 40, 751-753.
Discusses the incorporation of a pilot money management project with case management services with 89 homeless mentally ill persons. The results indicate that the addition of the money management program can aid in the stabilization of client's lives.

1583. Stretch, J.J., Hutchinson, W.J., & Searight, P. (1989).   Networking services with the homeless. In R.I. Jahiel (Ed.), Homelessness and its prevention. Baltimore, MD: Johns Hopkins Press.

1584. Stretch, J.J., & Kleing, A.M. (1984).   Continuum of services for homeless families in St. Louis. Paper presented at Homelessness Study Group, Committee on Health Services Research, Medical Care Section, American Public Health Association, Anaheim, CA, November.

1585. Stretch, J.J., & Kreuger, L.W. (1987).   Multidimensional networking.   Paper presented at the Annual Program Meeting of the National Association of Social Workers, New Orleans, LA, September.

1586. Stretch, J.J., Kreuger, L.W., Johnston, A.K., & Hutchinson, W.J. (1988).   The homeless continuum model: Serving homeless families. St. Louis, MO: The Salvation Army.
Provides a comprehensive description of homeless families served by the Salvation Army Emergency Lodge in St. Louis, Missouri over a five year period from 1983-1988 as well as a description of the program components and day to day operation of the homeless continuum model developed for serving homeless individuals and families.   The authors conclude with a discussion of future program and policy research issues.

1587. Tabler, D.L. (1982).   Preliminary report: Emergency adult-at-risk shelter: A BCDSS demonstration project. Baltimore Department of Social Services.

1588. The Boston Foundation. (1987).   Homelessness: Critical issues for policy and practice. Boston, MA: Author.
Sections of this report address homeless families, homeless street youth, alcohol abuse, the homeless mentally ill, sheltering the homeless, providing health care for the homeless, and state initiatives addressing homelessness. Included is a listing of organizations and other resources involved with homelessness.

1589. The Boston Foundation. (1988). <u>The fund for the homeless: Final report</u>. Boston, MA: Author.
Describes the purpose and types of funds provided by a private-sector initiative on behalf of the homeless. Funding has been primarily for capital projects, for which state funds are not available. Also discussed is a new corporate-sponsored initiative, the Shelter Technical Assistance Project, which works with a small number of shelters to provide organizational assessments, technical assistance, and low interest loans to support fundraising.

1590. Thomas, Y. (1987). <u>Cleveland health care for the homeless: Update project summary</u>. Cleveland, OH: Federation for Community Planning.

1591. Toff, G.E. (1988). <u>Self-help programs serving people who are homeless and mentally ill</u>. Washington, DC: Intergovernmental Health Policy Project.
Summarizes proceedings of a NIMH sponsored meeting to study self-help programs for the homeless mentally ill. The report includes guidelines for program development and synopses of existing self-help programs.

1592. U.S. Comptroller General. (1987). <u>Homelessness: Implementation of Food and Shelter Programs under the McKinney Act. Report to the Congress</u>. Washington, DC.

1593. U.S. Conference of Mayors. (1986). <u>Responding to homelessness in American cities</u>. Washington, DC.
Community programs to serve the homeless in 21 cities across the country are summarized. Summaries of the programs, including programs for the homeless mentally ill in Charleston, South Carolina and San Juan, Puerto Rico, are provided.

1594. U.S. Conference of Mayors. (1987). <u>Local responses to the needs of homeless mentally ill persons</u>. Washington, DC.
Describes programs to serve the homeless mentally ill in 14 cities. Case studies are provided.

1595. U.S. Conference of Mayors. (1988). <u>A status report on the Stewart B. McKinney Homeless Assistance Act of 1987</u>. Washington, DC.
This is a description of the provisions of the Stewart B. McKinney Homeless Assistance Act and a summary of several programs for the homeless that have been funded under this act.

1596. U.S. Department of Health and Human Services. (1984). <u>Helping the homeless: A resource guide</u>. Washington, DC: Department of Health and Human Services.
Provides an overview (e.g., defines homelessness, provides estimates of the incidence of homelessness, discusses causes of homelessness, etc.) of homelessness in America. Also, public (e.g., federal, state and local) and private sector initiatives on behalf of the homeless are discussed. Federal programs are given special attention, especially entitlement programs and other programs for the poor that could be used to assist the homeless. Further, the report suggests a public/private sector partnership to aid the homeless.

1597. U.S. Department of Health and Human Services. (1984).   The homeless: Background, analysis, and options. Washington, DC.
This is an overview of homelessness and a review of private and public initiatives, with special emphasis on federal programs and initiatives. The argument is for public and private sector cooperation in resolving the homeless problem.

1598. U.S. Department of Health and Human Services (1983). Plan for carrying out the emergency food and shelter program. Federal Emergency Management Agency, Federal Register, 48(88), 20014-20019.

1599. U.S. Department of Housing and Urban Development. (1989).   Homeless assistance policy and practice in the nation's five largest cities. Washington, DC.
Discusses local attitudes towards the homeless, funding of local programs, local shelter capacity and types of services made available to homeless persons in five cities.

1600. U.S. Department of Housing and Urban Development. (1989).   Homeless assistance programs. Washington, DC.

1601. U.S. Department of Housing and Urban Development. (1988). SAFAH grants: Aiding comprehensive strategies for the homeless. Washington, DC.
Twelve programs funded by SAFAH grants representing the diversity of community responses to the crisis of homeless families are described. Services provided under these grants include: (1) transitional housing, (2) support services for families and victims of domestic abuse, (3) housing for chronically homeless elderly men, (4) day shelters for children, (5) employment and housing counseling, (6) case management to link homeless individuals and families to community resources.

1602. U.S. Department of Labor. (1989).   Synopses of homeless job training demonstration projects. Washington, DC.

1603. U.S. General Accounting Office, Division of Human Resources. (1983). Federally Supported Centers Provide Needed Services for Runaways and Homeless Youths. Report to the Chairman, Subcommittee on Human Resources, Committee on Education and Labor, House of Representatives. Gaithersburg, MD: General Accounting Office.

1604. U.S. General Accounting Office. (1985). Homelessness: A complex problem and the federal response. Washington, DC.
Reviews homelessness in the U.S. and a criticizes the accuracy of estimates of the numbers of homeless provided by both federal agencies and others. Discussion also includes the major reasons for homelessness and defines the role of the Federal government in providing aid to cities and counties to meet increased service costs.

1605. U.S. House Committee on Education and Labor. (1982). Oversight Hearing on Runaway and Homeless Youth Program. Hearing before the Subcommittee on Human Resources of the Committee on Education and Labor. House of

Representatives, Ninety-Seventh Congress, Second Session. Washington, DC: U.S. Government Printing Office.

1606. U.S. House Committee on Government Operations. (1985). The federal response to the homeless crisis: Hearings before a Subcommittee of the Committee on Government Operations. House of Representatives, 98th Congress, 2nd Session. Washington, DC: U.S. Government Printing Office.

1607. U.S. House of Representatives (1987). Stewart B. McKinney Homeless Assistance Act. Conference Report To Accompany H.R. 558. House of Representatives, 100th Congress, 1st Session.

1608. U.S. House of Representatives Committee on Education and Labor. (1987). Oversight Hearing on Jobs and Education for the Homeless. Joint Hearing before the Committee on Education and Labor and the Select Committee on Aging. House of Representatives, One Hundredth Congress, First Session (Los Angeles, California, March 20, 1987). Washington, DC: U.S. Government Printing Office.

1609. U.S. Senate, Committee on Appropriations (1983). Special hearing on street people. Washington, DC: U.S. Government Printing Office.

1610. U.S. Senate Committee on the Appropriations. (1983). Street people: Hearing. Washington, DC: U.S. Government Printing Office.

1611. United Way of Los Angeles. (1983). Emergency assistance programs: An exploratory survey. Los Angeles: United Way.

1612. Upshur, C.C. (1986). The Bridge, Inc. Residential Independent Living Project Evaluation. Second Year Follow-Up Report. Paper presented at the 94th Annual Convention of the American Psychological Association, Los Angeles, California.

1613. Van Tosh, L. (1989). Project ACT NOW: Curriculum and overview. Philadelphia, PA: Project OATS.
Describes a training and employment project for mental health and homeless consumers which has successfully placed trainees as staff in programs serving the mentally ill and homeless populations.

1614. Van Tosh, L. (1989). The training and employment project: Overview, curriculum, and summary report. Philadelphia, PA: Project OATS.
Describes a demonstration project designed to train homeless and homeless mentally ill persons to work in social service or advocacy agencies that serve the homeless and homeless mentally ill. A discussion of program design and client outcomes is included.

1615. Vuyst, A. (1989). Self help for the homeless. The Humanist, 49, 3-49.

1616. Witheridge, T.F. (1991). The "active ingredients" of assertive outreach. New Directions in Mental Heath Services, Winter, 47-64.

1617. Wright, J.D. (1985, July). The Johnson-Pew health care for the homeless program. Paper prepared for the National Institute of Alcohol Abuse and Alcoholism Conference on the Homeless with Alcohol Related Problems, Bethesda, Md.

1618. Youssef, F.A., Omokehinde, M., & Garland, I.M. (1988). The homeless and unhealthy: a review and analysis. Issues in Mental Health Nursing, 9, 317-324. Argues for improving systems of coordinated services and case management to link the homeless with the service delivery system based on a review of the literature.

11

Housing

1619. Alisky, J.M., & Iczkowski, K.A. (1989). Barriers to housing for deinstitutionalized psychiatric patients. Hospital and Community Psychiatry, 41, 93-95.
Findings from a study of barriers to housing resources for discharged mental patients suggest that mentally ill persons have trouble finding adequate housing due to lack of available units and high rents and discrimination by private landlords.

1620. Allard, M.A., & Carling, P. (1986). Providing housing and supports for people with psychiatric disabilities: A technical assistance manual for applicants for the Robert Johnson Foundation and U.S. Department of Housing and Urban Development Program for the "chronically mentally ill." Rockville, MD: NIMH.
This manual describes the development of housing resources for the seriously mentally ill. The need for stable housing for those with psychiatric disabilities is discussed within the context of current shortages of affordable housing and a number of innovative approaches towards housing and rehabilitating the mentally ill are presented. Also, Federal, State, local, and private approaches to financing housing for this population are explained.

1621. Alter, J. (1986). Homeless in America. In J. Erickson & C. Wilhelm (Eds.), Housing the homeless. New Brunswick, NJ: Center for Urban Policy Research, Rutgers University.

1622. Appelbaum, P.S. (1988). Housing for the mentally ill: An unexpected outcome of a class-action suit against the SSA. Hospital and Community Psychiatry, 39, 479-480.

1623. Atencio, A.R. (1982). Emergency housing in the City and County of Denver. Denver: Department of Social Services.

1624. Axelroad, S.E., & Toff, G. (1987). Zoning issues in the development of housing for homeless people who are mentally ill. Washington, DC: NIMH. Reports on a meeting of experts in developing and operating housing services for the mentally disabled sponsored by NIMH. Issues discussed relate to the role played by zoning laws in the establishment of community residences for homeless mentally ill people.

1625. Baxter, E. (1986). The heights: A community housing strategy. New York: Community Service Society of New York.

1626. Bijlani, H.U. (1988). Strategies for urban shelter: The improvement of slums, squatter settlements and sites-and-services. Habitat International, 12, 45-53.

1627. Bogue, D.J. (1986). An introduction to Chicago's skid rows: Survey results. In J. Erickson & C. Wilhelm (Eds.). Housing the homeless. New Brunswick, NJ: Center for Urban Policy Research, Rutgers University.

1628. Bureau of Planning. (1986). Status report on low-income single room occupancy (SRO) housing in downtown Portland. Portland, OR.: Author.

1629. Carliner, M.S. (1987). Homelessness: A housing problem. In R.D. Bingham, R.E. Green & S.B. White (Eds.), The homeless in contemporary society. Newbury Park, CA: Sage Publications. Discusses homelessness in the context of the housing situation in the United States and argues that extending existing government housing programs and creating new ones seem to be the most viable solutions to the shortage of low-income housing.

1630. Coalition for the Homeless. (1982). Federal housing programs and their impact on homelessness. New York: Author.

1631. Coleman, J.R. (1986). Diary of a homeless man. In J. Erickson & C. Wilhelm (Eds.), Housing the homeless. New Brunswick, NJ: Center for Urban Policy Research, Rutgers University.

1632. Confluence St. Louis Task Force. (1988). Housing for low-income families: The crisis and the challenge. St. Louis, MO: Confluence St. Louis.

1633. Cuomo, M.M. (1983). 1933-1983: Never again. A report to the National Governor's Association Task Force on the Homeless. Albany, NY: State of New York.

1634. Cuomo, M.M. (1987). The state role: New York State's approach to homelessness. In R.D. Bingham, R.E. Green & S.B. White (Eds.), The homeless in contemporary society. Newbury Park, CA: Sage Publications. This chapter discusses innovative approaches developed by the state of New York to remedy the homelessness problem. Among the programs discussed include a transitional housing program for homeless families, reconfiguration of the state mental health care system, and several other initiatives aimed at improving existing housing, especially SRO hotels, or providing housing assistance for the homeless.

1635. Emergency Food and Shelter National Board Program. (1985). Study of homelessness. Washington, DC: Public Technology.

1636. English, J. (1972). Homeless near a thousand homes. Urban Studies, 9, 143-145.

1637. Erickson, J., & Wilhelm, C. (Eds.) (1986). Housing the homeless. New Brunswick, NJ: Center for Urban Policy Research, Rutgers University.

1638. Friedrichs, J. (Ed.) (1988). Affordable housing and the homeless. Hawthorne, NY: DeGruyter.

1639. Green, L.L. (1986). Task force on homelessness: Final report of findings and recommendations. Nashville, TN: Metropolitan Development and Housing Agency.

1640. Greer, N.R. (1985). The homeless: An urban crisis of the 1980's. Architecture, July, 56-59.

1641. Greer, N.R. (1986). The search for shelter. Washington, DC: The American Institute of Architects.

1642. Greer, N.R. (1988). The creation of shelter. Washington, DC: American Institute of Architects.

1643. Hartman, C. (Ed.). (1983). America's housing crisis: What is to be done. Boston: Routledge & Kegan Paul.

1644. Hartman, C. (1986). The housing part of the homelessness problem. New Directions for Mental Health Services, June, 71-85.
Discusses the relationship between the low-income housing crisis and contemporary homelessness. It is suggested that solutions to the homelessness problem include: (1) increasing the supply of low-income housing units, (2) rehabilitation of SRO hotels, (3) increasing tenant protection against eviction, (4) establishment of a national "right to shelter," and (5) improving housing options for the homeless mentally ill.

1645. Heskin, A.D. (1987). Los Angeles: Innovative local approaches. In R.D. Bingham, R.E. Green & S.B. White (Eds.), The homeless in contemporary society. Newbury Park, CA: Sage Publications.
This book chapter describes several innovative approaches to develop both short- and long-term housing in Los Angeles. The projects described include: (1) a housing program designed with the participation of street people, as well as, government and human services representatives, (2) transitional housing programs, and (3) a program which purchases and renovates SRO hotels. The author suggests that the experiences of the city of Los Angeles in addressing the homeless problem could be excellent models for programs in other cities.

1646. Hirschl, T.A. (1987). Finding shelter in Cortland county: A local housing market study. Ithaca, NY: Cornell University, Department of Rural Sociology.

1647. Hoch, C. (1986). Homeless in the United States. Housing Studies, 1, 228-240.

1648. Hope, M., & Young, J. (1986). The politics of displacement: Sinking into homelessness. In J. Erickson & C. Wilhelm (Eds.), Housing the homeless. New Brunswick, NJ: Center for Urban Policy Research, Rutgers University.

1649. Hopper, K. (1984). Whose lives are these, anyway? (A comment on the recently issued report on the homeless and emergency shelters by the Department of Housing and Urban Development.). Urban and Social Change Review, 17, 12-13.
Critiques a 1984 HUD report for its use of faulty statistical methodology and thereby underestimating the numbers of homeless people in the United States. It is also critical of the report's failure to recognize the scarcity of affordable housing as a cause of homelessness.

1650. Huttman, E., & Franz, M. (1989). The effect of housing affordability on single households and one parent households. Paper presented at the Annual Meetings of the American Sociological Association.

1651. Kanter, A.S. (1984). Overcoming obstacles to housing for people who are mentally disabled and homeless. Clearinghouse Review, 18, 955-964.
Among the obstacles to housing for the mentally ill, are: (1) inadequacies of Medicaid and SSI as sources of funding, and (2) zoning laws utilized to exclude mentally ill persons from neighborhoods. The author also reports on several litigations seeking to establish a right to community mental health services for the mentally ill and provides recommendations to improve the service delivery system and reintegrate the homeless mentally ill into the community.

1652. Kasinitz, P. (1984). Gentrification and homelessness: The single room occupant and the inner-city revival. Urban and Social Change Review, 17, 515-518.
Traces the history of gentrification from a small, grassroots movement to active social policy in many cities. The effects of gentrification (e.g., loss of SRO hotels) in New York City and others is discussed. The author cites gentrification as one of the primary causes of increased homelessness and suggests several alternatives for single, inner city poor left homeless by gentrification.

1653. Kasinitz, P. (1986). Gentrification and homelessness: The single room occupant and the inner-city revival. In J. Erickson & C. Wilhelm (Eds.), Housing the homeless. New Brunswick, NJ: Center for Urban Policy Research, Rutgers University.

1654. Kondratas, S.A. (1986). A strategy for helping America's homeless. In J. Erickson & C. Wilhelm (Eds.). Housing the homeless. New Brunswick, NJ: Center for Urban Policy Research, Rutgers University.

1655. Levine, A. (Ed.). (1988). Housing for people with mental illness: A guide for development. Princeton, NJ: Robert Wood Johnson Foundation.

1656. Lumsden, G.H., Jr. (1984). Housing the indigent and evaluation research: Issues associated with the Salvation Army sit-up shelter programs. Paper presented at the annual meeting of the Southwestern Social Science Association, Fort Worth, Texas, March.

1657. Main, T.J. (1983). The homeless of New York. Public Interest, 72, 3-28.

1658. Main, T.J. (1986). The homeless of New York. In J. Erickson & C. Wilhelm (Eds.), Housing the homeless. New Brunswick, NJ: Center for Urban Policy Research, Rutgers University.

1659. McEntire, D. (1959). Relocation plan: Slum area labor market, Sacramento. Sacramento, CA: Redevelopment Agency of the City of Sacramento and Federal Housing and Home Finance Agency.

1660. Momeni, J.A. (1987). Housing and racial/ethnic minority status in the United States. Westport, CT: Greenwood Press.

1661. Murray, H. (1984). Time in the streets. Human Organization, 43, 158-159.

1662. Murray, H. (1986). Time in the streets. In J. Erickson & C. Wilhelm (Eds.), Housing the homeless. New Brunswick, NJ: Center for Urban Policy Research, Rutgers University.

1663. National Alliance to End Homelessness. (1988). Housing and homelessness. Washington, DC: Author.
Describes the size of the homeless population and the needs of the major subgroups within it concludes with a discussion of housing strategies used to both, provide housing for those currently homeless, and to prevent further homelessness.

1664. National Housing Task Force. (1988). A decent place to live: The report of the National Housing Task Force. Washington, DC.
This is the final report of a privately initiated and funded task force created by Congress to study the country's housing policy. The report discusses lack of affordable housing for low-income persons and families and makes several recommendations for policy change at all levels of government.

1665. Nelson, M.Z. (1986). Street People. In J. Erickson & C. Wilhelm (Eds.), Housing the homeless. New Brunswick, NJ: Center for Urban Policy Research, Rutgers University.

1666. New Jersey Bureau of Housing Services. (1988). New Jersey homelessness prevention program: Fiscal year 1988 report. New Jersey Homelessness Prevention Program Report 39.

1667. New Jersey Homelessness Prevention Program. (1987). Assisting people in crisis. New Jersey Homelessness Prevention Program Report 41.

1668. New York State Department of Social Services. (1984). Homeless housing and assistance program: Report to the Governor and the Legislature. Albany, NY.: Author.

1669. Paterson, A., & Rhubright, E. (1986). Housing for the mentally ill: A place called home. Human Resources Series. State Legislative Report, 11, 1-21.

1670. Paul, B. (1981). Rehabilitating residential hotels. Washington, DC: National Trust for Historic Preservation.

1671. Philip, K. (1984). Gentrification and homelessness: The single room occupant and the inner city revival. Urban and Social Change Review, 17, 9-14.
Describes how gentrification has forced the occupants of single room occupancy hotels, rooming houses, and shelters that serve marginal populations, into the streets, contributed to the growing numbers of homeless people.

1672. Randolph, F.L., Lauz, B., & Carling, P.J. (1987). In search of housing. Burlington, VT: Center for Community Change Through Housing and Support, University of Vermont.

1673. Raubeson, A. (1988). Single room occupancy housing corporation: Annual reports. Los Angeles, CA: SRO Housing Corporation.

1674. Ridgway, R. (1988). Coming home: Ex-patients view housing options and needs. Burlington, VT: Center for Community Change Through Housing and Support.

1675. Roanoke City Manager's Task Force. (1987). No place to call home: A study of housing and homelessness in Roanoke, Virginia. Roanoke, VA: Task Force on Housing and Homelessness.

1676. Sanjeck, R. (1986). Federal housing programs and their impact on homelessness. In J. Erickson & C. Wilhelm (Eds.). Housing the homeless. New Brunswick, NJ: Center for Urban Policy Research, Rutgers University.

1677. Schneider, J.C. (1986). Skid row as an urban neighborhood: 1880-1960. In J. Erickson & C. Wilhelm (Eds.), Housing the homeless. New Brunswick, NJ: Center for Urban Policy Research, Rutgers University.

1678. Schneider, J.C. (1989). Homeless men and housing policy in urban America. Urban Studies, 26, 90-99.

1679. Schulte, L. (1988). Inn-Between: A manual on transitional housing. Cleveland, OH: THI Consulting Service, Inc.
This is a practitioner oriented manual for planning, funding and operating transitional housing programs. It is based on the author's experiences in operating transitional housing programs for homeless women and includes samples of many forms, worksheets and questionnaires developed for a transitional housing program.

1680. Siegal, H.A. (1986). A descriptive portrait of the S.R.O. world. In J. Erickson & C. Wilhelm (Eds.). Housing the homeless. New Brunswick, NJ: Center for Urban Policy Research, Rutgers University.

1681. Somerville, P. (1989). A critical comment on Saunders and Williams. Housing Studies, 4, 113-118.

1682. Southeastern Virginia Planning District Commission. (1984). Emergency housing survey. Chesapeake, VA.: Author.

1683. Sprague, J.F. (1986). A manual on transitional housing. Boston, MA: Women's Institute for Housing and Economic Development.
Describes essentials of planning and development of comprehensive transitional housing programs for homeless women and children in order to bridge the gap between emergency shelter services and permanent housing. Included are summaries of several successful transitional housing programs from across the country and a discussion of the service needs of sub-groups of homeless women, including: (1) life planning services, (2) personal counseling, and (3) parenting skills training.

1684. Sprague, J.F. (1988). Taking action: A comprehensive approach to housing women and children in Massachusetts. Boston, MA: Women's Institute for Housing and Economic development.

1685. Stretch, J.J. (1988). Transitional housing for homeless families. Chapter in Tulane Studies in Social Welfare, 25th anniversary issue. New Orleans, LA: Tulane University.

1686. Struening, E.L., & Rafferty, M. (1987). Housing preferences of homeless people. New York, NY: New York State Psychiatric Institute.
Discusses the housing needs and mental health status of the homeless population as well as the housing preferences of New York City shelter residents. Homeless persons find unsafe and unhealthy living situations most objectionable and prefer housing conditions similar to those offered by not-for-profit SRO hotels. The authors conclude by arguing that the further development of such housing arrangements may be the most practical solution to the problem of housing the homeless currently available.

1687. Thurman, J.A. (1991). Providing adequate housing in the "Courts" section of Harvard, Nebraska by starting a Habitat for Humanity affiliate. Dissertation Abstracts International, 52, 2600 A.

1688. Tucker, W. (1989). The excluded Americans: Homelessness and housing policies. Washington, DC: Regnery Gateway.

1689. U.S. Department of Health and Human Services. (1986). Program design and management. In J. Erickson & C. Wilhelm (Eds.), Housing the homeless. New Brunswick, NJ: Center for Urban Policy Research.

1690. U.S. Department of Health and Human Services and U.S. Department of Housing and Urban Development. (1983). Report on federal efforts to respond to the shelter and basic living needs of chronically mentally ill individuals. Washington, DC: Department of Health and Human Services.
Provides an overview of the numbers of chronically mentally ill that are homeless and critiques the appropriateness and adequacy of many of the

institutional and community settings in which the chronically mentally ill reside. The report stresses the need for a continuum of housing resources for the chronically mentally ill and describes DHHS and HUD programs and demonstrations that provide services for the chronically mentally ill. Recommendations for provision of housing and basic living resources through federal initiatives are presented.

1691. U.S. House of Representatives Committee on Banking, Finance and Urban Affairs, Subcommittee on Housing and Community Development. (1982). Hearing on shelter for the homeless. Washington, DC: U.S. Government Printing Office.

1692. U.S. House of Representatives Committee on Banking, Finance and Urban Affairs, Subcommittee on Housing and Community Development. (1984). Homelessness in America II. Washington, DC: U.S. Government Printing Office.

1693. U.S. House Committee on Banking, Finance and Urban Affairs. (1987). Rental Housing Affordability for Low- and Moderate-Income People. Hearing before the Subcommittee on Housing and Community Development of the Committee on Banking, Finance and Urban Affairs. House of Representatives. One Hundredth Congress, First Session. Washington, DC: U.S. Government Printing Office.

1694. U.S. House of Representatives Committee on Banking, Finance and Urban Affairs, Subcommittee on Housing and Community Development. (1984). Hearing on shelter for the homeless. Washington, DC: U.S. Government Printing Office.

1695. U.S. House of Representatives Committee on the Budget. (1988). Effect of Our Nation's Housing Policy on Homelessness. Hearing before the Ad Hoc Task Force on the Homeless and Housing of the Committee on the Budget, House of Representatives. One Hundredth Congress, Second Session. Washington, DC: U.S. Government Printing Office.

1696. U.S. Senate Committee on Agriculture, Nutrition, and Forestry. (1987). Nutrition for the Homeless. Hearing before the Subcommittee on Nutrition and Investigations of the Committee on Agriculture, Nutrition, and Forestry. United States Senate, One Hundredth Congress, First Session. Washington, DC: U.S. Government Printing Office.

1697. U.S. Senate Special Committee on Aging. (1978). Single room occupancy: A need for national concern. Washington, DC: U.S. Government Printing Office.

1698. U.S. Senate Committee on Banking, Housing and Urban Affairs. (1987). The Need for Decent, Affordable Housing. Hearing before the Subcommittee on Housing and Urban Affairs of the Committee on Banking, Housing, and Urban Affairs. United States Senate, One Hundredth Congress, First Session (Los Angeles, California, July 2, 1987). Washington, DC: U.S. Government Printing Office.

1699. Vanderkooi, R.C. (1967). Relocating West Madison "skid row" residents: A study of the problem, with recommendations. Chicago, IL: Chicago Department of Urban Renewal.
Reports findings of interviews with 210 skid-row men conducted to ascertain their view of the problems they might face with impending urban renewal. The development of a "half-way community" where relocated skid-row residents would have access to greatly upgraded services and facilities is advocated.

1700. Vegare, M.J., & Arce, A.A. (1986). Homeless adult individuals and their shelter network. New Directions for Mental Health Services, June, 15-26.
Based on a literature review, the authors argue that the diversity of the homeless population poses many complex problems in design and implementation of effective housing programs for the homeless. Most current services address only the emergency aspects of the problem while failing to address the long-term needs of the homeless population.

1701. Walsh, G. (1987). Resolutions Adopted by the International Labour Conference; Shelter for the Homeless: Signs of Promise. Labour Education, 68, 5-15.

1702. Watson, S. & Austerberry, H. (1986). Housing and homelessness: A feminist perspective. Boston, MA: Routledge & Kegan Paul.

1703. Wright, J.D., & Lam, J.A. (1987). Homelessness and the Low-Income Housing Supply. Social Policy, 17, 48-53.
Based on data from 12 cities with declines in low-income housing supplies, the homeless are becoming increasingly female, non-white, and younger. The authors suggest that affordable housing is a first step in addressing the problems of the homeless.

Author Index

(Entries are citation numbers rather than page numbers.)

Subject Index

(Entries are citation numbers rather than page numbers.)

About the Compilers

ROD VAN WHITLOCK is a community psychologist in private practice. He is a co-compiler with Bernard Lubin of *Family Therapy: A Bibliography, 1937-1986* (Greenwood Press, 1988).

BERNARD LUBIN, Curator's Professor, University of Missouri at Kansas City, is the author of *Psychosocial Aspects of Disaster* (1989), *Comprehensive Index to Writings in Group Psychotherapy* (1988), and *Ecological Approaches to Clinical and Community Psychology* (1984) among other books and articles dealing with clinical and community psychology.

JEAN R. SAILORS is a graduate student in the Department of Psychology at the University of Missouri at Kansas City.